also by the author:

, *Even Recent Cultural History:*
　　place, art, and poetry in ordinary life
Thinking Sound Music:
　　the life and music of Robert Erickson
Why I Read Stein
How I Saw Duchamp
The Company of Strangers (travel)
Getting There: the first thirty years (memoir)

with Virgil Thomson and Margery Tede:
Everbest Ever: Correspondence with Bay Area Friends

with Charles Strong and Gerald Nordland:
Uncompromising Vision: the Art of Jack Jefferson

ROMAN LETTERS

CHARLES SHERE

With thanks to Rosella, Gabriella, Franco, Marta, and Richard
for their continuing hospitality and friendship

Healdsburg : Ear Press : 2007
©2004 Charles Shere
ISBN 978-0-61-516600-1

printed and bound at Lulu.com

ROMAN LETTERS

*observations from two months in Italy,
January and November 2004*

CHARLES SHERE

₤

HEALDSBURG : EAR PRESS : 2007

CONTENTS

JANUARY IN ROME

Arrival	page 1
Roman hours	3
Disorientation	5
Crowds and colors	9
Random impressions	12
Alla tavola!	16
Aim Hot	19
Conversation in Orvieto	22
City life	28
We took the bus	32
Roman Martinis	37
Jazz in the basement	41
Always more	45
How we eat	50
Cold weather	55
Speechless	60
Guidebooks	63
Money and trees	67
Innocence abroad	73
Who broke this stuff?	79
Pickpocket!	83
Rain	86
Perilli	89
Bread and breakfast	93
Mozart and starlings	97
Finale	100

POLITICS AND PASTA

Arrival	page 107
The Salone del Gusto	111
Terra Madre, 1	115
Terra Madre concluded	119
Bagna cauda	122
Agricultural school	127
Wines I have tasted	131
Highways and hotels	137
Pure heart and paranoia	142
Roman arrival	147
The Curse of the Zivnys	151
Further tribulations of the apartment	156
Street Life	160
Italian comments on the American scene	164
Winter and teeth	171
Cecilia and bagna cauda	176
An uncomfortable moment	180
Haircut (not mine)	184
Ou sont les neiges	189
Demonstrations: Palestine; farmers	194
Jump in mouth	199
God and Cod	206
A Day in the Country	211
Politics and pasta	215
Haircut (mine)	220
The Parmesan lesson	225
Se vuol ballare	229
Epilogue	234
Appendix: Restaurants in Rome	239

JANUARY IN ROME

a month in Trastevere

Giuseppe Vasi: Monastero e Cheisa di S. Egidio in Trastevere, 1765. Our apartment was in the building on the extreme left.

We landed in Rome on January 2, 2004, having decided we need a month in a city every now and then, just to remind ourselves of what it is to be civil and urbane. Where better to attempt such virtues than the Eternal City? What follows is the e-mails sent home to a group of friends, lightly edited.p

Arrival

Rome, January 3 2004 —

THE MOOD AT THE AIRPORT in San Francisco was a little subdued on New Year's Day. I asked a cop where I could mail some letters, and he was cheerful enough: but when I asked how things were going, he looked a little concerned. So-so, he said. A little tense. And the weather was miserable, gloomy and wet. And there seemed very little traffic.

Next morning we were flying in over the North Sea, blue and calm below us, and the first land we saw was Holland, covered with snow. I'd never seen it so before, or at least I don't recall it if I have. Those my age, who grew up during black and white photography, are immediately thrust back into childhood by snowy vistas; from the air everything is white white white, with black or dark grey lines of railroads and highways, and long shadows, even toward noon, thrown by steeples and lines of bare poplars and elms. The occasional spot of color is always shocking: a John Deere green, or stoplight red, to remind you there is visual excitement as well as fascination.

Then back into the clouds and rain over Belgium and Germany, and only a glimpse through storm-clouds over the Alps, and back into rain for the landing at Rome, and a long wait at the wrong baggage carrousel before finally finding the right one, and the easy train trip to Trastevere and an only slightly less easy taxi trip, patiently explaining the route to the cheerful driver, to our apartment.

We are in the piazza Sant' Egidio. We could be in a village, and I suppose in fact we are: Trastevere is a subset of Rome, a little like the crooked-street area of New York's Greenwich Village, or San Francisco's North Beach. It was dark when we arrived, but the streets were glowing in a soft peach-beige-rose light cast by unseen lamps, the dark cobblestones glistening wet, the air cold but thankfully dry.

We're on the second floor: eighteen steps up to the first, seventeen to the second, all of them stone of course. Our knees will be in good shape by the end of the month, unless we're cripples. The apartment is perfect: the kitchen ample, the sitting room snug and sophisticated; the bed firm but comfortable. The computer works, as you see.

We went out for a few provisions, just in the neighboring street, getting oil and garlic and lettuce and such, and Lindsey whipped up a pasta *agliolio*, just garlic and oil, and that and a salad was enough, with a bottle of the soft barely spritzy local white wine, to send us to a long winter's nap.

I got up at 8:30 this morning and crept out for a cappuccino and a *Herald Tribune* for Lindsey and a couple of pastries. The morning is clear and cold and glorious; it's a shame to waste it here typing this. So we're off for our first morning, to the Campidoglio I think, and I'll check in later.

Roman hours

Piazza Sant' Egidio, January 4—

A LONG NIGHT AND A SHORT ONE, the morning when finally we put out the lights, and proceeding by quarter-hours. Along with even prettier hair (though lamentably less curly) and the gimpy knee increasing maturity has brought me heightened jet-lag. There was a time I could cross the continent and the Atlantic with little dislocation; that time is in the past. A week that begins in Barstow and ends in Rome, begins among range-fed Barswetians and ends in a Trastevere trattoria, simply provides too much ponder-provender to accommodate an honest night's sleep.

And then there are the bells. We encountered them on our first trip to Europe, thirty years ago, when we spent a night in a hotel attic conveniently alongside a belfry in Maastricht. Here in Trastevere the bells are somewhat more remote; Santa Maria is a good block away and our walls are thick; but they are easily heard, telling the hours and the quarters. Three deep bells at three o'clock; the same three and a single higher one at quarter past; the three and two higher ones at half past, and so on. Three; four; five; six.

Night thoughts while listening to Mahler. I have not read the book of that title, but I often meditate the thought at night; I think I know what it mean. Of course the Mahler must be the adagietto to the Fifth Symphony, though that is not what I would have chosen, I would alternate between the finale of the Fourth, in the rare cheerful mood, and the opening of the Ninth in my more usual moroseness. This was one of those nights.

Rome is big enough to encourage extremes of mood. Respighi should have written a fourth tone-poem, to introduce his *Pines* and *Fountains* and *Holidays*: a *Moods of Rome*. (Of course he did, in a way, in his *Church Windows*, insufficiently performed.) Yesterday the *passeggiata*, the evening stroll throughout every Italian city, provided a Shakespearian spectacle of young adolescent lovers, strutting actors in the prime of life, aging onlookers, and old men and women helped on by younger attendants. The Roman streets provided, too, what Shakespeare rarely considers: children, laughing, running, gripping parental hands or silly toys, and always taking everything in with that mixture of incredulity and perplexity and inevitability that makes them so reassuring. Life goes on, as Mahler seems at the end unable to remember. He should have listened more to Haydn.

The night is quiet, except for the bells, and it is utterly dark, dark as only an Italian bedroom can be, with its thick walls and heavy shutters. I think of these usually as guarding against heat, but it occurs to me they also wall out reality. The night thoughts turn as they always do to mortality — one thinks of Keats consulting his mortality here, in his pink room on the Spanish Steps, and then proving it — and the Italian sickroom, Gianni Schicchi's or Gilda's (I know, it was in Paris, but most successfully described by the same Italian composer); and how these rooms must have held their sleepers safe from malaria, or safer yet for the Black Death.

For God's sake, I can hear dear George say on reading this far — and he would have stayed with it; he was a loyal reader — for God's sake, Charles, cheer up: and I will, and do. This mood is simply an accompaniment to the others, *besciamella* to the fettucine. But it would be dishonest to hide it, and perhaps it has its utility, sharpening appreciation for the more vivacious aspects of Rome, the flea markets, the crowds, the spritz and sharp tastes that counteract the eternally present eternal.

Venice, a city clearly dying, curiously presents a more lively face than does the Rome of my present mood. Rome, a city clearly alive and powerful, is not so much weighted by its past; it is built on its past, crushes it into not-quite-oblivion by its very weight. But as Venice sinks into mud so Rome presses down into age.

Or so it does, at any rate, while I should be sleeping. It's nearly eight now; time soon to make a pot of coffee for the sleeping Lindsey, my Roman beauty who moves with so much more assurance than do I among these eternities...

Disorientation

Sant' Egidio, January 5—

OUR BED HERE RUNS EAST and west, crosswise to convention. (Our convention these days, anyway: at home it is north and south, or nearly so.) Perhaps that is why the house seems backward; or perhaps it's simply another result of beginning a week in Barstow, closing it out in Rome.

Barstow backs itself up against a ridge running east and west, like our present bed, and tilting itself a bit resentfully into the desert. It has the entire Mojave Desert to spread out in, but the climate is discouraging, the Mojave River mostly dry.

Rome's another matter. It has been both drained and irrigated for twenty-five hundred years; built on a drainage-sewer and watered by aqueducts, like California, but so far with greater success — because it is purely metropolitan, at least now, and needn't concern itself with sustainability; it has the world to sustain it. One wonders if this will last; the world is changing.

Still in bed, still fighting jet-lag, I contemplate the map of Rome in my mind. The Tiber doesn't help. Like the Seine in Paris, the Tiber draws a louche "S" across its city, turning it ninety degrees from what it should be, at least for me: so it's always a surprise to see the sun rising or setting or doing whatever it does in an unexpected direction. I'm a country boy, conditioned by skies open enough to be honest with morning and evening. In the city the light is too generalized; the unemployed have only their appetite to determine time of day, while there's any light at all.

(Getting up for a nocturnal trip to a small room confusingly at the front of the apartment, not the back where the bedroom is, it's somehow fitting that the green blank hour blinks insanely from the oven door, like a videotape player perpetually in need of setting.)

Piazza Sant' Egidio is just north of Santa Maria in Trastevere, one of the few Romanesque buildings to be found in Rome, a fine brick shed of a church with confusingly Venetian or Byzantine gilded mosaics on its fascia. But the three streets leading out of our piazza seems to me to incline it northeast toward the river, toward the convenient Ponte Sisto footbridge — old and friendly precisely because of its convenience — and the Farnese and Campo de' Fiori beyond.

The river divides the city, in fact. Old Rome thrust up against the Tiber from the east, I don't know why; it must have begun on the island just east of us, and then climbed up the Capitoline hill, the most convenient height for Romulus to build his house on, needing no doubt to be on the lookout for rebellion from within as well as invasion from without. I mentioned the other day that Trastevere, our side of the river, is like Greenwich Village, or North Beach; it is also like the Latin Quarter in Paris, though confusingly on the right bank of the Tiber — not that you can really think of the Tiber as having left and right; political terms are too subtle here for such a generalization.

Though its faucets don't allow it to run quite as free, the bathroom here is like the Tiber: it interrupts the orderly layout of the place. From the staircase hall you step right into the dining-area of the kitchen: bedroom's on the right, at the back of the apartment, with its handy computer desk and bookshelf; bath's on the left, to the left of the little *salotto* with its couches and television set, at the front of the apartment, and overlooking the piazza.

During the evening *passeggiata* the piazza is noisy with talk and laughter, and we like that; we've come to a city to be citizens for a month; the enjoyment of public conversation and laughter is a civic obligation. But the apartment has only four windows, one to each room, and they are small windows letting in little light or noise, heightening the sense of dislocation.

Yesterday — Saturday, I mean — we walked up Michelangelo's ramp to the Campidoglio and looked down from the pine-strewn hill across the Forum. The weather was fine and there were plenty of tourists — most of them Italian, and many, I think, Roman, reacquainting themselves with the history and significance of their city. We reconfirmed the existence of cats in the Area Sacra, that otherwise silent and mysterious footprint of temples and latrines from two millennia ago; and we walked through the Campo de' Fiori to pay our respects to Giordano Bruno, a man who was better than his times and therefore persecuted.

It's the first time we've been here in fifteen years, and while the city is immensely cleaner and somewhat more prosperous it remains curiously confused. The Renaissance rebuilt it after a thousand years of neglect and decay; but like so much of Italy it slipped away from the mainstream of history — apart from the Vatican, of course — until quite recently. Italy wasn't a country, after all, until a little over a century ago.

I suppose it was Mussolini who shouldered Rome into a semblance of modernity. (What more modern than fascism, more fascistic than Modernism?) But doing so required yet another Hausmannization, adding better and more open lines of transportation; and this hasn't really been accomplished. I think Rome has a great deal of inertia. Power is aggressive abroad, but stodgy at home.

So Rome remains a jumble of periods, and the amazing thing is that with very few exceptions there is a real sense of ensemble. This rises partly from the generally even color of the buildings by day, the warm lighting by night, and partly from the height limits, which keep out skyscrapers and preserve the low but uneven rooflines of past centuries.

There are exceptions — the Victorian-baroque Monument to Vittorio Emmanuele in particular. Nicknamed The Wedding Cake and The Typewriter (think of an oldfashioned upright manual one), it gleams in lustrous white marble unlike anything around it. I suppose it recalls the Lincoln Monument: and why not? It celebrates the reunification of a great country at about the same time, the late middle 19th century.

We approach it not centrally, from the piazza Venezia, but cornerwise, exploring the little park, again set about with towering but open pines. Seen out the corner of the eye even this monument takes its place, coldly eyeing the distant Vatican like the cooperative enemy it was, rising above the commercial fray of the piazza, yet maintaining an attitude of some modesty, even deference, to the imperial Campidoglio of the Caesars and the Renaissance which, in turn, looks over it.

But then we turn our backs on all this and walk back to Trastevere, a town of people rather than memories or institutions. In the evening, after a nap, its streets are still lit with Christmas ornaments, stars suspended over the pavements, and strings of lights spelling out AUGURI (greetings) — which, seen from behind, becomes the more enigmatic IRUGUA, as if a mythical South American nation were being introduced to the Romans.

Dinner right next door, at La Tana de Noantri — nothing to write home about, so I will: good hot vegetable soup; veal Marsala for Lindsey, *penne arrabbiata* for me, the tomato sauce thick, hot, and spicy; a side of green beans, a half bottle of Corvo: forty bucks. Cheap, Rome ain't.

And now off to the flea market to shake the moodiness, and onward toward Tuesday's big holiday. Hope you're well and happy!

Crowds and colors
S. Egidio, January 5—

PIAZZA IN AGONIA, that's the etymological derivation of Piazza Navona. Because it was at one time a racetrack where games, in Latin-Greek *agonia*, were played, generally with Ben Hur-like chariots and such.

Today, the eve of Epiphany, it was agony simply to walk across the piazza, usually the work of a minute or less, in these circumstances almost impossible. The piazza is set about with market-stalls selling toys, creche equipment, and various forms of inedibles — huge doughnutlike things, cotton candy, hot dogs.

And the crowds. Men women and children, a few dogs, a few strollers (I mean the kind kids ride in, not saunterers, no one is able to saunter in such a scene). Police, undercover agents, pickpockets, tourists, television journalists, pitchmen. And, of course, the Living Statues. This year they run to the Egyptian style; there were two done up like King Tut, and another making a brave attempt at Cleopatra, unless it was Elizabeth Taylor.

(It's a sign of the times that street performers get by with metallic makeup, cheap flashy costumes, and absolute motionlessness. There was a time when they'd have been acrobats, jugglers, dancers. Now there's enough fast motion on the streets in cars, neon signs, and milling crowds; the performers are the more startling for being still.)

In such circumstances, indeed perhaps in all circumstances, it is not normal in Italy to queue up, or alternate turns, or hang back in any way. If you make way for one person, say a little old lady with a plastic bag containing a pound or two of small sharply-pointed objects of some kind, then the next hundred will follow right on her heels. The situation is impossible.

But it is a sight to be seen, and now we have seen it, and checked it off.

We have been here three full days now and our impressions are as overloaded as the Piazza Navona. There is no overriding single impression, unless it is that of variety. There have been really only two constants: our apartment, which is snug and friendly and provides all the comfort we want (except a bathtub, for which there's really no room); and the river Tiber, dividing our quarter from what we generally the Seven Hills. Even the Tiber's not that steady; its quality shifts with the light, from fine and serene to somber and moody.

Yesterday we took a tram tour, after first walking up from our apartment, through the Janiculum park, and across the Vatican (crowded as always). The little streetcar was nearly empty: just us and half a dozen middle-aged Filipino women. It crossed the river and soon reached the Borghese, a fine park housing a number of museums and the city zoo. We crossed it to reach a complacent upper-class residential quarter, and I thought of the streetcar suburbs of Portland, distant suburbs until the automobile came along: the terrain here is rolling, the houses set apart with fine gardens and a number of trees — welcome to us; until now we've seen only the few pines around the Vittorio Emmanuele Typewriter and the lanky sycamores reaching spindly arms way way up to grab at the few remaining crisply dying leaves.

We got off at the Piazza Buenos Aires to explore an amazing quarter, the Coppedé neighborhood, anchored at the piazza by a fine if eccentric church setting the mood for the architectural excess just down the street.

Here there are blocks and blocks of villas built in the 1920s in a style that manages to merge the finest aspects of Art Nouveau with the margins of Cubism and hints of Bauhaus Modernism to come. It sounds stage-set-like, but it isn't: these buildings are well thought through and consistently achieved, and they are set about their narrow, curved, rolling streets with a true sense of ensemble. I suppose the closest American equivalent would be the early Frank Lloyd Wright manner, except that he exaggerates the horizontal, taking up lots of room in the American way, where these buildings are essentially cubical (though their faces much broken and relieved, with both decorative flourishes and functional space-gaining bays and balconies).

We've been conducting a casual comparison of guidebooks: only one, the Cadogan, has much (or anything at all) to say about this quarter. But I would think it an important part of any architectural visit to Rome, because although its period is narrow the quarter is pure and its design is fascinating. We spent a half-hour or so strolling the neighborhood in the twilight, taking photographs, meeting very few people on the streets. Some of the villas are now embassies; two or three seem to be foundation offices; a number are undergoing restoration, perhaps turning into condominiums.

Then back to the streetcar, past the boring Mussolini architecture of the university, a couple of nearby brand-new glass-box buildings (one housing the local Blockbuster videorental); past the Colosseum brooding in the gathering night; past the pathetically majestic pyramid Cestius build for his tomb; past the grass field that is the Circus Maximus.

And then on foot, out of a traffic jam, and across the Tiber again exactly in the *heure bleue*, the Vatican dome a distant spot of light, the serene silver surface of the river meditating on the bare trees marking it off from the sky hovering in blue velvet.

There were other things — morning in the flea market, beset by gypsies who had to be beat off; conversation with an old lady with a pretty face, pleased that we were pleased with Italy, but mourning its declines in comportment and values; dinner at home, beginning with Lindsey's re-creation of her grandmother's antipasto, a nostalgic blend of tuna, *giardiniera*, and tomato paste.

And, most of all, the incredible skies and light and colors of the Roman surfaces and edges — stucco, stone, paving; all those things cities are made of, and our usual days lack utterly in the countryside. But this is surely more than enough for one day.

Random impressions
S. Egidio, January 7—

LET'S SEE, WHAT HAVE we been doing? Today Rome began to return to normal after its twelve days of Christmas. I suppose: in fact I have no idea what normal is in Rome, never having spent much time here before. The decorations are still hanging over the streets; I haven't been out tonight to see if they're lit. But people are returning to work: I was able to get a haircut this afternoon with no trouble at all. It doesn't take much Italian to be able to say *non troppo corte*, not too short. *Ma anche non troppo lunghe*; but not too long, either.

We walked the via Giulia this morning, in a very leisurely manner, looking at everything the DK Guide recommended, and noticing thereby things other visitors apparently missed. We assumed they too were visitors; they stood in corners consulting maps, then looking about as if to get their bearings. But they did not look closely at the arch that spans the narrow street, an arch designed by Michelangelo — the beginning of a project, never pushed further, to span the entire width of the Tiber, on order to connect the Farnese Palace to the Farnesina.

We checked out the frescos and the plaques; the foundation stones and the portals. Like most Roman streets the via Giulia lacks sidewalks, and this part of town hasn't changed much to the casual eye since, say, the Renaissance, if you ignore the traffic, which you'd better not. The buildings are big and blocky and set right against the street and one another, but through their portals you catch glimpses of big interior courtyards and gardens; and you're reminded that the ancient mailboxes had names like Cosmo de' Medici on them.

Except for the churches, of course, and the jails. The New Jail is here, ordered up by a Renaissance pope intent on bringing a measure of humanity to a penal system with a long history of unconcern for human rights. Today the building is no longer a jail, but a government office: according to its plaque, the Office Against Mafiaism.

We stepped up onto the porch of San Giovanni at the end of the Giuilia, and a young Italian boy, sixteen or so, came up to us and asked if we knew of a statue of Giordano Bruno. My first thought was to tell him we were tourists ourselves, that we didn't speak Italian, but immediately I knew how to explain to him that poor Bruno was standing in the middle of the Campo de' Fiori where he had been burned at the stake five hundred years ago, and the boy left in a hurry, whether at my Italian, or the thought of the execution, or in anticipation of some sweet rendezvous, I couldn't say.

We sauntered back along the via Pellegrino which is, oddly, the only street I really remember from the last time we were here, fifteen years ago, when we arrived unexpectedly, and couldn't find a place to stay, and I recalled Therese saying that if you needed a room you should always go to the Campo de' Fiori and ask, you will surely find one there; and we did: I asked in a barbershop if anyone there knew of a room available, and they said Go to the Albergo di Sole, so we did, and found one of the most memorable rooms we've stayed in.

But that was fifteen years ago. We walked this morning past the same barbershop but it was closed. So we bought some potatoes and *puntarelli* and *insalatina* in the Capo, just under Bruno's statue, and walked on home for lunch and a cup of tea.

I read a little more in my novel. It's interesting how much more easily you can read Italian in Italy than at home. Of course I understand perhaps half of Moravia's beautifully wrought sentences, but the novel — his first, *Gli Indifferenti*,— unfolds so easily, so like any number of other narratives of its period (the late 1920s) that the impression is clear, and a few useful words, a very few, stay with me after each reading.

So I was fairly secure when I walked down the via della Scala in pursuit of a haircut. Ah, said the hostess of the salon, I speak English, it is good that I, mmm, repeat it when possible. So we spoke a little of this and a little of the other. I explained that yes I speak a bit of Italian well enough — I always have this explanation ready, the kind Italians are so quick to complement anyone's broken attempt at their language — but that I don't understand it.

How is it possible, she said reasonably enough, that you might speak a language and not understand? Oh yes of course, it is one thing to express...

I explained that my wife understands but does not speak; I speak but do not understand. You should have brought her, she said. Oh no, I replied, she doesn't like to come to *parruchieri*. She's just like me, the young woman said eagerly, She doesn't like to part with money, oh no, I never do the shops, I hate to buy, it makes me sweet. We looked at one another uncomprehendingly. It makes me sweat, she corrected herself.

Yesterday we walked through the Forum without looking at it. It's best to sneak up on these things, I say. We did pause at the Temple of Portunus, a little square Greek-style temple as close to perfect as these things get; and we admired the Church of St. George, which I must visit one day at the equinox, as it's clear the sun will then shine right through the round window over the front door, bounce off the white marble floor, and illuminate the amazing mosaics in the apse, if that's what it's called.

(But of course perhaps it won't be there again. It was badly damaged by a bomb just ten years ago, and has been painstakingly restored.)

We walked through the Forum and up to the Esquiline to see a huge show of paintings by de Chirico, Carra, and Morandi, with a few others thrown in — a panorama of Metaphysical Modernism. Fascinating the way the familiar Twentieth Century is seen completely differently by other cultures: here in Italy, Willem de Kooning is part of the Metaphysical movement. (I exaggerate: but a fine painting of his was in fact included, as having been influenced by Chirico's sense of futile, neutral, oppressive emptiness.)

We were in the show for over two hours: it was huge. Among the paintings were three or four splendid ones, modern as all getout, from the national art museum in Tehran. How little we Americans know of the nations of the Middle East! How much more fascinating, even-valued, and alive the world is seen from other than categorical American perspectives!

But it was an exhausting visit, and the walk back took us through very crowded streets, especially around the Trevi Fountain, where a memorably beautiful young woman, say twenty-two or -

three, pushed her garbage cart and swept up papers and trash, uncomplainingly aware of a few pair of eyes following every move. We took a cup of gelato — *crema* and *fior di latte* for me, thank you, I pursue a rigorous research program — and walked home for dinner (leftovers); then stepped out once more, again across the Ponte Palatino to see the Temple of Portunus under the full moon.

And now I step out once again for another look at the full moon, and so I leave you for another day or two. There are only so many full moons; the Chinese say we get only a thousand. It's best not to let any go by unvisited.

the Temple of Portunus

Alla tavola!
S. Egidio, January 8—

AND WHAT DO YOU EAT, some of you are wondering. Well we eat at home; at least so far; at least except for one meal. Today for example I got up and made coffee as usual: we're drinking Lavazza Rosso, a medium-good coffee, I like it better than Illy, but not as well as the delicious coffees we had in Venice.

Rome has two cafes famous for their house brand of coffee: the Caffé San Eustacchio, whose espresso has an absurdly thick and creamy "crema," and is famous for it; and Tazza d'oro. We have tried so far only the first, and I immediately dismissed it from mind. It's a trick. The barista works furtively; there's a sort of metallic curtain surrounding the machine; you can't see what he's up to. The espresso arrives, a little cup perhaps a third full of espresso (as should be the case); floating on it a dense layer of froth, exactly the right cinnamon color and smelling of nothing but espresso. But in the mouth it's clear there's something funny going on. Egg white, I said; Lindsey wasn't so sure — but then how much experience does Lindsey have with egg whites? There could even be a bit of gelatin in it, I think: but Lindsey thinks it's primarily sugar. Could be: there are sugars and sugars. The whole thing reminds me of the phony mystique surrounding Orange Julius, when I was a boy; the secret formula and all that, the refusal to let people know what's going on. And the coffee wasn't all that good.

We'll try Tazza d'Oro one of these days. In the meantime I like Lavazza; it's a huge company, I suppose the Folger's of Italy. But it isn't the Starbucks of Italy: that would be Illy.

Anyway breakfast was a glass of pineapple juice, coffee with hot milk (yes, ultra-pasteurized, why not, we just heat it in the microwave anyway), and bread. There's a splendid bakery just down the street: the Panificio Arnese. It was featured in the special issue the magazine Gourmet devoted to Rome, last March; but we found it independently. The women behind the counter are as dry and cold as they come, but the bread, the yellow cornmeal cake, the *brutti ma buoni* are absolutely wonderful. We get the half of a *ciabatta*: the tall thin angry woman snatches a loaf up out of a basket on the floor, rests one end on a worn table, grabs a knife as if she hated it, and guillotines the loaf, carefully handing us the very slightly smaller of the two halves. We take it home and eat it avidly.

Then we walked down to Santa Cecilia to see the fabulous Cavalini frescos. In reproductions frescos always bore me; they look flat flat flat, like candybox covers. But these, seen in the flesh so to speak, looked like high-resolution color photographs taken in the 13th century. The faces on these angels and apostles were perfectly three-dimensional. Except for their nightgowns and the extravagantly colored feathers of their wings they were people I've been seeing on the street. The sense of immediacy was breathtaking.

In the basement we spent an hour or so in Cecilia's 3rd-century apartments, looking at her root cellar, her collection of broken columns, the holes in the ground where she kept her Roman meal, and (guiltily) her steam-closet, where she was imprisoned for three days as a kind of slow execution, but she did not die, she sang through it all; then was put to the axe, again three times, again almost without result — but she was finally martyred, for having converted her husband Valerian; and now there she is in her church somewhere, which is special to all musicians for she is after all the patron saint of music.

And then up the street to the Piazza S. Cosimato where there is an outdoor market every morning. Here we were immediately accosted by a dark young man carrying plastic bags of garlic, which he was selling for two euros the bag, a euro a head of garlic. Too much, I said, and offered one. We settled on one fifty. He tried to speak English to us, but neither of us could understand a word of it; his Italian was clearer — he was from Bangladesh, and made his living selling garlic, probably black market garlic. No one seemed to mind.

We bought a couple of chicken breasts, and a slice of Fontina, and a couple of handfuls of Romano beans, and then walked the few blocks home for lunch: bread and coppa and the delicious local white wine, well not all that local, I think it comes from Naples, but it's slightly sparkling and goes down like water and costs about two fifty a bottle.

And then a long walk window-shopping, perhaps four miles altogether, which took us up and down the Corso, and over to the Spanish Steps where we spent twenty-five dollars on two cups of tea, I kid you not; and then back by way of the Pantheon, which will always be the single most amazing building I have ever seen, marred only by the arrogance with which one upstart mystical religion has shouldered out all other gods — to whom after all the most powerful civilization of its time had dedicated the building — and turned it over to only one, and that one a transplant from the Middle East desert. But I digress, and I fulminate.

Back, then, through the darkness, though some of the streets do still have their Christmas lights up, to have an aperitif watching Mr. Powell rededicate himself to the mysterious arsenal of Iraq; and then to cook our dinner:

- chicken valdostana: flatten, then salt and pepper the chicken breasts; saute them in olive oil; turn them; spread them with thin slices of Fontina and prosciutto
- Romano beans: just rinse them and steam them with a drop or two of oil
- green salad: *puntarelle* and *insalatina*, dressed at the table with oil and vinegar

And that's all you need to know. Our tea had cost twenty-five dollars, but dinner was about seven fifty, wine included. And now for a bit of chocolate and a tiny bit of Prosecco grappa, as smooth as the travertine sheathing that island in the Tiber.

Aim Hot

S. Egidio, January 9—

STREET OBSERVATIONS — THE ODD little unexpected things that you notice in spite of yourself. They come back every morning, an hour or two before waking up. This morning it was the perfect valley girl English we heard yesterday, over on the via Veneto. My theory is, female adolescent American English sounds the way it does because of orthodontia. Of course I could be wrong about this: we who grew up in poverty know little about orthodontia; only rich families could afford to straighten their kids' teeth.

But the word "way" comes out something like "waaa-ay," as if she set her mouth to pronounce the first syllable of "apple" but said "way" instead. Anatomy determines expression.

And I think much of Italian must be left-handed; that's why the signs are as they are.

ᙠ , for example: you see this very often, spelled out in big metal
A   letters hanging down the side of a building. Bilateral symme-
Я   try: there are six capital letters which, like Republicans, don't distinguish between going forward and going backward. A-H-I-M-O-T. Aim hot. Then the alphabet goes crazy; the next five letters, from U to Y, are all symmetrical, though they aren't good for much.

In the word B
A
            Я that central "A," symmetrical, anchors the thing, and you don't really mind that "B" and "R" aren't quite symmetrical; they're close enough. HOTEL works out pretty well too; by the time you get to the last two letters you know what's happening.

Why left-handed? Because of Leonardo, who famously wrote backward, as one can easily if one's left-handed, and has been taught to write right-handedly. My father used to be able to write with both hands simultaneously, and the amazing thing was that both hands wrote frontward, as if he were playing the piano. (I've often thought the piano would be a good deal easier to play if the left-hand part of the keyboard were arranged backward, so both hands could finger things the same way. But that's another insane divagation.)

We hear a certain amount of English on the street. Here in Trastevere there are lots of students; and then the American Academy is up the hill — we haven't been there yet, and won't get there today either; for the first time it's raining, and this will be a museum day.

Yesterday at Babington's Tea Room there were Germans on the right of us, a nervous thin dark-haired woman and her husband, big and bearlike, wild brown short-cut but unruly hair, studiously repairing his hearing aid with a small screwdriver. (On the left a table of four Italians, chain-smoking.)

(Babington's, by the way, is at the bottom of the Spanish Steps, is why our tea was ten euros a pot, not a cup: Lindsey reprimands me gently for having given you a false idea yesterday.)

We hear a little bit of Hebrew from time to time, and once I overheard some French. But mostly we hear Italian or, as I like to think, Roman; the sound is a little harsher, less lyrical than the Italian I'm used to from Torino, Milan, or Verona. (Not to mention Venice, where there's another kind of problem.)

Only once have I heard a woman, an older woman, speak Italian through her nose, as they tend to do in Piemonte. Perhaps like me she was from out of town. My own Italian is, as George used to say of his French, lamentable, but I doggedly speak it, and the person I speak to rarely resorts himself to English, partly because in many cases he can't. Italians are quick to compliment one's own bumbling attempt to destroy their lovely lyrical language: *Parla bene italiano*, they say; you speak it well. Privately they wonder, I'm sure, what the hell it is you intend to say.

I'm reading Moravia. It's amazing how much easier it is to read than to speak: you don't have to remember the words, they're right there on the page for you, printed out forwards, too. If you squint a bit and don't look at the individual words; if you read quickly; then you get the impression you know what it's all about. The newspaper's another matter, of course: colloquial and given to jargon and allusions, and full of acronyms. And these latter are spelled out in lower case, not in capitals as they are in English; so that the UNO (United Nations Organization) becomes Onu, for example. You have to be on your toes.

* * *

A note on yesterday's chicken *valdostana*. It's incomplete without sage, as I realized when we got home yesterday evening. So I rushed out to the little greengrocer on the piazza: *Avete poche foglie di salvia*, I asked, do you have a few leaves of sage? Of course, the man smiled, and took a bunch out of the refrigerator. No charge. I fried a few leaves in olive oil, the oil I used later to saute the chicken breasts; you can see the result on the webpage noted below. Chicken *valdostana* is, we think, one of the Hundred Great Dishes.

* * *

And now we're back from lunch, our second meal out — at a trattoria, no, an *osteria* around the corner, Da Augusto, paper tablecovers, casual in the extreme. The cooks in sweatshirts because their kitchen is so cold. Pots balanced on top of other pots on the stove, improvising a steam table. We had *baccalà*, with side dishes of spinach and roast potatoes, and a half liter of very cheap white wine, the whole thing about twenty-five dollars. At the next table two girls and their mother, all Americans, touring Italy, wondering if they can get citizenship since the mother's father was born in Italy.

Before lunch we sat out the rain in the museum across the street, where there's an exhibition fortuitously concerning Alberto Moravia — newspaper and magazine articles, first editions, typescript and manuscript letters, photos; also paintings from his own collection, very uneven but full of heart. The permanent collection contains dioramas portraying 18th-19th-century Rome; very kitschy and fascinating; and prints and watercolors from the same period. Except for people's clothes, which are now the same the world over, and for the fact that nothing is repaired any more, simply thrown out, and except of course for the damn cars and motorbikes, the streets haven't changed that much. The water still courses down the middle of these narrow cobblestoned streets when it rains. People still sit and drink in doorways, and ogle one another, and smile at the (very) occasional drunk, and squirt water into their mouths from the fountains, even though Lindsey does point out not everyone's hands are clean.

Conversation in Orvieto

S Egidio, January 12—

WE SPENT THE WEEKEND in Orvieto, after all my ranting about not leaving Rome for a moment. The idea was to immerse ourselves in City, after all. But the only way to visit Rosella was to run up to her town; she was only there another few days; the train only takes an hour; so off we went Saturday morning, taking the H bus from the piazza Sonnino a few minutes' walk from our house, then killing a short hour at the train station because, well, one's always a bit anxious when catching a train, one wouldn't want to miss it.

The Rome station always reminds me of the main station in Amsterdam: it has an enormous bus plaza out in front of it. Its architecture is very different, though: instead of ornate postBaroque Edwardian brick and terra cotta, it is very 1950s postwar Modernist, low and wide and white, all about the horizontal — which is appropriate to a rail terminal: trains don't like climbs.

And inside the station, on both street and basement levels, there are enormous shops. You can buy anything you want here as long as it's some sort of luxury: chocolate, alcohol, books, jewelry, all kinds of clothes. Well, not work clothes, unless your work is... Oh, never mind. There's a big Nike store: we stepped in, looked at shoes that ranged up to a couple hundred dollars a pair (for athletic shoes!), and stepped back out.

Orvieto, as you probably know, is set on top of a hill, really a single "plug," I think, left over after the surrounding volcano had been long since eroded away, either by the river draining that wide beautiful valley, or by centuries of farming and quarrying, or perhaps by the wind; who knows. You can drive up; I think there are two roads up; and six or seven thousand Orvietians live up there, looking down on the twenty thousand or so who live at the bottom, or in outlying villages and farms.

But we did not drive up: we took the funicular conveniently sited across the street from the train station. You pay your euro, surrender the ticket, and take a seat on a little wooden bench in one of the three or four private compartments on what is essentially a large elevator cabin sitting at a forty-five degree angle on its rails.

There is no operator. A buzzer sounds and the car moves slowly forward and up, passed halfway up by the other cabin coming down. It reminded me exactly of Angel's Flight, the cable funicular in the Los Angeles of fifty years ago; and of course it reminded me of the old Neopolitan song with its refrain "funiculi funicula": but I wisely refrained from singing it.

There at the top came Rosella, lovely exuberant Rosella, in the gray and graygreen corduroy she wears with such distinction, such flair; and off we marched up the main street, the Corso Cavour, and she pointed out the sights, the quarters into which the town is divided, the way of the People and the way of the Church, the clock tower, the city hall, the Duomo.

We stopped in at an artist's studio tucked into a building across from the Duomo to admired a number of abstract expressionist but figurative-based paintings and prints crowding a sort of exhibition space. A doorway led to the artist's studio, fragrant with the familiar scent of gesso: he was preparing a new canvas.

I was attracted by a prose-poem in longhand on a large sheet of paper with drawings, framed under glass and hanging in the doorway. The artist had by then appeared and was talking busily to Rosella, who introduced us. I asked him if he'd written much poetry, and he was happy to talk about his writing, and pointed to a stack of books on a high shelf, all identical, awaiting sale. He tried to pull one out of the stack but could not reach the top, so I stood on tiptoe and took one down.

He gave it to us: *Un Muro l'uccidio degli uccelli*, "A wall, slaughterer of birds." Like almost all of his work, the book itself, published in 1980, is a testament of Livio Valentini's lifelong testimony against violence. We asked him why, and he spoke of his adventures in the Second World War, ending with two years' imprisonment at Buchenwald. He spoke passionately against violence, but as I looked around me at the images in his painting I said "but you must admit that there is also a beauty in violence, a beauty that many find compelling and even a justification." He agreed immediately, Yes, there is a beauty, and we must contemplate it to counter it, to achieve a life full of beauty but devoid of violence.

Valentini is not young; he's fifteen years older than I, eighty-three years old. He shames me, though: he works every day, and I can't say that his work is merely a routine; he clearly re-dedicates himself to the joy and the beauty of it every day. The book, a catalogue of his first sixty years, contains his own description of that terrible war in a ten-page letter written, "without any pretense at making literature," to his mother, in 1951. It's compelling writing, but offset too by the panorama of small black-and-white reproductions of the work he did in the next thirty years — painting, mixed-media work, jewelry, prints.

We were really touched by this short but intense visit. He inscribed the book: *A Charlesy per un incontro d'arte e di amicizia*, for a meeting of art and friendship, and I like the double meaning, and hope to stay in touch. But we had other things to do, and walked on through the narrow streets and the surprising small hidden piazzas, admiring the odd light on the rough-textured sand-colored walls made of a curiously sandstone-colored local tufa. The railroad station had been socked in by dense fog, but we'd climbed toward the light on that funicular, and minute by minute the air was clearing, and the distant hills were coming into view, green and inviting through the mists.

Lunch was goulash that Rosella had made, and pecorino and pears, delicious, and we talked for hours, and went out shopping for the next day's midday dinner — she hadn't yet bought a Gorgonzola she'd fancied, because she wasn't sure we liked Gorgonzola. (It didn't take long to set her straight on that.)

We went to Dei Fratelli, a very impressive purveyor of "local and national gastronomical specialities of traditional quality and competence," and here we tasted five or six pecorinos and the aforementioned Gorgonzola, and a few hams and prosciuttos too just in case; and we admired the shelves of black truffles and the oils and I bought a bottle of local red wine and we exacted a promise that yes he'd be open the next day in the morning, up until noon, yes even though it was Sunday, and we went back to Rosella's for more talk and a rest.

And then went out to dinner at the Trattoria del orso, where we admired small drawings hanging on the wall, drawn by a friend of the guys who run the restaurant, not an artist but a microbiologist (or something like that, if there is anything like that that isn't that) who does these only for himself and a few friends; and we had a delicious meal, not ordering from a menu because the cook prepares only what he wants to, from whatever is available that day. We had a delicious vegetable soup, Lindsey and I, subtly flavored with fennel seed; and then she had *strozzapreti* with mushrooms and black truffles and I passed up guinea fowl, a favorite of mine, for three wonderful lamb chops simply grilled and salt-and-peppered and brought to me with a piece of lemon; and afterward a fine cherry *crostata* which he'd bought at a nearby *pasticceria* because, he said, he does not bake, he cooks; and he made no apology for this since he was talking, after all, to an important pastry chef.

His kitchen is tiny and he does everything in it, and his dining rooms are not very big though there are after all two of them, and his friend does all the waiting on tables, or did the night we were there. They close three days a week, and two and a half months of the year, and I don't know how long they'll stay with it; I'm sixty years old, said the cook — Gabriele Di Giandomenico — and this is a lot of work. He speaks perfect American English; he lived for years in New Jersey. But he spoke perfect Italian too, and he and Rosella jabbered happily about the Costa Smeralda in Sardegna, and life among the rich and beautiful, while Lindsey and I and the waiter talked happily about food.

A long night's solid sleep, then, since we were over four hours at the restaurant; and the next morning a walk around the town, to find that the delicatessen was closed, of course; it had quality but its competence was sadly lacking that morning I thought; and the Duomo was off limits as well because after all services were going on, so we took a coffee in the second-rate cafe, not the first-rate one we'd gone to earlier with Rosella, where she'd bought her cake for today's lunch, the only cafe people go to to be seen in, since after all we'd already been seen there, and we thought we'd see who was to be seen in the other one. And that turned out to be a young couple with back-packs who were just finishing their breakfast and were examining their banknotes as if they weren't sure what continent had issued them.

I was reading Valentini's book when Rosella came back from Mass with two friends who were joining us for lunch — really midday dinner: Gisella, a writer and food person who makes frequent trips to the U.S. (especially Texas and the San Francisco area) to give demonstrations on Italian regional foods, and Adriana, a member of old Roman society (she has an apartment on the Piazza Veneto and was the widow of a painter in the Futurist movement). An interesting lunch: Gisella brought *rotelle* she had made, circular tortellini-like filled pastas with an intriguing, complex filling; we had a mountain of *porchetta*, the cold sliced roast pork the Italians do so well; there was the Gorgonzola and a fine pecorino; and then the *millefeuille* — excuse me; *migliafolie*.

This was a many-layered pastry (hence the name, of course), filled with pastry cream and all covered with big shavings of white chocolate: it looked elaborate and special and tasted sublime, though it resisted even Lindsey's efforts — she was delegated, of course — at cutting it into portions without breaking it into shreds. And a bottle of white, and a bottle of red, and a half bottle of *limoncello*, and so on.

Adriana told a funny story: she had seen, in the Piazza Venezia, a man in a big expensive car carefully maneuvering it to get into a small parking space in the crowded lot, when a couple of kids in a Fiat Cinquecento, smaller than a VW beetle, zip into it before his irritated eyes, lock their car, and leave, calling out to him *Cosi fanno i giovani*, That's how youth does it. He got out of his car, walked over to theirs, and beat dents into it while they looked on astonished. *Cosi fann'i ricchi*, he said, giving them his calling card, That's how the rich do it. I thought (but did not mention) that movie *Fried Green Tomatoes*, with a very funny sequence exactly similar, and wondered if Adriana had seen it, but did not ask.

The conversation: food, mostly, on our side of the table, with Gisella; art and Italianicity, on Adriana and Rosella's side. I had the previous evening asked Rosella what she thought was the chief characteristic of the celebrated Italian quality of daily life, and the first thing that came to her mind was the pace — not necessarily a slower pace, certainly not in such cities as Milan and Rome; but a more capacious pace, a pace that not only allowed but actually encouraged discursiveness. You see this in the long meals, in the evening strolls, in the detailed, loquacious conversations. You see it in the newspaper articles, which one of our guidebooks warned us tended to go into long and detailed investigations of the opinions and history behind events.

I think what it comes down to is that Italy is a land of voce, of voice. When I first began reading Moravia's *Gli indifferenti* I was struck by his fabulous opening sentences, almost Proustian; I was so struck by them that I read one aloud to Emma, because it sounded, to me, like narrative song. And at the end of the volume containing that first novel (and the next few as well), among the editor's notes, I find the surprising information, well perhaps not so very surprising after all, that he composed this novel over a period of three years or so, while he was shaking a case of bone tuberculosis in various mountain sanitoria; and that he never wrote any of the paragraphs down until he had worked them out speaking them aloud. The entire novel is the written record of a story told aloud.

That I think is the essence of the Italian genius: it is given to expression, to shared expression. An American like Hawthorne goes to Rome and writes an interior novel, really a sort of meditation, on his reaction to this Italian genius for publicity: but it reads like a monologue, however fascinating it is — a monologue or the transcription of notes to himself by a professional witness, a therapist, say, or a judge. Even a Henry James reads like this: you can see the sentences being reworked with a pencil, between the lines. (Though it is true all his later novels were dictated, and this of course has a great deal to do with the rather sudden irruption of his celebrated later style, more convoluted, more discursive.)

Our entire dinner conversation went like this, mostly in Italian though with recourse to English when necessary — entirely too often, of course. And then we had missed our train back, and had to rush to catch the next one. Adriana drove us down to the station; she was driving off to her country house anyway, on a ridge off across the valley. She drove us down the narrow road and its hairpin turns, a proper but scintillating woman in her mid-80s, a woman whose husband had been among the great Modernists of the first decades of the last century; she drove us down to the station in her small practical car a dozen years old or so, and angled into a no-parking spot to let us out.

Cosi fann'i ricchi, she smiled, and we grinned too, and took our train back to Rome and dinner with Richard and Marta who have come down from Verona to spend a few days with us.

City life
S. Egidio, January 15—

SOME OF YOU HAVE WRITTEN enviously of our opportunity to get to know Rome rather well, but assure yourselves: we're not making the most of the opportunity. We are carefully observing the duties of modern city life, spending leisurely days with friends, talking in the kitchen, strolling the streets, taking lunch and dinner in restaurants or at home, lingering over coffee in the cafes. This is perhaps not the most studious approach to The Eternal City, but it is pleasant.

We walked up the Botteghe Oscure yesterday, on our way to another trip up Michelangelo's ramp to the Piazza del Campidoglio, and I remembered a copy of the literary quarterly of that name, found in the middle 1950s at Creed's Books on Telegraph Avenue in Berkeley, a thick square book on rough creamy paper in subtle brown covers, containing stories and poems, perhaps an essay or two as well, I don't remember now, in English, French, and Italian. It was the beginning of my fascination with modern languages, unknown languages concealing unimaginable stories of intelligence and sophistication.

I just read one of them, Moravia's "Delitto" — how to translate that? "in a tennis club," about the murderous joke played by a group of slightly older men, say in their late twenties, rich and spoiled members of a decadent 1920s Roman society. It is, of course, dated; hardly worth reading now except as background to his novels.

Constantly at the back of my mind is the inescapable comparison of our society at the beginning of the 21st century with that of two thousand years ago. Yesterday our president announced, in all seriousness, that we will set up a permanent base on the moon, and then go on to land on Mars. The American flag will begin a journey throughout the solar system.

There was a headline in an Italian paper the other day, predicting this announcement. "Bush promises voters the moon and Mars," it read, with a fine sense of irony. I don't know that you have to be across the ocean from New York and Washington to sense the arrogance of the promise, but perhaps it helps to see, on every side, evidence that a great civilization (if in fact it was civilized), a great power inevitably collapses of its own weight, of the impossibility of sustaining itself when its power and its delights depend on the exploitation and suppression of others.

There's a small ruin near the Theater of Marcellus — an old floor or more likely sub-floor, a rough wall say twenty feet long rising about chest-high, and three beautiful symmetrical marble basins set against the wall. Floor and wall were probably once veneered with marble, long since pried off to decorate some other installation. Each great period wears old clothes. There are iron rings set into the wall, perhaps to tie horses to if this was a rich horse stable, perhaps simply towel-rings if, as I think more likely, it is the remains of a restroom.

What's interesting is the basins, any one of which would fetch a good price in an antiquities market, would make a stunning birdbath or holy-water font. They are two thousand years old and priceless works of art. But they are also clearly simply the product of some factory: three identical marble basins, three of what must have been thousands, scattered throughout the cities of the Roman Empire, from Constantinople to London.

Who made them? Were they freemen or slaves? What did they eat and drink; what were their habitations? How did they make them? Were they somehow turned as if on a lathe? Were they roughed out by prisoners or apprentices, then shipped to a finishing shop where experienced eyes and hands reduced them to this degree of interchangeability?

What kind of global trade agreements underlay the Roman Empire, I wonder, and, if (as I suspect) a great deal of the labor involved was less than completely willing, how was order and subordination maintained? There are lessons to be learned here, if anyone in Washington is interested.

I have the feeling, though not the language skills to confirm it, that much of today's Europe is aware of the historical evidence that the future, any future, is not on the side of the arrogant, and particularly of the arrogantly demanding. London, Paris, and Rome — I have not yet been to Madrid — are among other things pathetic witnesses of the transience of Empire. Empires cannot live in peaceful competition, it seems; but when one finally rises to overwhelming dominance it cannot sustain itself either. Durability lies not in the imposition of power but in submission to the constraints of sustainability, of wanting and using only what can be produced and replaced at home.

The City is what we've come to observe from within, and the question I keep asking is whether The City doesn't represent the nut of the human problem. We need to live communally, apparently; there are so many delights in community. In the last few weeks we've been to concerts and museums and theaters and restaurants, here and at home, whose existence simply requires a prosperous community. And the subtler delights, requiring leisure and education to appreciate, perhaps require that larger class of workers willing to make them possible — the dishwashers, the taxi drivers, the janitors; but also technicians in generating plants, engineers supervising water distribution networks, government administrators and the like.

You walk down an old street faced with 16th-century buildings and notice someone in a jumpsuit poking a screwdriver into the nest of wires behind a set of doorbells. The telephones work, the ATMs spit out money, the streets are lit (and beautifully!) because of people like him. Does he care if the concert of recent chamber music is well programmed, or well played, or well attended? It's all very well to concede that the discernment of this music is analogous of the wires behind those doorbells, or the intelligence that wiring represents, but does that finally serve Empire, or even the simple sustainability of a civil society?

The concert was night before last, in the University, by an active group founded twenty years ago by our friend Marcello, and much of the music was really quite fascinating (to the point that it suggested I get back to work myself!). The concert hall was in one of Mussolini's university buildings, with travertine walls detailing the precise clarity of the acoustics, and a fine big mural behind the musicians showing workers and scientists and, yes, militarism all contributing to an ideal fascist society. I was introduced to Petrassi's widow, a fine handsome woman in a fine handsome fur; and to the conductor of an affecting piece, for children's voices, setting aspiring passages from Jonah, Pinocchio, and *The Divine Comedy*.

Afterwards we all five of us bundled into Marcello's little car and he dropped us off at a trendy pizzeria up near the Borghese, the only place still open in this fashionable part of town near the Piazza del Populo. We had pretty good pizza and then grabbed a cab to cross the river to Trastevere. We dropped Richard and Marta off at their hotel, not far from St. Peter's, and then went on down to our quarter, considerably less aspiring in its architecture, its streets, its shops.

It was well after midnight. The narrow pedestrian streets around our piazza were alive with crowds, young people for the most part, some children even, dogs, students, eating at pizzerias and cafes, walking about talking about things. The vitality is really quite amazing, and, somehow, reassuring. The City I like is a city of continuing present, not aspiring future. It's here in Trastevere, I think, not in the ruins.

We took the bus today, oh boy

S. Egidio, January 16—

I WROTE SYMPATHETICALLY last time about the common man and his indispensable place in society. Yesterday we took the bus to Tivoli and back. It made the trip from Barstow to Bakersfield — was it really only a little over two weeks ago? — look like a picnic.

We caught the infamous Bus H at the Piazza Belli. The letter "H" is never sounded in Italian, and the bus H should never be seen. And in fact it rarely is seen, especially when you're waiting for it; and when it did arrive it was unspeakably full.

I did finally get a seat. A young man took one look at my grizzled head and offered it — the seat, I mean — to me, out of courtesy or perhaps contempt, I thought at first, but it quickly became clear he simply didn't want to sit there. In front of me was a family right out of that horrible old Italian movie *Brutto, Sporco, e Cattivo* (Ugly, Dirty, and Bad), a disgustingly crude man standing gripping the stanchion, his fatigued and resentful wife, and three wretched kids, all under six, all disfigured by varying degrees of dirt, neglect, impetigo, and bred-in wary meanness.

The man, in his thirties I suppose, amused himself grabbing his wife's nose with his right hand and threatening to put out her right eye with the index finger of his left. She moaned and complained. The kids squirmed and coughed. The man sneezed, never covering his mouth. It was probably a blessing he had no handkerchief to drag out of a pocket; he would have flourished it about and made matters worse.

Finally we pulled up at the end of the line, at the train station, and I got off as quickly as I could, so quickly I left my hat behind. They of course were quick to seize any opportunity: the man called out to me *Hai lasci cappelino*, Ya left yer cap. I looked back at the crowded bus. *Il piccolo luporta*, he added, The kid's bringin' it. I took it from the kid and thanked him. The father held out his hand for a tip. I dug out a twenty-cent piece, the only change I had, and carefully gave it to the kid, who immediately put a strong fist around it, then plunged it into a pocket. The father cuffed the kid, shouting at him to thank me.

Then he turned to me and asked for more. You can't even buy an ice-cream with that, he said. The kid looked at me aggressively. I turned on my heel and left the pack of them behind and we all went to the metro station for the next leg of the trip.

The Rome metro is pretty clean and efficient, disregarding its route which is conceived for Rome commuters, not tourists. We got out to the end of the line reasonably soon, and waited only five or ten minutes for the bus that would complete our trip out to Tivoli. And it too was reasonably clean and efficient, for a local bus; it lumbered along the highway past an appalling stretch of discount stores, auto agencies, apartment-house complexes, warehouses, light industry, and all the other blights great cities tuck away on their margins. Venice has its Mestre; Paris its beyond-the-beltway Zones; why should Rome be any different.

At one point the bus travelled a sort of causeway across a stone quarry, an amazing and depressing sight perhaps a half-mile square and at least sixty feet deep. It was white as, well, as marble; its floor was flat as a pancake; the squared-off walls looked as if they'd been constructed of masonry; and where they bounded the quarry you could see how thick the soil above it was, under the scrappy lawns and gardens of benighted suburban houses perched right next this enormous dig.

I have no idea how old this quarry is, but I'd guess some of it goes back quite a way. There's an unbelievable amount of tufa, limestone, marble, travertine, porphyry, and granite in this city, and it's logical that most of it came from as near as possible: even slave labor must have cost something, and this stuff is heavy. It's true that a considerable amount of stone came from North Africa and Egypt, and some fine marble from Greece. But when you see the amount of stone in Rome, and consider that much of even Ancient Rome was built on landfill, or had sliced the tops off hills, you're aware of the incredible amounts that had to be brought in.

The history of mankind is among other things the history of material being dug out of the ground only to be piled up elsewhere. I've often though a wonderful film could be made following one stone from its formation millennia ago through its various locations and uses throughout human history. This could be depressing, of course: many statues were burnt, even in Imperial Rome, to make slaked lime for concrete; many buildings were knocked down and the fragments turned into landfill. The Colosseum is built on a city dump which itself had filled in a marsh.

We took the bus and metro on an outing to Tivoli, there to see the ruins of a couple of Roman temples and the garden at the Villa d'Este. There's not much point in going out to Tivoli for only half a day; I wouldn't do it again: the town needs a couple of days: one should spend the night. But we had time to wander up the main street to the far end of town, where the temples were, have lunch, and spend a long hour in the garden afterward.

Lunch was at the Sibilla, named for the prophetess whose temple was just outside the dining room. Lunch wasn't bad, though the green beans had been cooked long ahead of time, perhaps for another occasion. The restaurant would after all be forgiven for resting on its fame; there are plaques — in chiseled marble, of course — noting previous illustrious customers going back two centuries or more; writers, poets, composers, but mostly heads of state — princes and princesses, kings and queens from Japan, Africa, the European nations. (Our presidents were notably absent.)

The garden was marvelous. We were very nearly alone in it, and we walked at our leisure down the back-and-forth side aisles admiring the many fountains; then along the paths of the lowest terrace astonished at the ancient trees; then back up the center in the gathering twilight, taking up conversation with two gardeners who were clearly ready to end their workday — the place closes at twilight — but generous with time and talk, explaining various things, how long the chestnut withes of the retaining walls last (ten years), why the garden is no longer illuminated (broke down in 1985, no money to fix it), and confirming our guesses that yes the garden is laid out to make a special effect on the equinoxes and yes that is St. Peter's there on the horizon.

The sunset was memorable. First the sun stood behind a single large cloud, throwing its shadow up into the sky above to make a luminous goblet in the air; then it descended slowly to touch the horizon, then more quickly. It was dead quiet. The cypresses and pines were black. We didn't say much.

We did on the bus back, though; it was trapped for many minutes in a terrible traffic jam. It would move perhaps three or four feet, then stop for five minutes. People were both angry and resolutely resigned. I asked the guy ahead of me if this were normal, Yes, of course it's normal, it happens every day, there are all these people getting off work, going out shopping, it all happens at the same time, it's tied up for five kilometers, it takes hours to get through it.

The bus was a few feet from a bus stop, and two or three people were waiting to get off. Open, open, a woman shouted up to the driver, but he did not open, open the door. Her telephone rang. What do you mean where am I, I'm on the bus, she said, in Italian of course, and she said a lot more too that I didn't get. The bus moved a foot or so, then stopped again. After quite a while her phone rang again. What do you mean where am I, I'm still on the bus, it's at the stop, no he won't open the door.

Finally enough ease for the bus to slide over to the curb, open the doors, let the people off. And then miraculously the way was clearer, and we inched our way past the woman, running up the sidewalk, telephone to her ear.

We were about seven hours on buses and subways for the four hours spent in Tivoli. We realized how insular we'd been these last two weeks, walking, strolling really, in what is oddly a very quiet Rome, quiet at least in the neighborhoods we've chosen for the most part. Of course it's crowded in the shopping streets, but many of them have been pedestrianized. Rome has very few boulevards, and we try to stay away from them.

We walked today around, but not into, the Palatine, ending at San Clemente over near the Colosseum, and taking our lunch up at the Ostaria Nerone on the advice of one of our guidebooks (which got the telephone number wrong, but was otherwise right). It's Friday, so Lindsey and I had salt cod, and with it a buttery-soft but nicely textured artichoke, and the four of us had a fine Ceretto Dolcetto, and I had a delicious ricotta cake. And then a cab up to the Museum of Contemporary Art, closed of course; and then a long wait for a nonexistent bus to the Piazza di Spagna, and a walk down the Condotti, and an experimental Martini (Italian vermouth is not really dry, even when it's white and says it is, and the man put only a tiny splash of gin into it, and garnished it with a slice of lemon), and then a walk across the river to the Piazza Cavour and a bus back to our apartment to eat in tonight: some coppa on levain bread Richard had borrowed from his hotel breakfast for us, a couple of big salads, and that pleasant cheap white wine that comes unlabeled from the plaza greengrocer.

If you stay off the buses it's a pleasant life.

Rome from the Quirinale

Martinis in Rome

S. Egidio, January 17—

THIS IS THE CENTRAL DAY of our stay in Rome. The first week, as I look back at it, was a matter of getting settled. See here a movie process shot: dog turning himself round and round, nose following tail, atavistically beating down the long grasses to make a nest in which to be comfortable. That's basically what we did.

Then a weekend in Orvieto, and then a week with two dear friends who'd come all the way down from Verona to be with us. With them we've walked the streets, poked into a few churches and museums, auditioned a few restaurants, filled a few wine bottles with the local air, talked and talked.

Tonight was the celebratory dinner for that, at least as far as I'm concerned; tomorrow we'll have another day, perhaps seeing some more museums if the weather's gloomy, or walking in the Aventine if it's not, in any case cementing further a friendship, recalling visits years ago, marveling at our different takes on the proper way to investigate a museum, wondering why one person likes Picasso and another Matisse (substitute here Joyce and Lawrence, Schubert and Schumann, veal and beef, *puntarelli* and *spinace*), kidding one another about weaknesses or enthusiasms, helping one another on our common paths to... but enough of that.

What I really want to tell you about tonight is Martinis. I like, as some of you know, to have a Martini on Friday and Saturday evening. I think enough about the subject to capitalize it. Yesterday was Friday, the third one of this trip. I'd missed it last week, and the week before we were just arriving, not a chance we'd go out looking for a drink. But yesterday we were in a very fashionable quarter, walking away from the Piazza di Spagna, and we stopped in at one of those storefronts with the promising, if backward, sign on it. It was Martini time.

Lindsey said she'd have a glass of Sherry. Richard and Marta said they'd have, let's see, a coffee, no, Marta changed her mind. I asked for a Martini. We were standing at the bar at the back of the cafe: at the front was a coffee-counter with a few pastries and the like; at the back where we were was a real bar.

I looked up at the bottles on the shelves behind the bar. On the right-hand side were a number of bottles of various wines and vermouths: yes, among the four or five different Martini & Rossi bottles there was a "dry Italian bianco" vermouth. And yes, among the bottles in the section to the left, where the Johnny Walker and the rums and the grappas were, there was a bottle that might have been gin. But you couldn't be sure, because its back was decorously turned to the room.

Martini, signor, the barman said politely, *Martini e Rossi? Mezzo-mezzo?* No, I said, also politely, *Martini cocktail, con gin, per favore*, pointing to the bottle I suspected of having gin in it. He looked at me curiously. Gin, I repeated, *e vermut, tre di gin, uno di vermut*. He looked at me a little more closely.

And, I said, um, *hayrez, Jerez*, sherry. *Avete Lei di Sherry?* By now he was beginning to look a little disconsolate, as if he were wondering why he'd transferred here from some more comfortable job elsewhere. *No*, he said uncertainly, *mi dispiace*, I'm sorry.

I reported the bad news to Lindsey, who thought it over. What's that artichoke aperitif called, she asked me, asked Richard, asked Marta. Carciofo, I said, and turned to the barman: *Avete Lei di carciofo?* He was more reluctant than ever. *No, signor, mi dispiace.* Okay, I said, resorting to one of the universal languages, *per me un Martini, per la signora un bitter.* Any bitter.

He reeled out a number of brand names and I seized on one of them, Montenegro. By now Marta was interested in bitters, and she too stipulated one, a Ramazzotti I think. Richard was gone off looking for that room he always hides in at such moments.

Barman got out glasses and got down bottles and began pouring, looking at me out of the side of his unnecessarily round face, as I thought it. *Martini*, he said to me, a little uncertainly. *Si*, I said, *Martini, con gin, tre parte gin, una parta Martini bianco.*

We looked at one another steadily for a few moments, and then he kindly requested me to sit down at the little table where the others already were. I think I'd made him nervous. I know he'd made me nervous. I explained to my friends, Lindsey included, that I wanted to watch him make it, not because I was concerned that he do it properly, but out of pure intellectual curiosity as to what he might be doing.

Martinis in Rome

Why did you order a Martini, Lindsey asked with sweet adversariality, we're here in Italy, why didn't you ask for something Italian. What, I responded with swift wit but certain self-destruction, like a sherry, you mean. I did ask for something Italian. I asked for a Martini as it would be made in Italy. You have to appreciate my sense of experiment, of investigation.

Three usual sorts of drinks arrived soon enough at our marble table, three usual glasses and one anomaly. My Martini was in a big green plastic glass with a logo on it: Yoga.

Inside was the damnedest thing I've tasted. Once when our youngest daughter Giovanna was younger than she is today I told her what the perfect Martini was, and she got it wrong, and made me one that was three parts vermouth to one part gin. This was a little like that, except that there was a certain amount of water in it, and a nice slice of lemon, and the whole thing was in this plastic glass with a couple of modest ice-cubes doing a sort of dead-man's float in the whole apparatus. There was not much to appreciate, visually, on the palate, or in the nose. Everyone thought it a good joke, and we ate the potato chips, and I managed to make the best of whatever you might call the drink, and we walked on.

Tonight we ate at what I think was the best restaurant so far, but I won't describe it; I'll save the restaurants for a sort of supplement, except to note that its incongruous name was Paris. But that's not tonight's point: Tonight's point is that we waited for Richard and Marta, who were walking down from their hotel a few hundred meters north of here on the same side the Tiber, in the bar-cafe downstairs from our apartment, the Ombre Rosse.

Ombre Rosse means Red Shadows, and the term means red wine, cheap I suppose red wine, the red wine of poet's muses and young romance. But that is not what we had, Lindsey and I. It was Saturday night, and she had a Frascati Superiore — because, she said, she wanted to know what a superior one would taste like, after all the ordinary ones we've been drinking — and I had a Martini.

You're a glutton for punishment, Lindsey said. No, I said, it's a matter of intellectual curiosity; it's investigation. Suppose I write a travel article about Martinis in Rome: I'll want to have done some research, even if I am a journalist of sorts.

We waited for quite a while. The Ombre Rosse was full, as it always is at eight o'clock, or from then until midnight; it's a trendy place, a café serving all kinds of drinks and coffees and also light meals. The bar menu had long lists of wines by the bottle, by the glass, cocktails including my Martini and a few siblings (vodka, with weird juices, etc.); and also a number of tropical drinks; even a number of variations on the Caipirinha, Julio will be glad to know. (But the Caipirinha was the most expensive of all, no doubt because of the labor involved.)

Ultimately Richard and Marta appeared, and then so did our drinks. The Martini came in a beautiful glass of the correct size and shape, its stem flaring elegantly into its angular cup. The olive was green and had its pit and did not put fake anchovy or pimento flavors into the affair. The gin was present but not overwhelming; the vermouth was Italian and subtle and ingratiating; there wasn't a hint of water let alone ice; the drink was cold as justice and fragrant as a baby's cheek.

Afterward I went to the bar and told the fellow what I thought of it, and this Friday, God willing, I'll be back.

Jazz in the basement
S. Egidio, January 18—

WELL, NOT REALLY JAZZ in the basement; it was on the ground floor, but in the Ombre Rosse which serves as our own ground floor, or at least the little ten-table dining room does where the jazz was. I read about it in *Repubblica* today — the first paper I've bought in a while; it was a lucky coincidence — and after walking Richard and Marta up to their hotel in a gentle rain, to see them off in a 3:30 taxicab to catch their 4 pm train back to Verona, and after walking back home in the mist under the sycamores alongside the Tiber, and after doing the laundry for the first time, and after resting up a bit, I went down to see what the action was.

I like the Ombre Rosse, and not only because it gave me a perfect Martini last night. It reminds me of San Francisco fifty years ago. Inside the front door is the bar, running down the left-hand side, with three or four cafe tables scattered about; off to the right, at the back, is the dining room, with perhaps ten tables.

The walls are a sort of ochre color, quite clean; the place is well lit; there are lots of paintings on the walls that remind me of the Beat paintings of the 1950s, though they're sunnier, more lyrical. The place was full, but there was a seat at the bar, so I took it and asked for a white wine, which came with a couple of canapés and a small bowl of peanuts, and before I'd dented any of that a table emptied in the dining room right in front of the combo, so in I went.

In front of me Elisabetta Antonini perched on a high stool with a microphone in her hand, scatting her way through a Gershwin song, accompanied by guitar and contrabass — electric guitar, acoustic bass. She was damned good and as soon as there was a break I stepped outside to telephone Lindsey to come down, then quickly went back in to reclaim my seat.

What a pleasure to hear good jazz, especially vocal jazz, in a small room, sitting right up close to the music! Lindsey arrived in the middle of the first song of the second set, "My Funny Valentine," which Antonini introduced in a quietly spoken short talk referring to Chet Baker; and she quoted some of his version of the classic in her performance. There was a bit of formula to the trio: she would sing the chorus of each song, with standard chord-and-bass backing; then usually break into scat-singing for an extended second chorus.

Then the guitarist took over, often reminding me of George Shearing's guitarist — modest, unexciting, but very pleasant indeed — and then the bassist, who was capable of really quite impressive extended improvisations, always in tune, always suggesting the beat. (The beat was left to the imagination, of course; this trio has no drums.) Then Antonina would return for a closing chorus, but sometimes this would be quite distorted — deliberately, of course — or lapse into further scat-singing; and sometimes the group would sidetrack into a long coda, often wandering off into an unrelated key before coming back to order.

She sang standards — But Not For Me; Valentine; stuff like that. She's rather small, dark hair, say late twenties, dark sweater, jeans; and she sang with understated facial expression and gesture. Her English sounded pretty good, but she spoke only Italian as far as I could hear, to members of the audience congratulating her afterward, and to her guitarist and bassist when they occasionally consulted between numbers.

We sat for an hour or so nursing our wine — a nicely full-bodied one from Sardinia — and nodding our heads and occasionally pointing a finger to her complex rhythms; and then we went up to our apartment for a salad and some Pecorino, and then out to the Piazza S. Maria, around the corner, for an ordinary but quite acceptable gelato, the place we'd intended to try being closed this Sunday evening.

It was an uneventful day. We'd had dinner at midday, or nearly so, at home: semolina gnocchi Lindsey had whipped up a couple of days ago, and salad, and pastries, and a bottle of Sangiovese, and coffee — a farewell dinner for Richard and Marta, who've entertained us the last week. The laundromat was the other entertainment for the day, figuring out how to trade euros for tokens, watching the clothes tumble, talking to the kid who runs the place — whose English is fluent and American-accented because, it turned out, he is an American, though he's been here for five years. The whole area here in Trastevere seems to be bilingual; eavesdropping on the strolling couples in the streets you hear both English and Italian, either often accented by the other, and it doesn't seem to matter which language you start out in.

There's a considerable police presence. There's always a police car parked outside the Ombre Rosse, next to the movie theater, and there're always two cops sitting in it. Around the corner in S Maria tonight there were the usual two, a squad car and a sort of mobile police office; and a couple of other squad cars cruised the piazza while we stood eating our gelati.

Across the river the police presence is even greater. Carabiniere are stationed at the corners of the block taken up by the Synagogue, and often they stand with their fingers on the triggers, which makes me a little nervous — I recall too easily the night six or eight squad cars converged on me in San Francisco, and the cops jumped out and threw me against the wall, ordered me to raise my hands and to remain absolutely still, then asked for my identification, confusing me as to what to do, all the while pointing guns at me. It's a scary experience: but I suppose we should be grateful for their protection.

The newspapers are full of stories about the primaries. All of Italy knows more than I do about the intricacies of the Iowa Caucus, and frequent news stories assure us that the Democrats haven't a chance: they're a party without vision, without money, without leadership. It's curious to read about American politics in terms of a Christian Right and a Center Left. I get the feeling that Europe, or certainly Italy, is perplexed at the drift of our country toward monarchy. And of course Italy has its own national crises; Berlusconi has just been robbed of his ex post facto law exonerating him for fraud or whatever it is his citizens object to in his character, and the Parmalat affair rivals our Enron case, and children are demonstrating against reductions in school hours, and last night the Piazza S. Maria was full of milling eco-bicyclists protesting automobile traffic and its attendant pollution.

We have a little more than two weeks left, and two years of sight-seeing to do. Our pace will quicken now that we're on our own. We came for companionship, of course; we have friends here and wanted long conversations and leisurely walks. But we came for Rome, too, and now it's her turn. And it's time to plan tomorrow's action.

On the Palatine

Always more

S. Egidio, January 19—

RAIN TODAY, OR AT LEAST threatening this morning, so we plan a day carefully, to be maximally indoors. "Maximally" is very Roman; everything here is maximal; maximalism has even infected the words these eight fingers press out of the keyboard, as it has affected my poor ankles, swelling valiantly to absorb the constant pounding against stone floors, the incessant little adjustments to be made against the cobblestones.

Anyway down the Lungaretta to the Via and across the Ponte Garibaldi to the Argentina to hear the youth symphony play Petrassi, Ravel, and — unless we escape it — Tchaikovsky's Violin Concerto. But we are late; no doubt they'll begin the concert with the one thing we want most to hear, the Petrassi. We run into the lobby to find it deserted except for one attendant who directs us to another building to buy tickets — wait — no, that's not right — just a moment — she looks up another attendant: is a ticket needed at this point? Perhaps — the subject's worth a few minutes' discussion — well, no harm in getting one — we duck out into the light rain to the next building and into the ticket counter, where we are informed that yes indeed we're a little late, the concert was yesterday, we've lost another day of our lives.

But we've gained an hour. What to do with it? And not only has it stopped raining, the sun's breaking through: so we walk up the Via Corso, that long straight road laid out two thousand years ago, then revived five hundred years ago for a racetrack. Jew races, hunchback races, cripple races, naked old man races. When I mention that last one Lindsey gives me a funny little look; I can see her seeing me whipped into line with all the other naked old men. The thought is not pleasing.

I duck into a bookstore for a final definitive assault on one of my few projects here: to buy a copy of Picciardi's *Dizionario della gastronomia*, which some lying lazy clerk guessed the other day must be out of print, since he couldn't find it on the shelf. Here at Feltrice, a definitive bookstore, I consult a clerk whose bespectacled appearance projects quiet competence, even authority: she will know where to find it. She looks at the computer, finds the title quickly: *ah no signor, e definitivamente esauro.*

Esauro and *restauro*, the twin terrors of the Italian vocabulary: out of print and in restoration. Every book I want to buy is *esauro*; every site I want to see is in *restauro*. We go on, like characters in a Beckett novel; we go on.

We go on to ice cream, to be exact, because we find ourselves in front of Giolitti, famous for its gelato. We could eat lunch here, but it seems a little early, and I'm not in the mood for what looks like a humdrum sandwich in a glorious setting. But the gelati look fabulous, and I have the usual, a scoop each of *crema* and *fior di latte* — wait — they have *riso*! Rice-flavored ice cream is a hobby of mine, so I substitute it for the *crema*, and the *fior* here is not *di latte*, milk, but *di panna*, cream. But then we decide against it: it's too early: we'll come back later.

We go on as far as the piazza della colonna and then turn south as I want a coffee. This is another project: to sample as many coffees as possible always with the object of confirming my prejudice against Illy and Pavel's preference for Tazza d'Oro. The Pantheon is nearby, and with it Tazza d'Oro. En route we realize we are hungry. In my pocket are lists of many restaurants to try, but none is near enough; we pass a trattoria in whose window a family is eating; a bored little girl looks wistfully through the glass at us; I make a mental note. Rome is full of omens, or at least I find it so; and no omens are more, well, ominous than birds and children. I suppose I should include cats as well: all three species are full of life and enigmatic intelligence; they move unpredictably but are capable of long periods of motionlessness; they are somehow comforting in the concept but often abrupt and unsettling in the moment.

Tazza d'Oro is as perfect as ever, in every way. The coffee itself is dark and deep, redolent on the palate; it speaks of latitudes nearer the equator, of a slower tempo. So many coffees are merely assertive, even nerve-wracking; Tazza d'Oro is more supportive in character, like that rare friend with whom one never argues, whose tastes and interests are always in parallel with one's own. I ask if it can be bought by mail; of course it can, on the Internet: the URL is www.tazzadorocoffeeshop.com. I will persevere in my project;

there are many more coffees here to try. And we have a fair amount of Lavazza Rosso in the kitchen to finish, so I don't buy any Tazza d'Oro at the moment. But I'll be back.

Time now for lunch — we seem to be doing everything backward today. Back to La Scaletta, then. The little girl is now sleeping and her parents and uncle, if that's the configuration, are lingering over their coffees. Lindsey and I are the only other diners; it's only one o'clock. Big high-ceilinged room, tables covered with green plaid tablepapers, a simple but extensive menu. I'll have a *spaghetti carbonara* here, Lindsey announces, as a sort of benchmark against which to judge other places. I adopt the same strategy to a *saltimbocca*, and we order water and wine (white for her, red for me), and there follows a perfectly ordinary, perfectly satisfactory twentyfivedollar lunch a few steps from the greatest building ever conceived.

That would be Hadrian's Pantheon, of course, which we visited the other day. It isn't raining, still, so we don't go in again; one of the luxuries of being here a whole month is walking past the Pantheon without going in. We go instead to the Galleria Pamphilj, whose final long "i" always delights me, and spend too much time gawking at too much art — paintings hung in tiers of three and four; statues and urns; a 17th-century harp; velvets and parquet; gilt tables and satin-brocade chairs. Lindsey listens to an Acoustiguide; I saunter, a little unwillingly, hands in pockets.

There's always more, always more. We finally emerge and it is now definitively raining and we don't have umbrellas. Time to go home. Toward the Argentina a fellow steps up with a number of umbrellas and an irresistible smile. *Quanti costa*, I ask, Five euro, he replies, instantly knowing my language. I take one, unsheathe it, press the button, unfurl the thing, inspect it, hand it to Lindsey. I give the man his five euro. Where you from, he asks with genuine interest and friendliness, London? No, I say, California. Where are you from? Bangladesh, he says.

I met your cousin last week, I tell him, Selling garlic in Trastevere. Oh yes, he smiled happily, That could be him. What about you? He's genuinely concerned that the one small umbrella will leave me in the rain. I embrace my sweet wet Roman matron to demonstrate that we can share it, and his smile lights up the entire

Argentina.

We jump on the streetcar, ride two stops, and jump off. We'll have to backtrack a little to buy groceries, but it's stopped raining seriously. Our stores turn out to be closed, though — it's Monday afternoon — so we go home to watch a little television, read a little more, and eat an inspired meal Lindsey manages to put together:

> *bread and Pecorino*
> *antipasto*
> *Sangiovese*
> *pears*

The antipasto, as we always call it, is Lindsey's grandmother's recipe: a jar of pickled little vegetables (*giardinera*), a can of tuna, a squeeze of tomato paste from the tube; and preferably a day or two in the refrigerator. It's delicious.

The television is about elections, in Iraq and Iowa, two four-letter words beginning with "I," I can't help noticing. I'm reading Eleanor Clark's essay on Hadrian's Villa, because we plan to go out there again one of these days, and I run across one of her felicitous sentences, in which she's comparing Hadrian's compulsive building with those follies of 19th-century American eccentrics — think Mrs Winchester:

"The main thing is to keep building, for one's very point of rest to be always in motion, a thrusting out of the ailing ego which must have recognition and more and more is forced to make it for itself, in its own empyrean; if it stopped building its own temple it would die."

And Bush's man Frist tells us the State of the Union address will be upbeat and positive, that we are moving forward; and I realize again that our own country is imperial and a folly; the United States today finds its point of rest always in motion; that we are always after more, because to be content and stable and sustainable is somehow monotonous and certainly no way to make money.

We are lucky to be in on this glorious decadent period, though, in a way; we're able as have few been in history to see where we are, poised between the glories of the Renaissance, or the Age of Reason, or Modernism, and the chaos that has already begun to engulf those glories, and is perhaps their inevitable result.

But in the meantime we have several ice creams to try, and I'll try to report on them soon.

Vicolo del Cedro

How we eat

S. Egidio, January 20—

ACTUALLY THERE ARE TWO things on my mind tonight, I mean two that are pushy enough to shove their way to my fingertips, one is what I've written above, How we eat, the other is the difference between seen-from-above and seen-straight-ahead.

(There's a third one, noticed when I typed that date above: time is growing short, we have only two weeks left, there's a lot to be covered... but the hell with that.)

I spend a lot of time looking at a plastic map of central Rome, inconveniently divided between This Side and The Other Side. Whatever I want is most likely on the other side. Occasionally it's even worse, it's exactly on the divider. This map, one of those Streetwise things, gives a little bit of overlap. But still.

Then there's the problem of finding things in indexes. We have about nineteen hundred guidebooks here. I wish I could recommend one: so far I can't. One of the irritations is the indexes. Say you want to look up a church: is it under "Church," or "Chiesa," or "S." (for San, or Santa)? Is it under the name of the saint for whom the church is named? Most indexes settle on one system or another and maintain it fairly consistently, but I can never remember which book does it which way.

And the street names. Typically a street in Rome is either a Via or a Viale or maybe a Vicolo; all three are abbreviated "v." If the street is widening out a bit it might be a Largo, or it might be a Piazza. If it gets elephantiasis it turns into a Piazzale. There is even one Campo, the Campo de' Fiori, or is it dei Fiori?

In any case, after Via or Piazza or whatever you come to the actual name of the street. If you're lucky it's a single word, like Via Aurelia, or Viale Glorioso. But more likely it's either someones' name, like Via Nicola Fabrizii — I'm taking all these at random, from just one side of Streetwise — or perhaps a date, like Via 4 Novembre. Well then of course you have to wonder, will it be indexed by the guy's last name or his first name, which I generally call (because I was so brought up) his Christian name, and that generally works here. Or, if it's a date, will it be indexed by the month, I hope, or by the day; and in that case will the date be spelled out Quattro, or listed numerically 4.

And then there are the streets whose names are preceded by prepositions, like the via della Scala that leads to our Piazza Sant' Egidio.

But all this is beside the point, which is that I spend a lot of time looking at the Map, Seen From Above (and that schematically, it need hardly be pointed out) and trying to translate it, for two reasons at least, into what I learned in a logic course at San Francisco State was a very different thing, the Territory, Seen Straight Ahead. I do this partly because I'm concerned about distances — one wants to get there as efficiently as possible, by now, because Time Is Growing Short. And partly because I'm curious about terrain: there are after all seven famous hills in this city, and a few more that are generously uncounted, and they interfere with all sorts of things.

And partly because with a very few exceptions there are no streets that go in a straight line if they can possibly avoid it, and they can.

All that is Reason One. Reason Two is not practical at all; it's much more important than that: it's emotional. I know that it's unlikely I'll do this again, spend a month here I mean, and I want to have it all as fully in mind as I can. Ideally I would carry a videocamera with me and catch every day's itinerary, as hopelessly chaotic and improvised as it is, so that later I could savor the thing, not that I would of course; life is so full of living there's never much reason or time or inclination to re-live any of it. But I do want later to be able to look at the goddam map and see the goddam straight-ahead view, if you see what I mean; to see in my mind's eye the facade of this church or that, this piazza or that, so that when I look at the map — or read an address in a Henry James novel, or an issue of *Gourmet*, or on a travel mailing-list website — I'll be able to recall this magical month.

But all that's beside the real point here, which is that I expect that by now some of you will be curious as to How We Eat.

Today after breakfast — the usual: coffee from the little stovetop espresso pot, hot milk, toast, juice — we went out shopping. There's a small market three piazzas away, which is about three normal city blocks, maybe four. It's January, so not all the stalls are open; a lot of people close down for a few weeks after Epiphany. But we have maybe four or five vegetable stands, two fish, two meat, one cheese, one pots and pans, one ceramic items, and one miscellaneous household (where we buy toilet paper, for example).

Here we bought stuff for tonight's dinner: a small head of *romesco* or whatever it's called — that spiral leaf-green thing that's neither broccoli nor cauliflower — a bag of *puntarelle*, a couple of blood oranges, and some fennel. The latter was an afterthought. Let's look at these last two stands, I said; Oh, Lindsey said, we have to buy some of this fennel, look at the man who's selling it. He was tall, handsome, had been ruddy and blond in the Venetian manner, and had a good many of his teeth. He wore a red-and-white baseball cap. He was the cheerfullest man in the market, I thought, and that was saying something, as there were a good many cheerful people there.

We did not buy any meat, though the pork chops, the veal, and the rib-eye looked good. We had after all bought a couple of delicious chicken breasts there a week or so ago. But it seems likely we'll be eating at a few restaurants in the next two weeks, and that'll be the logical place for meat; it's too much trouble cleaning up after a broil in our apartment.

But I do want to write something here about the meat-counters in the market: they seem absolutely clean and attractive. Of course it's winter; there's no hot sun, no flies, no mosquitos. Even so I think the market would be neat and clean. You do of course see whole animals; there were several whole lambs on one counter, hardly larger than a toy poodle (though much more attractive to me!), heads hooves and all.

The other day someone was fretting about this on a travel website I happened across. I'd forgotten that we simply don't see whole carcasses at butcher-shops any more. Americans eat meat, but take their meat from small Styrofoam trays; it doesn't look like part of an animal, it looks like part of a dinner, like sliced cheese, or packages of something. I think that if you're going to eat meat you should be reminded it's an animal.

And then in the last few days we've seen so many paintings and sculptures of carcasses, human ones, or semidivine; men and women who have been steamed, or boiled in oil, or grilled on an iron (we saw St. Laurence's gridiron just yesterday), or nailed up, or hacked apart. It seems you can't be Christian unless you dwell on these things; and Christians are conventionally carnivores, except on Fridays; it's logical that they be reminded of mortality; transubstantiation depends on it.

Oh well. On the way home we stopped in at the local *pastaficio*, a tiny place dominated by the refrigerated counter housing *strozzapreti*, ravioli, *raviolini*, gnocchi, *malfatti*, *penne*, and three or four other things, all made by hand (and a single small electric rolling-out machine) in an adjacent room, glassed over so there could be no secrets.

I was attracted first by a hand-lettered sign on the door: *Pace si; no alle guerre*. Peace yes; no to wars. Then I was attracted by a jar of honey that could only have come from Sardinia, and I noticed a bottle of Sardinian wine on a shelf. *Tutti qui viene di Sardegna*, I asked; yes, it's all Sard; *Perchè*, I asked, because we are Sard, the nice lady answered. So we bought some raviolini stuffed with mushrooms.

Further along the short way home we went into the local CRAI mini-super, where we bought a bottle of water and a bottle of milk; and then I stopped into the greengrocer on our own piazza, guilty at not having bought vegetables from him, and got a bottle of the white wine from Campania we drink, light and a little spritzy and very cheap.

And then it was out for the day's touring, which I won't bore you with. Well, a little: we spent the afternoon at S. Giovanni Laterano, the mother church of the Christian world, looking at marvelous mosaics, a fragment of a Giotto fresco, a delightful cloister, and an impressive baptistry going back to Roman times. What am I saying? They're ALL Roman times: I mean paleochristian times.

Lunch was at a little dive, the Fly Bar (God knows why so called), a ham sandwich for L., a *tortellini in ragù* for me with a glass of red wine, and a bottle of water and a coffee; €12.50 altogether, and worth all of it and no more.

And then back for more sight-seeing, and home to fix dinner. Lindsey made a favorite of ours, slicing peeled blood oranges thin, intercalating them with thinly sliced raw onion, and dressing them with oil, salt, pepper, and vinegar. Then we had the raviolini with just oil and fresh-ground pepper and a little salt. Then we had salad, the puntarelle and a half a small radicchio tossed with vinaigrette *ma façon*, as the French would say. And with it a slice of bread, and most of the bottle of white wine.

Puntarelle are, as far as I can see, the base and stem of chicory heads, the leaves all removed leaving only the stems, those then slit vertically into very fine fingers all still attached at the base, and the whole machine put into ice water to make it curl and stay firm. There isn't a trace of bitterness. It's crisp, firm, bright — a little like celery without the celery flavor but with considerable lettuce flavor. Mixed with sliced radicchio (which lends the needed foil of bitterness) it's absolutely wonderful, and the oil and garlic, the salt and vinegar only push the whole thing into high relief, like the fine carvings we saw in the cloister.

Like what I hope will happen, ultimately, to *Streetwise Rome*.

Cold weather

S. Egidio, January 22—

THE OLD WOMAN at the tram-stop was in a swivet, and who could blame her. We were waiting for the #3 to Circo Massimo, because that's the closest Metro stop. We'd taken the #8 down to the #3, because we were a little bit lazy, and a little bit more in a hurry. We're spending the day at Hadrian's Villa, and there's no time to lose, and it's already eleven in the morning — it takes time to get started, you have to make coffee, make phone calls, make appointments; and then, we tend not to get started until past eight o'clock; it's so nice to snuggle down for an extra half-hour.

The old woman in the swivet has noticed that three #3 trams have gone by the other way, but none has come back our way. Further, we've all noticed that each of the last six trams to come our way was a #8. What can this mean? The #8 has only three or four stops to go before it comes to the Argentina, the end of the line! We've probably seen the same car go by two or three times, in both directions!

The old woman mutters, then complains, then expostulates. This requires a good deal of arm-waving, and she's right to do it. Each arm goes out away from the shoulder: she is expressive. The man next to her answers with his right hand, which circles expressively clockwise. A younger woman in a fur agrees, thrusting her chin up and to the right, in the direction all the #8s go, and we expect to go finally on our #3, if it ever comes.

It is COLD! We aren't used to this. At home it gets cold at night, colder than it does here, but it always warms up some once the sun's up, even if the sun's not out, if you see what I mean. Here it's just cold, cold. This has its advantages: the air is clear and it's not raining. But it's hard to deal with.

For one thing our apartment is toasty warm all the time. I'm not sure how it's heated or how the heat is regulated. I could find out; it must be in the house notes our capable landlady has provided; but there's been no need to adjust anything, chiefly because in fact we like it toasty warm.

The trams are warm, too, when they finally show up. But the tram stops are all outside, next to the tramtracks, and they are cold. So you're constantly adjusting things: gloves, scarf, jacket zipper. Most of the people around me do this with considerable grace and panache; I do it clumsy and slow.

It was cold out at Hadrian's Villa, which we spent the day visiting. There was ice on the cobbles, particularly of course in shaded areas; and it wasn't always visible. You have to be careful. Like so many places we've visited Hadrian's Villa is full of staircases and steps. There are quite up-to-date concessions to the handicapped, but they're only in the form of blue plaques pointing out wheelchair routes. These of course bypass all the interesting aspects of the Villa, by which I mean everything except a few gravel paths among the olive trees.

Those areas are pleasant too, of course, but you can have them just about anywhere. What you can't have just about anywhere is Hadrian's Villa. Though even that is not technically true: you can have built it anywhere you want — if you're a Roman Emperor. Our guidebooks go into frenzies of speculation as to why he built it where he did, at the foot of the low mountain on which was, and is, the town of Tivoli. Everyone else built high on the mountain, partly to get above the malaria belt, partly for the view.

Not Hadrian. He bought up cheaper property, not down on the plain but on a low shelf above it, and there he built what was apparently something like San Simeon, something like Palm Springs, something like the Metropolitan Museum. We spent a half day poking around. We'd armed ourselves with a guidebook dedicated expressly to the purpose, but even so we were almost immediately disoriented: it must be the cold.

I wrote last time about my insane desire to be able to translate Seen-From-Above into See-Straight-Ahead. Forget it. Rome exists in four directions, after all, and none of them is easy. I can usually orient myself fairly easily: at noon, my shadow points north. But here at Hadrian's Villa there are so many shadows! The ruins exist in three or sometimes four storeys above ground, and two or three (or God knows how many more) below. All the above-ground ruins cast shadows, and they're cast onto quite rumpled terrain.

There's not a natural hill among the Seven Hills of Rome, nor among the rises, ridges, swales, declivities, hummocks, wallows, or humps of Hadrian's Villa. Everything here, everything for hundreds of miles around, has been leveled, heaped up, hollowed out, filled in, built upon, scooped out, excavated. So much for shadows.

And on top of the three normal dimensions there's that final, exhausting, murderous one: Time. What we walk on has been put on something a thousand years old; and that was put on top of something a thousand years old, and that in turn was put on top of something a thousand years old. Yesterday on the Palatine hill we tried to make sense of some of this. All I wanted to see was Romulus's hut, which was actually identified not too long ago from postholes the archaeologists found, or said they'd found, on top of the hill, or maybe it was under a few layers of hill that later settlers, farmers, builders, developers, emperors, plunderers, and archaeologists had piled on top of the original holes.

I think they exist. There's a model of the whole thing in the Capitoline Museum, and We Have Seen It. That was itself a triumph, just finding the Museum, which was in fact an imperative, as it was pretty likely there would be facilities there, facilities which are otherwise few and far between.

(I'm told there was a day when Rome, like the Paris I used to know, was supplied with reasonably well-distributed public facilities for at least the stronger sex. *Pissotières*, I mean. No longer. There are neither *pissotières* nor those dreadful J.C. Decaux machines that have replaced them in Paris. There are only parked cars in narrow streets. But I digress.)

There is no natural vertical dimension to be found here, except that you know that in general the lower you go the further back in time, unless you're taking the Metro. From our piazza, for example, you walk slightly downhill along the Lungaretta toward the river. Fine; you expect a river to be lower than the city on its banks. But when you get to the river you climb up, of course, because Rome walled the river in, maybe a little over a century ago, to keep it from occasionally flooding the city. So then you cross the bridge and look down on the island, the island we have yet to explore though it's only minutes from home. And on the other side you walk downhill to the temples and the cattle-market that were once on the level of the riverbank and a respectable height above its waters.

I'm a simple guy, I grew up in the country, I expect the terrain to be pretty much as it was before White Man got there and began messing it up. Furthermore I have enough intellectual curiosity to mess me up when I'm trying to deal with things like Rome. So all this confuses me utterly.

Yesterday's plan was simple: Explore the Palatine Hill. Today's ditto: Hadrian's Villa. It would take months and a graduate seminar to scratch the, um, surface, not that the surface has been much more than scratched, of either.

So we take solace in the simple pleasures. Tram, metro, and bus got us out to the Villa in a little over an hour. Then we walked fifteen minutes or so through some town or other, I don't know its name, to the Villa; bought our tickets, and walked another five or ten minutes up a gentle hill to the Villa itself. There we found one the facilities, and a Dutch couple from Amsterdam, who told me what I wanted to know about the current Dutch political situation (prime minister eager but untrained, Queen patient but constitutionally forbidden from ruling) while I waited for someone.

A few hours walking about the ruins, accompanied by a very sweet marmalade-colored cat.

A short half-hour in a corner bar waiting for the bus. (Here we continued our scientific research into Bitters, it being too cold for Gelati. Lindsey had a Ramozzotti, warmed by running steam through it from the espresso machine — thanks, Marta, for that lesson. It was bracing, like a very slightly alcoholic tea. I had a simple Averna. *Normale?* asked the barman, wondering if I wanted it steamed. *Si, normale*, I answered, *perchè io son normale*, because I'm normal. He agreed and poured it out.)

A conversation with the couple seated ahead of us in the bus when it inexplicably turned 180 degrees away from Rome to climb into a tiny village where no one got on the bus or off. Do you know where you're going? he asked me in good American English. Yes, I said, To hell in a handbasket, thanks to my leader. The couple turned out to be from Monterey; he's a waiter in Big Sur; they only come to Italy in January when they can get a vacation.

A longer conversation with the Bus Police who wanted to make sure I had a ticket for the bus. Failure to prove this: €51, which is getting close to $70. My wife has it, I said, shouting at her to come back. She rummaged through her purse for five minutes looking for it. Six bored cops stood around giving one another very big eyes. Then I remembered that I had them; I showed them to the cops; they agreed they were probably valid; we went on.

Dinner at home: rigatoni with oil and pepper and parmesan, salad, Perotti's Dolcetto. And so it goes.

Teatro di Marcello

Speechless
S. Egidio, January 23—

STRUCK DUMB; SPEECHLESS; at a loss for words. Not my usual state. As Rossini says: *freddo ed immobile, come una statua* — cold and motionless, like a statue. It may have been the influence of all those statues we've been seeing; it might very well have been the cold.

But in fact it was the young man who walked up to us purposefully in the portico of S. Maria Maggiore, where we had spent a pleasant hour or more alternately reading fine print in dim light and then gazing at almost splendid mosaics as long as the euro-in-the-slot meter would allow, and who addressed us directly in lightly accented English: Would you mind signing our petition?

I looked at him a full ten seconds without moving. Why was this guy speaking to me in English? Lindsey then answered, something, it didn't register on me, I was still standing cold and motionless, and the young man was clearly enjoying himself.

Where are you from, he went on, California? Northern California? I finally answered him: why are we speaking English? Well, he said, reasonably, you look like you're from San Francisco. Do you know City Lights Books? Of course, I said, everyone knows City Lights Books. You look like Ferlinghetti, he said, are you Lawrence Ferlinghetti?

I detached myself from Ferlinghetti. No, I said; I'm no poet. He seemed a little disappointed. Do you like San Francisco music, he wondered. What would that be, I asked; Jefferson Airplane, Grateful Dead, he answered, his accent thickening up on those words.

I told him that in fact I had known Phil Lesh in the old days, and his eyes widened; I think he began to think I was lying about not being Ferlinghetti.

We signed the petition, which was against AIDS and for human rights, and put a little money in the box — it all seemed quite legitimate — and walked out into the cold cold gathering twilight. I was a little annoyed. The Italians, in my experience, don't speak to you in English unless they have heard you speaking English, and then they rarely do; partly because they don't always speak English themselves, partly because they're Italian.

When I really need to know something from someone I usually start out by asking if they speak English. Once in a while they do; they really do. People in the computer business; the young woman in the architectural bookstore; the telephone operator at the opera company. More often they either do not, or else they speak English imperfectly, about the way I speak Italian. In that case we speak English, but soon we're speaking Italian; it just seems easier.

I'm often surprised at the American surprise that other nations are different, have their own languages and agendas. An e-mail list I read has been commenting on the recent French decision to ban Moslem head-scarves and other religious personal paraphernalia from public schools. This is about on a level, it seems to me, with our banning prayer from public schools: it's simply an affirmation of a secular government. The schools are governmental institutions; hence religious observation is excluded from them.

The Italians, I'm told, agreed completely with the French, until someone pointed out that in that case there should be no crucifixes in schoolrooms. No crucifixes; how could that be? Crucifixes are standard issue; they belong in rooms just as do light-switches, or doorknobs. Walls demand crucifixes; no self-respecting hotel bed lacks one, any more than its bathroom lacks that mysterious pull-cord in the shower, or over the bathtub, pulling which is said to bring paramedics panting into the most intimate of moments, because you must have just slipped on a bar of soap and fallen and broken your neck.

The day started out in a couple of local museums, the Farnesina with its amazing frescos and then the Palazzo Corsini with its dark brooding paintings and cold and motionless statues. The Farnesina guards let us in without paying: we're over 65. The very nice lady at the Corsini, who complimented me on my Italian — it's a frequent compliment, to which I always respond that I may speak it well but I don't understand it at all — regretted that she had to charge us, as we were from the United States, and there is no reciprocal agreement between the two countries, as there is among all the European Community members.

I said I was sorry to be an American too, these days, and she assured me that our foreign policy was not my fault, there are governments and then there are citizens, a distinction that should be made more often.

Outside the Corsini windows it was snowing, large feathery flakes that drifted down so slowly that at first I thought they must be ash. They didn't stick, but they looked cold. We walked through this odd weather to a local trattoria for salt cod, it being Friday, and to sit out the snow.

The afternoon work consisted in buying concert and opera tickets. We'll hear a youth orchestra Sunday noon at the Teatro Argentina, where Rossini's *Barber of Seville* was laughed off the stage at its premiere. (Maybe that's why *Freddo ed immobile* is on my mind.) Then Wednesday we'll hear a Respighi opera, being given its first ever performance, ninety years after its composition. And another orchestra, the chief one in this city, the Accademia di Santa Cecilia, is playing Sibelius and Bruckner, and that beckons, if we can get tickets.

Rome, I read today in the guide we finally bought and should have had all along, in spite of its fine print, the TCI (Touring Club Italiano) guide, now has close to two and a half million inhabitants, so it's no surprise there's a music scene. Theater too: there are about seventy legitimate theaters — well, maybe some aren't quite so legitimate — listed in the weekly where-it's-at directory.

I may have suggested to some of you that we thought a month would give us a chance to get to know this city, at least its surface. Wrong. As I've written, it has no surface; it's all depth and complexity. We're all too aware that the remaining time is dwindling, and though we're cheerful about ruling some things out — theater, the Vatican, expensive restaurants — there's still a lot we'd like to do.

Well, we'll just put on an extra pair of socks and head out across the Tiber and follow our noses. We may be cold but we're not motionless, and unlike many of the statues here we have our noses, at least for the moment.

Guidebooks
S. Egidio, January 24—

WE CAME HERE ARMED with any number of guidebooks — some borrowed, some bought for the trip. And we arrived to find a number more in the apartment we'd rented — one, in fact, written by the woman who owns the apartment, a very pleasant New Yorker transplanted lo these many years to this city.

Of course the ideal guidebook has yet to be published. Only Borges could write it, as it would have to be magic, to know exactly what you want to read, to exclude all else. Then after Borges had written it it would have to be perfectly illustrated. Two kinds of photographs: those showing the area as it is, and those showing it as it was. (There are guidebooks like this, and they're very interesting. You see, say, the Colosseum as it looked when it was new; then you lift the clear plastic overlay on which the reconstruction is printed to reveal the present appearance. The change is not always for the better.)

And maps: the map would show not only the area you're interested in, with the street-names clearly legible and street-numbers provided (this is very important, Roman street-numbers are a little bit confusing); but also the two best ways to get from where you are to where you want to be, both on foot and in public transportation. (And the latter would be annotated to advise you as to whether the tram will if fact arrive, and whether track-work will keep it from going to where you want to arrive.)

Ideally all this would be available both as a small book, easily slipped into your pocket, and as a file you can put on your Palm or whatever handheld computer you prefer. And it would glow in the dark, of course, so you could read it at night, or in the church in question, or the restaurant.

And, speaking of restaurants, it would include lists of them arranged by area, by price, and most important of all by whether they are actually open or not; and an indication of the general quality wouldn't hurt either.

What we've been using for the most part are these:

- *National Geographic* guide, because our landlady wrote it, and the prose is good, the selection of sites useful, the photos inspiring.
- *DK*, because the exploded illustrations showing city blocks and walking itineraries seems realistic. (But oh dear it's heavy.)
- *Access*, because it leads you to shops, restaurants, historical sites, and museums with equal nonchalance, reinforcing the idea we already have that all such categories are of equal value.
- An old (1980) *Blue Guide*, because it has detailed information about the historical sites. But of course it is out of date, not so much about the history, that doesn't change that much, but the hours and accessibility and all that have changed in many cases.
- *Lonely Planet*, because it's compact, has useful information about phone numbers and restaurants and such, and provides a fair amount of historical value.

But yesterday I finally found and bought the best guide so far, the Touring Club Italiano (TCI) guide. I'd been lusting after it for quite a while, but 1) I couldn't find it when I wanted it 2) When I could find it I was suddenly aware of the need to economize, and it costs €15. But finally yesterday there it was at the big Feltricinella bookstore on the Argentina and I by God bought it.

Last night looking it over I discovered that there was a production error. The other side of page 705 was not 706; it was 912 or something; and the next page was 913; then it went back to 708. Thirty-two pages on, same kind of problem; repeating for hundreds of pages. Clearly the signatures had got messed up, and it wasn't a binding problem, it was a problem in how the pages had been photographed, or computerset, or whatever. This as you can imagine irritated me vastly.

This morning I called TCI to advise them of the problem. They didn't seem too happy to hear the news. They requested I pay them a visit. Since the place in question was on today's itinerary I obliged. They looked at my copy, disappeared with it, and then provided me with another, identical in every respect except for the errors.

I thanked the nice man with great humility and sincerity and then asked if many copies had appeared with this same problem. Oh no, he said, very few; very few. But if you buy a TCI *Rome* I would advise you to check into this.

Well, it isn't really a guidebook; it's a reference book. It is based on the very observation I was elaborating a few dispatches back: Rome is four-dimensional. It begins by advising you to walk from east to west looking at recent history, then from south to north thinking about imperial Rome. This is after 140 pages of introductory Roman history.

There follow hundreds of pages organized by the various quarters or neighborhoods, with Blue Guide-type detail in the descriptions of the great public buildings, and considerable detail concerning history, political movements, and the like. There are really only two problems: the book is in Italian, and it provides no help with restaurant choices. (It doesn't glow in the dark, either, and its type is small; but at least it is fairly compact, given its 1006 pages.)

Today the weather was glorious, though cold, and we took a very long walk, from the Argentina to the Piazza di Spagna, then to the Piazza del Popolo, up into the park overlooking that piazza, back down again and across to the Tiber, down the river to the Mazzini bridge, and across to the Botanical Garden. This took about five hours, including the conversation at TCI, stops at a couple of cafes, and long pauses here and there.

It was exactly the kind of day I love. The city was populous, especially around the Spanish Steps, but not pocketpickingly tight, if you see what I mean. All the shops are having sales, so lots of people are out buying things, or at least windowshopping. But the city's not beset by tourists; these people are mostly all Romans. You don't even really have to reserve dinner at trendy restaurants; they're not full.

So the Piazza del Popolo, for example, was empty enough that you could really drink in its architecture, both down in the piazza itself and from the belvedere up in the Pincio Gardens to its east. We strolled about the gardens, taking care not to slide on occasional icy patches, and were amused at a Hobbit Fair with tents set up serving mulled wine and "medieval lunch," and young people dressed as gladiators and princesses, and little children pedaling around on rented pedal-cars.

And we struck up a long conversation with a guy selling "watercolors," who explained the topographical layout of the city and its parks, the orientation I mean, and told us what were the best times to visit (May and October), detailing the meteorological advantages, and finally sold us a watercolor after dropping the price to a sixth the original without our having done any bargaining at all.

The walk along the Tiber was marvelous, the tall sycamores leafless but somehow benevolently protective above us, the frequent bridges going this way and that across the river because of its reverse curve in this part of town.

The Botanical Garden is not at its best in January; the roses and iris are only fond memories, but the bamboo forest and the ferns are remarkable, the redwoods and Torrey pines pleasantly familiar, the palms and agaves exotic in this setting but reminiscent of home — and the vistas from the heights of the garden, across the river and the rooftops to the snowy mountains all around to the north and east, were really quite memorable.

It is clear we will be back. I don't know why we've put this off so long, but I'm not regretful that we did; we can enjoy it now without pressure; we're old enough to merge our own tempo, our own values even, with the eternal ones here. I still don't like cities, but I like Rome. There's a saying: *Roma non basta una vita*; for Rome a lifetime is insufficient. I suppose that's true. But for a lifetime Rome is perhaps, in some sense, required; I mean, with Rome a lifetime begins to make some sense. Especially if the pages follow one another in an orderly way.

Money and trees
S. Egidio, January 24—

THE RECEIPTS PILE UP uselessly in my top dresser drawer, migrating there every from the desk every Friday morning, when we have to clean the house for the house cleaners. Lindsey says: be sure to give me all those receipts, it's the only way I have of knowing the cash expenditures. I say: You'll have to wait, I have to log them, so I know where we were when, and what we bought.

Why do you want to do that, she says, it's a waste of time. Yes, maybe, I answer, but it's a discipline, it's what I do. It's a poor discipline, she says; yes, I say, but it's the only discipline I have. You'll have to wait.

In fact for years now every Italian cash-register has printed out the time and date, the name and address, and of course the amount, of each transaction. And in Italy it's a crime, probably a Federal or whatever the national government is crime, not to have a receipt for a transaction. If you don't have it you might have stolen it, is one way of looking at this law: but if you don't have it, another reading goes, you might have paid for it under the table, there might be some kind of tax bypassed. The association of governmental supports and paranoia is boundless.

My glass is half full most of the time; it is rarely half empty. I like to try to be as optimistic as possible in this most present of all possible worlds. So we don't really have that much bad luck on these travels. Nevertheless there have been little glitches lately, rain, missed busses, trams that don't show up. And suddenly I realized I haven't been giving money to beggars.

Not only that: I've been feigning not seeing them. This occurred to me quite forcefully yesterday on a bridge, when I averted my eyes from a woman, I guess it was, sitting on the bridge, with her hand out. It's not a common sight; I mean you don't see a beggar every block or so, but there are certain places where they're not out of place: especially the porches of churches and important bridges.

I guess without going into the matter too analytically I would say there are now three orders of beggars here in Rome. There are the gypsy types, like the woman I ignored yesterday on the bridge. These are miserable. They often bend alarmingly if standing, or shake as if palsied. They wheedle and, well, beg. They wear headscarves and colorful but dirty or faded outer garments; they tend to be shapeless and their faces are invisible. You have no idea how old they are.

I don't know which would be worse, I told Lindsey, to be permanently bent over like that, or to bend over like that deliberately from nine to five in order to make a living. Either way it's lamentable.

(There's a subcategory of this order, the clearly crippled, or burnt, or loathsome. Fortunately we've seen only one or two of these on this trip.)

Then there are the people whose job it is to beg. I mean they make a social contribution of some kind by begging, just as others make social contributions by writing music reviews, or cooking dinners, or building houses. At the top of this group, for me, are the musicians, I mean the ones who don't use electricity, the real musicians. But these vary enormously on the skill axis. Some are really quite good; others are so-so; some really only pretend to be musical.

Now and then on the tram or the subway there'll be a musician, usually playing the stomach Steinway, but sometimes some other instrument. Yesterday on the Metro there was a violinist: this seems really dangerous on a crowded subway car. An upbow could blind an innocent bystander, turning him into a Beggar Type One. But the guy was careful, and it was easy for him to bow carefully, because he was no violinist at all; he repeated the same phrase from "Carmen" over and over, like a demented Steve Reich. Fortunately our stop came and we got off without ever actually having to deal with him.

Another time there was, believe it or not, a cimbalon player. This must be the instrument least suited to the job: it's big; it's clumsy. The cimbalon is a sort of small piano without its keys or case. You hammer on its strings with little spoon-ended sticks, one in each hand. When you're not playing, at least if you're this guy, the cimbalon folds up against your chest; when there's room, you hinge it down and have at it. He wasn't really bad, though the repertoire was, again, limited. I don't know how he collected his pay:

with all that apparatus, and both hands busy hammering away at Lady of Spain, it's hard for the tin cup to come into play.

Two or three weeks ago we heard a guy playing passable violin on the Argentina, and his wife banging away on a rattle to accompany him, or maybe she was urging him on, or at least urging him to keep to the straight and narrow. She was playing a sistrum. This is an ancient instrument, a sort of big two-tined fork with jingle-bells strung between the tines. You see it being played by angels in thousand-year-old mosaics, but you don't see it in the usual modern dance-band or symphony orchestra. She played with a will, and he played with a certain amount of grace and fantasy. But they were across the street, and we didn't contribute.

We haven't contributed to very many of these people, and that was beginning to get on my nerves today. Partly I haven't been contributing because of the annoying presence of the Type Three beggars, the ones who look perfectly well-bodied and competent but who would rather live under bridges with dogs, often Labrador retrievers, and play at playing the guitar or something, than do something productive. But who am I to know what their situation is, or how they got there, or how supportive their parents, or families, or Church, or government, is, in their particular case? So even there you have to think: either I give money from time to time, and to hell with whether it's deserved or not, or else I make an excuse to justify myself, and keep my spare change in my pocket.

And then you see the Type One who has a sign: *Your pocket change means nothing to you; it means something to eat to me.*

So I've begun, a little belatedly, separating the small change in my pocket. The one- and two-euro pieces go in my change purse, to be used for purchases; the others, even the fifty-cent pieces, are loose in my pocket. When I see one of these people I slip a coin into the hand, or the cap, or the basket, or the violin-case. It may be a nickel, it may be a half-dollar. That's up to chance. Maybe they "deserve" it, whatever that means, maybe they don't. That too is up to chance.

By and large people here are honest. I saw a guy running out of a bar and down the street yesterday, calling out to a departed customer: *Signor! Signor! Ha lasciato questo!* He was waving a coin, so it couldn't have been more than two euros, and he was running down the street to give it back. You couldn't help but think of Abraham Lincoln.

Tonight we went downstairs to the Ombre Rosse, on the ground floor of our building, for an aperitif. Martini time. The Martinis here are just right. It was cold, even under the propane burner on the street, but it was full inside, and besides we wanted to watch the world go by, or the tiny part that ambulates the Piazza Sant' Egidio; and besides the sky was a magnificent deep cerulean blue, and a thin fingernail of a moon hung over the museum across the street.

Lindsey pointed out a guy sitting down at the other end of the terrace. He wore an unnecessarily big beret rakishly draped off one side; he had tortoiseshell glasses; he smoked a pipe; he ostentatiously read a newspaper on a stick, one of the cafe's newspapers; he drank from a demitasse.

He was me, I realized, forty years ago. I saw myself sitting out in front of the Piccolo Espresso, where today's Mediterraneum is, on Telegraph Avenue. Strange to see forty years parade past over a Martini. On the whole, I told Lindsey, I don't regret these forty years; they've been good.

The waitress had charged six fifty for our drinks, and I gave her a ten-euro note, wondering what the hell was going on. Sure enough she came back a little later, with a long apology in Roman Italian. I may still be wearing my black fedora, but I don't look like a Californian at the Ombre Rosse, not even like Ferlinghetti. She spoke Italian to me, and apologized that she'd forgotten to ring up Lindsey's Frascati superior, which brought the bill right up to ten euro, six fifty for my excellent Martini, three fifty for Lindsey's wine. I left a euro extra.

Tipping here runs say eight or ten percent, at least that's what I do. The whole thing has changed alarmingly in the last few years. It used to be that service was included, but the Americans have ruined the system here as they have in France. They misunderstood the system and went on tipping anyway, fifteen or twenty percent, ostentatiously. Since things are cheap (well, except for Martinis), why not leave more change on the table? But that of course distorts the whole equation, and the equation must needs inevitably recover its balance.

That's been done here, as often in France, by abolishing the *service compris* system. You almost never see *servizio incluso* on the bill these days. I don't know how the service staff is paid; I'll have to try to find that out. In the meantime it's back to tipping, which I hate to do. It seems, somehow, to make beggars of the waiters. Next thing you know they'll be wearing cimbalons.

But what has any of this to do with trees, you reasonably ask. It's just that while sitting in the Ombre Rosse we were admiring our piazza, the Piazza S. Egidio, with the pink-stucco'd museum across the way, where we saw that interesting Moravia show, and the dark flank of S. Maria in Trastevere up to our left, and the handsome grey building down the other way that closes off the bottom end of the piazza.

Lindsey said, suddenly, And there are trees in our plaza. And it's true. There are trees; you can see them right there softening the stucco buildings and the cobblestone pavement. There are not that many trees in Rome. You see pines in odd public corners, like at the corners of Piazza Venezia, and if you look up in the sky you occasionally see them in roof gardens. Of course you see them in the Botanical Garden, wonderful trees; there are a couple of Sequoias, and there's a sycamore said to be getting on toward four hundred years old. You see them in the other big parks — Rome has a number of parks — the Pincio, the Borghese, the Celian, the Palatine.

But you don't see trees on the streets, with very few exceptions. The Viale Trastevere is bordered by trees, which rates a mention in the TCI guide. The river of course is bordered by trees. But we can walk from our house, down the via della Scala, up the Lungara, maybe half a mile, without seeing a tree.

The restaurants and cafes mostly all have "terraces" outside their doors with a few tables and chairs, and if it's not actively raining (or snowing) there'll be people sitting there — we took our drinks at the Ombre Rosse outside tonight, we took that photo from our table, and we were wearing gloves and mufflers even under the heaters. And around such terraces there is often greenery, little shrubby things in big terracotta pots, or pots that look like terra cotta but are in fact plastic, the terra cotta breaks when it freezes, or when someone hits it with a hand-truck delivering a few cases of wine or artichokes, or when a car or a motorbike runs into it rather than hit a pedestrian. But such shrubby things are not trees.

Day by day I recognize that the other axis — I mean the one that counters the axis of Time — is an axis of Rural-Urban. The declivity, as I see it, from pagan times to monotheism is in fact simply the movement from rural life to urban. People need trees, as surely as they need skies and water. I think when street trees are vandalized, as they so often were in our part of Berkeley; when kids or hoodlums deliberately break them, break off branches or even break the saplings at the ground, they do so because they resent not the tree but the paucity of trees. And so we appreciate them the more when we see them, here in our Piazza S. Egidio; and we seek them out when we need to relax, to come back to ourselves, on days like today, after days of overstimulation by the city, by its people, its ages, its hierarchies, its repressive history.

Santa Maria in Trastevere

Innocence abroad

S. Egidio, January 24—

YES, I KNOW, Mark Twain's book was called *Innocents Abroad*. I haven't read it. (The shelves of books remaining to be read are infinitely long.) But I like the idea of innocence abroad; innocence is what we two country bumpkins have, in spades.

Today, for example, we went to a concert. The program was interesting: Schubert's Fifth Symphony, which I like very much, and Shostakovich's First Symphony, which I tolerate more than the fourteen or so that followed. For one thing, he was only seventeen or so when he wrote it; you have to admire its precocity, if nothing else.

But what was most stunning of all was the concert hall. What an incredible pleasure to hear music in a place like the Teatro Argentina! We didn't really know what to expect. We climbed to our seats, two chairs in a little room of our own, three tiers up the seven or eight tiers of similar boxes, all rising perpendicular like shelves in a horseshoe-shaped cabinet. Lindsey hung her purse on the back of her chair and draped her jacket over it; I got out of my hat and my scarf and my jacket and my sweater; and we gaped at the hall, cream and red and gold as the inside of a jewelbox, brilliantly but subtly lit by lamps attached to the fronts of the boxes.

Below us, on the orchestra floor, perhaps four hundred armchairs were arranged in generous rows, staggered so that each person looked between the two ahead toward the stage. We were early but the orchestra section filled pretty well; it was amusing to see that perhaps a third of the audience was reading the sunday paper — a photo would have made good publicity for *Corriere della Sera*.

At 11:30 the orchestra came on stage to enthusiastic applause, rather a small orchestra for the Schubert; then the concertmaster, who stood to take the oboist's "A," repeat it to the string sections one by one, and then take his seat; and then the conductor, Nada Matosevic, a pleasantly pretty woman from Croatia. We knew from the moment the oboe sounded that "A" that these were exceptional acoustics, and the performance bore it out.

Schubert of course is utterly transparent, but you forget how inventive his orchestration often is — the unexpected solo appearances in the winds, the odd doublings, the skillful use of French horns. Matosevic urged the orchestra through quite brisk tempi, and the strings weren't always up to them. But what surprised us, what revealed our own naivety at this concert, was how fresh, clear, and immediate everything sounded. I've heard my share of orchestra concerts and then some, but I realized this morning that I'd never really heard an orchestra play (except for the very special sound of an orchestra heard from within, while performing as a part of the ensemble). Instead I've always heard a room with an orchestra playing in it.

The funny thing is that the hall was built as an opera house, not a concert hall; it has a proscenium stage (whose front curtain was never opened); opera is still played there often, and it's used for legitimate theater as well. But it makes a fantastic concert hall, and the many solos in the Shostakovich, for solo violin, viola, or cello, revealed that it would function equally well for chamber music.

And the other funny thing is, and this shows what an innocent I really am, that I've known all along that such halls are possible, we heard a magnificent performance of *Die Zauberflöte* once in a very similar hall in The Hague. But there's nothing as physical as actually hearing. The sound goes into your ears. You can do all the thinking about it, you can read about it, you can imagine it: but when it actually goes into your earholes and begins to interfere with your central nervous system, then you suddenly become physically aware.

So we heard the concert, and congratulated one another that we had heard it, and left the theater, waited at the light in the crowd, waited for the cars and the motorscooters, two guys each riding them, buzzing by close enough to touch you; and the light turned green and we crossed to Feltatrice to see if we could buy tickets to tomorrow night's concert. And, truth to tell, one of us wanted the facilities at Feltatrice, a very upscale bookstore with CDs and a box office and public restrooms. And while one of us decided to go to the box office the other of us said Where is my purse?

Well of course the other of us, namely me, I did not know where the purse was; I always assume the person who carries it knows where it is. I left it on the back of my chair, she said, her eyes wide with sudden concern and perhaps even fear. Go back right now, I said, and look for it, I'll go with you, you go to the box we had, I'll go to the office. But I realized it wasn't that simple.

She barged right past the doorman into the now empty theater. He looked at her, looked then at me, turned and looked at her again. I said to him, in the best Italian I could muster: she has left her purse, she is going to find it. I gave the two short whistles she always responded to and she stopped dead in her tracks and turned around like Orpheus (though she should have been Eurydice) and looked at me: Wait, I told her, he will go with her. I explained to him again what the situation was and they both went ahead of me.

I waited at the upstairs bar. I add quickly: I did not have a drink, I just lounged around. They were gone a long time. Finally I decided to go up to the box too, though I hadn't been invited. She was disconsolate: the purse was not there. The doorman said There is no purse, We must go downstairs. A woman in a green uniform was cleaning the halls with a vacuum cleaner. We went downstairs.

There is no office of things lost, he said. We went to the ticket office, where we learned there was no office of things lost. The purse was gone.

So we walked home and Lindsey thought about what was in the purse and she called one of the credit cards, the one that went with the checking account, and explained what had happened, and the card account was cancelled, and so was our checking account. She then tried to telephone our main credit card but our telephone card was now out of funds and the apartment telephone will not make long-distance calls so there was nothing more to do until we had another card.

I called the American Embassy because of course her passport was in the purse and the woman there sounded as if this happened every day and said that because of terrorism this was serious and we should go to the embassy tomorrow, Monday, and report it and make an application for a new passport. But she didn't ask for our names or anything.

Then I went downstairs to ask the police what we should do. There are always police downstairs in a car in the piazza, frequently the engine of their car is idling because the weather has been quite cold, this time it was idling and they were sitting there reading things as usual, I asked what to do and they said we should immediately go to the local police office, a five-minute walk away, and make a report, which in Italian is called *fa un denuncio*, which has the right denunciatory sound.

So we did that. The police station was colder than day before yesterday's scent, cold as a cigarette butt in the gutter. The cops were bored, arrogant, jumpy. We were buzzed past a steel door with a window in it and gestured to cold plastic chairs in a dim cold concrete corridor. Finally the specialist showed up and graciously invited us into his office, decorated with a large poster showing a man in a tuxedo embracing a woman in bikini underwear. He verified that we could speak Italian, since he spoke no English, and proceeded to interview us about the situation. He then shoved the *denuncio* form under Lindsey's nose, and she filled it out and signed it.

Then we went to the bakery and bought some pizza and a couple of jam tarts and we went to an internet office and bought telephone cards and went back to the apartment. Well I thought I'll call the credit card and block it but first I'll call the theater and make sure the purse hasn't turned up.

Of course it had turned up. So we ate our pizza and walked over to the theater. We'd been told to go to the stage door. There we found the usual security guard sitting at a little desk reading the newspaper. Draped over the partition next to his desk was another guy, the guy who actually had the purse, come with me he said, gesturing in that curious way Italians have of saying Follow me, they don't hold their hands up, palm to them, fingers up, and beckon rhythmically; instead they hold the palm down, level with the waist, fingers together, and wave rhythmically in a way that suggests, to an American at least, Wait right there. But we remembered this, and followed him.

We were led along dim corridors behind the scenes of the theater. There was a pair of kettledrums on one side, a string bass in its fiberglass case on another. Finally we reached his office. He beckoned us in. There was the purse: it was hers. The man looked triumphant. He never once asked us to describe something within it.

He pointed out all the things that were still there, and if you think I'm about to describe them to you, you're crazy. The checkbook; the credit cards; the various identity cards, the passport; all were there. He told us several times at great length exactly how he'd found it, but neither of us ever once could figure out what the hell he was saying. It was apparently on a staircase. Maybe she dropped it; maybe someone stole it and dropped it; maybe a cleaning person had taken it and had found out it was being sought and had dropped it: we'll never know.

The man's face had been beat up over the years and he smelled of red wine — but then it was just after lunchtime. He was like many people who work behind the scenes in theaters, maintaining a small and probably unnecessary but dignified job in a glamorous place. I gave him a small reward. I asked him about the backstage. He took us up onto the now empty stage. We discussed the theater. We left.

I'm not sure how Lindsey felt; I was curiously out of spirits. It was too late to do what we'd planned. We went on to Tazza d'Oro, the best coffeehouse in Rome, both for a badly needed espresso and for coffee for the kitchen. It was closed. We walked on home, planning to stop off for an ice cream. The route took us past the police station, and we stopped in to request a reversal of the denuncio. That wasn't so easy: the officer was concerned that the man who'd found the purse might have used the credit cards in the meantime, or taken a photo of the passport. This seemed extremely unlikely to me, and at risk of being subpoenaed by Mr. Ashcroft I assured him that we waived all rights in the matter and wanted to let bygones be bygones.

We went on to the gelateria on the piazza S. Cosimato which is known throughout all Rome for its chocolate gelato. It was closed.

But tonight we went out to dinner at a local trattoria, Trattoria da Lucia, thank you, Patty, and we had a wonderful dinner. Not the best, but perhaps the second or third best here, and cheap and homey and comfortable, and only a two-minute walk through the frigid night. And the best thing was that they don't take credit cards, so even though we still have one we didn't need it.

I've given considerable thought in the last few hours to the stories I could tell about lost credit cards. The lost wallet in New

York: I called and cancelled the cards; then the taxi came back to the hotel and gave me the wallet I'd lost. The stolen wallet in Torino: I reported the loss to the police and cancelled the cards; then someone phoned the hotel to say they'd found the wallet on the street; all the cards were in it. The time the credit card was cancelled because a woman in Greece had multiplied dollars by sixteen thousand to convert to drachmas, instead of dividing, and the bank cancelled the card when we assured them we hadn't spent $320,000 on flowers in Greece lately. And so on.

No harm done. What once was lost is now found, and we continue to leave the small change with the beggars and the musicians.

Who broke this stuff?

S. Egidio, January 23—

The tourist brochure suggested that one of the museums still on the list, the one with the big Antonio Gaudi exhibition, was not closed on Monday, so after a morning round of the market we walked over to begin a carefully planned day. The museum was, of course, closed. Oh well: we walked on to Tazza d'Oro for a coffee, and then down toward the Piazza Venezia, to see what the Time Adventure was all about.

Two young people were standing out on the Via Corso wearing outlandish costumes, a sort of Cosmicomix attempt at typifying Imperial Rome. One, female, held a flyer out to me: *No grazie*, I said, English, she asked, *Che pensa Lei*, What do you think, I answered. By now we were all three walking down the alley toward the Time Adventure, where we were ushered (huckstered?) through the front door to a ticket window.

After a short wait there were ten or twelve of us, enough for the show. We were shown into a small room, quite dark. The girl closed the door. The lights came up on a few wall panels stating the theme: all of Rome would be laid before our unbelieving eyes. It may not have been built in a day, but it could be covered in forty minutes. We digested this information, then turned around to face the other wall, on instruction. A series of blue spotlights careened across the wall, picking out plaster busts of Augustus Caesar and Michelangelo, maps of Imperial and Renaissance Rome, and a few other items that made no sense to me.

Caesar came to life and told us that he'd found Rome brick and left it covered with marble. Michelangelo came to life and laughed at Caesar's ruins and boasted of his own achievements. The blue lights wandered about aimlessly.

We were told we would soon embark on a marvelous scientific journey through Time, and that people with back problems, pregnant women, and those dedicated to motion sickness might not want to participate. We trooped into a small auditorium with four groups of ten seats, in two ranks of five, faced a wall with three screens. Behind was a row of fixed seats, presumably for the faint of heart.

Oh-oh, I thought, I've heard of these things. But it was too late. We put on our headphones, dialed "2" for English — except the people in front of us, who dialed "5" for Español — and waited to see what happened next. The panic bar jumped across our laps, as if we were in a carnival ride, and the journey began.

It was pretty hokey. Our seats were in constant motion. We "flew" over a riverbank forest to see the infants Romulus and Remus abandoned to the wolves, who looked a lot like German shepherds. We watched Nero sing, badly, to monotonous lyre accompaniment of his own improvisation, while a series of bonfires were superimposed on the photo of a plaster model of reconstructed Rome. We visited Michelangelo who was having a spat with the Pope about a few pagan intruders onto the Sistine ceiling.

Just as I was getting enough of the motion the show was over and we blinked our way out into the street. I asked Lindsey if she regretted our spending the time and the money; No, she said, it was interesting. What a fine woman I travel with! But I guess I don't regret it either; it's interesting to see these kinds of things now and then, to know what people are being sold. We saw a much better one in Tijuana years ago: the seats didn't move, but the projections were more sophisticated, film shot from the nose of a helicopter flying through the Copper Canyon, over the Yucatan jungle, past pods of whales, above mountain villages and huge Baroque churches.

We stopped in at the nearest bar for a Fernet to settle my stomach. We should have taken the Time Elevator next Monday, not today; we fly home next Tuesday, and any flight will seem more comfortable after sitting though this show.

Then, following our plan, we walked to the place the ArcheoBus leaves from, as the weather was uncertain, and an hour or two on a bus touring the city's major archaeological sites would be a pleasant way of sitting out any rain. We struck up a conversation with two men with the same idea, a guy from Antwerp whose native language was Dutch and his young friend who came from Toronto but whose native language was French from Quebec. The bus was due at two o'clock; twenty minutes later we gave it up to walk down Mussolini's Via Imperiale toward the day's main goal,

S. Clemente.

The bus showed up immediately, of course, but we were halfway across toward Trajan's Market. What a place! Half a small mountain — well, a pretty good-sized hill — had been hauled away so that Apollodorus could prove his architectural skill building a retaining wall to hold back the rest of the hill, a four-storey shopping complex, if that's what it was, and it sure looks like it to me.

These Imperial Romans had invented concrete, and they had a fine time with it. Vaults, arches, arcades, columns — there was nothing they couldn't do with it, it seems. The architectural style is repetitive, it's true; and being the postmodernists of their day it's a little too historicist for me; but you can't argue with its ambitions. But why is so much of it in such bad shape?

The whole historic center of Rome is a study in deferred maintenance. When you look down at the Imperial Forum — and you do look down, because the Rome of 2000 years ago was about thirty feet lower than today's — you see, scattered about the remaining marvelous pavements of marble slabs or mosaic designs, nothing but fragments of things. Columns, capitals, bases, staircases, pots and pans, basins and sinks, flowerpots, and all of them broken.

It's like the remaining statuary. The Romans didn't like modern art, they liked copies of Greek things, and they made them by the hundreds. But then, perhaps drunk or bored, they went around breaking the heads off the torsos, and the noses off the heads. Why did they do this? Or was it someone else?

On, finally, to S. Clemente — as the TCI guidebook calls it, "one of the most extraordinary and well conserved monumental palimpsests of the city." Richard and Marta had already led us here, a week or two ago, to see the frescos and mosaics, perhaps the finest we've really inspected; but on that occasion we'd lacked time for the basement. S. Clemente is a small basilica as these things go, but it's twenty times as big as our house or yours. And it was built on top of another, whose upkeep had got tiresome by 1100 or so. The Dark Ages didn't lack skill: they simply filled up the old basilica with rubble, of which there's an unending supply in Rome, and built this magnificent thing.

But what they'd filled with rubble was itself built on top of yet another layer, apparently of houses and a small temple or two. This had all succumbed to Nero's fire, a few years AD, so rubble was trucked in for the foundation for an early Christian basilica.

A few centuries ago the whole thing was given to an Irish Dominican order, I don't know why, and in the 19th century the resident top priest, who was smitten with a sense of history and an amateur's enthusiasm for archaeology, began digging. He found the paleoChristian basilica soon enough, but things went on past that.

We followed a couple of French tour groups around, eavesdropping, but our tempo was slower than theirs. The frescos, columns, and floors are fascinating. Saint Clement's history strikes me as dubious, but it's an enchanting story; it's always interesting to see these stories combining pagan mythology, northern fairytale, and political lesson all in one narrative designed to entertain and amaze and perhaps instruct a little bit — not unlike the Time Elevator, come to think of it.

But it was cold and dark and dank down there, even with our flashlight and sweaters and hat and scarves. When we emerged it was almost raining. The Number Three Tram was, amazingly, right there when we wanted it; we rode home in style and comfort; Lindsey roasted a chicken with forty cloves of garlic, and we've had another fine day. Just thought you might like to know.

Pickpocket!

S. Egidio, January 24—

HAVING JUST SENT one of you a reassuring e-mail concerning the loss of wallets and such I paid the price yesterday, or almost.

We were out near S. Maria Maggiore, not my favorite part of town, but an errand took us there, and we decided to take a bus home, having walked through our feet, ankles, and knees on the cold hard floors of two museums out at EUR. (An account, perhaps, for another day.)

There were four or five of us waiting for the bus, and I wondered when it would come. I almost asked a woman standing not too far from me; she looked alert and helpful; but she was busy with a younger woman, probably her daughter, a girl or woman of twenty or so who seemed to be disabled in some way.

Anyway the bus came in a few minutes. Lindsey got on ahead of me, as usual, and a few bystanders pushed their way on next, as usual, and then I stepped into the doorway. The two women were in the doorway, having just got on, and they were holding onto the grab bars, and I couldn't get past them. I excused myself, but the younger woman, stone-deaf, did not move; finally I pushed through and sat down next to Lindsey.

I patted my pockets as I always do. My wallet was missing. I told Lindsey; we looked on the seat between us; then I went right back to the door — the bus having in the meantime lurched onto the Via Cavour — and confronted the two women.

Give me back my wallet, I ordered, in bad Italian. The younger woman did not hear. I repeated myself. The older woman looked at me curiously and rattled off a couple of sharply worded sentences in fluent Italian. I repeated myself: One of you has taken my wallet: I want it back. The older woman opened her bag and took a couple of things out, saying Look, I don't have your wallet.

I turned to the younger woman: Give me back my wallet. She continued to feign deafness. By now some other riders had been alerted and were looking on curiously. I put my hand on her shoulder, and she abruptly turned her face to me: I don't have your wallet, she said.

I know you have my wallet, I said; give it to me. She looked toward a raunchy-looking guy on the back seat, a man who might have been her father except that he was shabbily dressed and ill-kempt. He said something to her. She gave me my wallet.

I went back to my seat, where I looked into the wallet. Everything there — except the cash. I had just made a cash withdrawal so I knew exactly the amount of cash that had been there. Another trip to the back of the bus to confront the sullen young woman.

Give me back my money, I said. I don't have your money, she said. I know exactly how much I had, I said; give it back.

I must have looked pretty threatening. She gave me a fifty. I took it and said Give me the rest. There is no more, she said. Give it to me NOW, I said, and she handed it over, a wad of banknotes she'd somehow crumpled together.

I went back to my seat and counted the money: twenty euros more than I'd had before getting on the bus.

We got off at the next stop, Lindsey and I, and walked a little, across the Piazza Venezia from Trajan's Column to the Piazza S. Marco. There I saw the bus stop and the two women and the man get off. I stopped to see what would happen next. They saw me and separated from one another, blending into a crowd at the bus stop.

Then another bus hove into view, a crowded one, and they all three waited until no one else was getting on, then jammed themselves into the doorway. I walked up quickly to the door and shouted into the bus: Watch your pockets, everyone!

The women looked at me with some irritation, and the other riders looked at me curiously. Watch your purses, I repeated, shouting, Watch those two women! And I pointed at them, and the doors closed, and the bus pulled away.

I suppose I should have gone to the police with the story, but I thought What would they say, your pocket was picked, you got the wallet and the money back, they've disappeared into the crowd. I regret, keenly, that I didn't have the presence of mind to take their photograph: I had my camera in my side pocket, ready to work. God knows what they'd have done if I'd photographed them.

Anyway the moral is: keep a hand on your wallet; know what's in it; be ready to confront people; stay off crowded buses. A taxi is cheaper than the loss of a wallet.

We walked took the tram home, a nice empty tram, and got off two stops beyond ours in order to go to a highly-recommended gelateria to try their ice cream. We'd gone there Saturday, but it was just closing when we got there. Sunday was their day off. They were wide open for business when we got there yesterday, but there was no gelato; I don't know why. Something about not making it this week; perhaps the guy who makes it is on vacation.

Home to brood, then, and catch our breath, and then out to dinner at Al Moro. Good, quite good; but I'll report on all these restaurants later on.

Mind your pockets!

Isola Tiberina

Rain

S. Egidio, January 23—

AND SO WE LEAN into the closing days, with only the weekend and Monday left to us. There are two ways to approach this: 1) go crazy about all the undone things, unseen sights, and try to cram in as many as possible; 2) say Oh the hell with it and have a good time. We tend toward the latter.

And then yesterday the weather didn't exactly cooperate. The morning was glorious, but I sat in front of this computer writing an opera review (available next week, I think, on "San Francisco Classical Voice" [www.sfcv.org]). The review will suggest further thought here about politics and history; it's fascinating to contemplate the years after the French Revolution, which seem to parallel those after the fall of the USSR, exactly two hundred years later. We spend perhaps too much time here watching CNN (whose treatment of the democratic candidates, especially Dean, borders on the criminally irresponsible; it's easy to see why CNN is thoughtful about the BBC affair), and the intersection of contemporary news with news from two centuries or two millennia ago continues to be meaningful.

But we also get out in the world, and yesterday took a bus up past the Vatican (which we have yet to visit, and almost certainly will not visit) to go quickly to the Piazza del Popolo. The bus was simple enough; we checked with a nice old woman, about five feet tall in a mock-Persian-lamb coat and a cloche hat and clutching both an umbrella and a reticule, and she smiled and said Yes, take this bus, then you can transfer; and then we struck up another conversation a bit later, and a slightly younger woman sitting in front of us joined in, and before long a regular imbroglio had begun between the two of them as to whether a tram or another bus was the correct strategy.

Oh well I said It doesn't matter, when you're on vacation any way you take is the right way. Yes, one of them said, Unless it rains. Oh well, the other one said, It can be very romantic when it rains. Romantic, I said, Imagine that, romantic, at my age. The woman smiled, perhaps at my Italian, and said Romantic, yes, at any age.

But in fact it was pouring when we got out a block from the Piazza del Popolo; it was no fun. We ducked into the Santa Maria to verify the tourguide's descriptions of the paintings, all of which can be illuminated for free with handy push-buttons. It was cold and damp. Why was no saint martyred, I wonder, by being forced to stand in the rain? Such a saint would do well here today. I imagine him tied to a post in the middle of a piazza, forced to gaze up into the rain... ah, but perhaps that's the reason: God would not send rain down on the innocent. Infidels provided flames and axes and lions and all that, but only God can provide the rain.

We hope He holds off today, and it looks as if He might. But yesterday was relentless. I stepped into the Borsolino store, hoping to find something on sale, but the obligatory sale shelf — for it's my understanding the twice-annual sales in Italy are almost legally required — held only a few knit hats for women. There was a hat I wanted, but it was over two hundred dollars. The hat will outlive me, I said to the bored svelte countergirls, who looked like rich languid movie stars; I don't want to leave such a hat to my son. (Well, I wouldn't mind, but I would like it to show some signs of wear first.)

On through the blinding rain, my own black rabbit-fur hat getting soaked of course, and into a cafe for two cappuccinos, one of them laced with grappa. Next to us two Japanese tourists drinking big glasses of beer with their white-bread ham-and-cheese sandwiches.

Then up to one of the best exhibitions yet, at the French Academy: a century of fashion. Here were scores of mannequins, the artificial kind, wearing Fortuny and Givenchy and Balmain and St. Laurent and Dior and Fath and even Quant and Gernreich, set out in rooms one or two to each decade. What an amazing parade this was, especially after seeing the fascinating collections of regional costumes a couple of days ago in the Museum of Folk Arts and Crafts.

Of course to my eyes the 20th century took a decided downward direction, in fashion at least, after the New Look. The highlights of the century are its first two decades and the late '40s and early '50s, with Dior and Balmain and Balenciaga always my favorites. One white wall was used as a screen for apparently haphazard projections of clips and stills, and there were Callas and Jackie and Audrey, as well as a number of anonymous starlets and models, all bright and optimistic in more innocent days when decadent capitalism was more fun and less dependent, or so it seemed, on the poverty and exertion of others.

We had taken a big lunch at a local Sard restaurant — again, I'll leave such details to a separate dispatch for the foodies — so it seemed logical to skip dinner, taking only a few pieces of fruit and a pot of tea in the evening. I began to think about how to sum up the restaurants, and also the museums, of which we've seen a fair number, though by no means all. I read the paper, *La Repubblica* today; nothing enchanting there. I took a look at the second volume of the complete Moravia, bought yesterday after searching a number of stores: over 1900 pages, worth any number of rainy evenings back home in Healdsburg. I reviewed the 457 photographs taken here so far this month — fewer in the last few days, when even Rome has begun to become an everyday experience.

And so to bed, for the usual kind of dream, in which unexpected friends look in on various events and processes involving recent experience — unsuccessful repairs to the pocket computer, dropped onto the tile floor; silly puns at the dinner table; books unread or unfound; trams taken or missed. You'd be surprised how many of you infiltrate these dreams; it's better not to write about it.

And now out into the sunshine for a final Friday (of January Rome, not final final), and a round of Etruscan statuary, and a gelato or two, and cocktails with a new friend, and so to bed.

Perilli

S. Egidio, January 30—

WE WERE NEARING the end of dinner at Perilli; it was nearly ten o'clock; the restaurant was beginning to fill up. The three men at the table to our left had finished and gone; I noticed one hadn't quite finished his little glass of grappa; there were a few raisins still in it.

Almost immediately the table was cleared, and three people arrived and were seated there. They were three of the four principle characters in Moravia's first novel *Gli Indifferenti*, which I learned last night had been translated into the American, in the mid-1930s, as *The Indifferent Ones*. (The phase doesn't ring quite as naturally in English.)

There was the mother, once pretty, now perhaps forty pounds overweight, the makeup a little extreme. She flung her fur over the back of the one chair that would be empty at their table, thought better of it — or, having made her gesture, now did the more careful thing; took the fur back up, folded it neatly, and set it on the seat of the chair. While seating herself she gave orders to the waiter, solicitously bending over her to help her to her seat.

There was the daughter, in her early twenties, thin, a bit anxious, intense, taking a seat opposite her mother; and there was the son, taking the chair next to mine, easy, self-assured, a little vacant, a year or two older or younger than his sister, bored.

The waiter appeared almost before they were all seated with a wooden platter on which was a sausage, say eight inches long, and a knife. The mother eyed it avidly, but waited for the waiter to leave; then descended, still chewing a bit of bread, to carve perhaps a quarter off the sausage for herself. She made no attempt to offer any to her children.

Her daughter continued to look at her malignantly. Well: that's perhaps too strong a word. Appraisingly, certainly. Is that me in twenty years, she was thinking; How do I avoid this. She waited as long as she could, not long enough, and then snatched up both sausage and knife and took another quarter for herself.

By now two more plates had arrived, plates of antipasto — sausage, cheese, pickled vegetables, something that looked like sushi but certainly could not have been. One was put down in front of the son; the other between the mother and the daughter. The mother tilted white wine from their half-liter carafe into her nearly full glass of water and drank distractedly, looking at the sausage. The daughter continued to eat, her eyes lowered, not looking at her mother. The son ate blandly, grandly, as if he had all the time in the world, as if the two women at his table were total strangers.

* * *

Earlier today we took a punishing walk, for it was a day of bus strikes. We took a tram three stops the wrong direction in order to transfer to the Tram 3, which would have taken us on a nice picturesque ride of half an hour or so to the Villa Giulia. But the Tram 3 never came.

A tall lanky guy in a cap, not that that distinguishes him, most men in this city who are not bare-headed are wearing caps, still he had an air of some distinction about him, muttered something in American English; it was clear the tram 3 would not come, there was some kind of strike. Where are you going, he asked; and when we told him, he said Walk, it's only forty minutes, I walked there yesterday.

So we walked, first stopping off at home, which was directly en route, to exchange my hat for a beret since it was windy. An hour later, plus perhaps twenty minutes for sightseeing and munching a grilled ham and cheese, we were at the Villa Giulia.

Ridotto, I told the ticket-seller, *Siamo pensionati*. But it didn't work: she asked for documents proving we were over sixty-five, and of course my documents are American, and the U.S. doesn't reciprocate in this arrangement. So we paid full price, and then learned a third of the museum is closed for restoration.

The museum itself is *ridotto*, I complained, Why can we not be. Oh, the woman smiled, There's plenty here even if some is closed, you'll see.

And we did. The Villa Giulia is the Etruscan museum, but I've decided not to describe the museums yet, any more than I'm evaluating our dinners. So I will only say that collections like this remind me of the Sears Roebuck catalogue. There is room after room filled with vases, jewelry, tools (which look uneasily like weapons), advertisements, interior decor. You can reconstruct an entire civilization from this sort of thing if you like. Much of it is extraordinarily beautiful, and nearly all of it is nearly unbearably affecting. We know so little about these people; at least I do; yet they are in so many ways so like us, and in so many other ways utterly enigmatic.

But it is all too much, and we have an appointment at five o'clock, and there is a bus strike. So we walk home, another hour and then some. We normally walk between four and five kilometers an hour, so this means today's walk is five or six miles, on cobblestones, in the cold; and the last half of the walk, though in the cold, is into a bright and blinding sun. But it isn't raining, and we know where we're going.

A quick change; then a taxi to our appointment, with a new friend in her hotel near the train station. We talk for a while, then cross the street to a meeting of her professional society in the wine cellar of a hotel restaurant. I look at hundreds of bottles of Barolo, the youngest from the 1980s, others going back nearly a century. None, of course, is opened; but we have excellent Frascati, and then a fine light red from Tuscany.

We talk to people we vaguely know, here from a number of countries for this meeting. One, recognizing Lindsey, elaborately kisses her hand in homage: I always like this; Lindsey's so important yet so modest; it always discombobulates her to get this kind of attention. Another is married to an architect who's building an elaborate house for a man our son Paolo knows near Healdsburg.

Wine and canapés are all very well, but I'm hungry. Several of them suggest Perilli, in a part of town we haven't investigated yet. I stop at the hotel desk and ask them to call and reserve a table.

Where, the man asks; Perilli, I answer, It's good, isn't it? Oh yes, he answers, very good, typical Roman food, the best. What time, he asks. Oh, let's see, I say, elaborately, in bad Italian, Eight thirty, it's early, but I'm very hungry, yes, eight thirty.

Very good, he says, I'll telephone, and the name? Consolini, I tell him. Consolini is the name we've been using lately; it's much easier on the telephone for Italian reservation-takers than Shere. Consolini, I tell him, and he looks at me in a bit of surprise and smiles just a bit. I always say Consolini, I tell him, it's so much easier. Consolini here in Italy.

He repeats all this to the woman next to him behind the counter who of course does all the actual work. She dials quickly. *Perilli? Due posti stasera? Otto mezzo. Il nome: Consolini.* And it's done, and we walk a half block to the train station and find — a miracle — the strike is over — we take a bus 75 right to the door.

Bread and breakfast
S. Egidio, January 30—

THE ROMAN BREAKFAST, various guidebooks inform me, consists of a cup of coffee or perhaps a cappuccino and a cornetto, which at its best is simply a croissant with a light wash of orange-juice glaze.

This happens to be my favorite breakfast too, but even though I have daily access to one of the best croissants in the United States I rarely eat them, because someone else in the house is opposed to them on principles of either health or morality, the two seeming to me to become hopelessly confused in such discussions.

So here too our usual breakfast is toast and coffee, the latter being made in the little stovetop espressomaker. These used to be called "Moka," which I think was the original brand name when the design was first produced in the mid-1930s. We had one for years but threw it out long ago; then a few years ago I found another in a yard sale in Seattle and we use it now when the antique piston-driven machine doesn't work ... but as usual I digress.

This morning we had no bread, and it was Saturday, and our last weekend here, so out at eight o'clock to get a newspaper and a couple of *cornetti*. *Semplice?* the countergirl asked, while I was distracted by careful silent analysis of her compelling beauty. Simple? meaning just a croissant, or *Speciale*, meaning one of the other pastries, say the round one with raisins and pine nuts. Both, I decided, and took the bag to the cashier, who asked *Cornetti?* Two, I said, are they the same price? Yes, they are.

I've often though it odd that American shopkeepers set so many different prices on things. At Berkeley's Monterey Market, for example, there might be fifteen or twenty different prices for apples, according to color, provenance, state of biosustainability, whether you got it inside or outside, and so on. I always suggest that they simple strike a mean or median or whatever it's called this year and apply that price to all apples. Hell: to all fruits. Why not? What difference would it really make to the consumer? And think how much simpler for the accountants, and the clerks, and the signmakers. But then mine is an unrealistic sense of money, I'm occasionally reminded.

Two newspapers, too: the *International Herald Tribune* for the one who really wants to know what's going on, *Corriere della Sera* for the one who really wants to improve his nodding acquaintance with Italian. I can't tell you what the IHT says, beyond the few items that get read to me while I'm trying to work my way through the *Corriere*.

I can report on a few items in the *Corriere*. There's the continuing unravelling of the Parmalat affair, which has as many intricacies as, well, a political crisis in Italy. There's a short report on yesterday's wildcat strike of half the bus drivers. (A half-strike is worse than a full one, because of the increased uncertainty.) There's an interesting commentary on the increasing polarization, American-style, of the Italian electorate, into two opposed camps of roughly equal size. There's commentary on other aspects of American politics, including its tendency to "reality show shop soap" (meaning soap-opera and reality-show), and its apparent intention to make consumerism a world hegemony.

(It's funny; we Americans hated the Russians because they wanted to impose their style of politics on the world; now we are doing exactly the same thing.)

There's the running account of a sensational murder of fifteen years ago, back in the news for some reason that eludes me because I lack interest in reading about it.

There are the substantial cultural pages, with mini-essays — what we used to call "Sunday think pieces" when I worked for the newspaper — on Etruscan tombs, or Van Dyck, or the Respighi opera we saw a few nights ago, or a new novel, or a new book about Dante or Mussolini or Shakespeare.

Many of these cultural pages are in fact full-page advertisements for the weekly special offered by the newspaper you're reading, for most of them, once a week, offer a book for a small supplemental fee to the cost of the daily newspaper. Most of these are in a series of some kind, since that traps the customer: there are encyclopedias, multi-volume dictionaries, collections of poetry, monographs on The Great Painters. One newspaper is currently offering compact editions of translations of great novels from other languages. I approve this democratization of culture, and in fact Italy, whose illiteracy rate was over thirty percent only fifty years ago, seems to me to be a remarkably book-oriented nation; I noticed this in small towns in Sardinia, even, fifteen years ago.

* * *

Back to breakfast: We're lucky in having quite a good bakery down the street, as I think I've mentioned — first-rate pizzas (what I call focaccias, big sheets of pizza *bianca*, which I'll get to in a bit, covered with marinated and roasted eggplant, or thin-sliced potato, or tomato and anchovy, or leeks, or any of a number of things); lattice-crusted *crostate* or jam-tarts, both individually-sized and large ones; various kinds of cookie including the ubiquitous *brutti ma buoni* or almond macaroons, variously flavored; and, of course, bread: *ciabatta*, whole-wheat *integrale*, and a few others that we haven't found in necessary to investigate.

(Once we also got some *pane giallo*, yellow bread, which was a slightly sweetened corn-based bread, almost like a pound cake; but I haven't seen it since; perhaps it was a Christmastime specialty.)

The apartment has all modern conveniences, including a fine toaster with those squeeze-the-handles-to-open-the-basket frames that drop down into the toaster making it impossible, or at least very unlikely, for bread to contact the heating element and burn. There's a microwave for heating milk. There's a full-size refrigerator where we keep the milk, even the superpasteurized milk that doesn't need refrigeration, and the excellent orange juice.

The juice, by the way, comes either *rosso* or *biondo*, red or blond. The red is of course from Sicilian blood oranges and they are tasty. The blond juice is in fact somewhat whiter than our normal yellow orange juice, and it too is very good; I haven't looked into its provenance; it might be Israeli or African or Spanish but I hope, sentimentally, that it is Italian.

Calling oranges "red" or "blond" is curious. The Italian language also specifies egg "reds," not yolks; "yolk" is a word related to "yellow," and the Italian egg-yolks are indeed darker, more reddish than the American, I don't know why, perhaps the chickens are fed something to encourage this color, which I find attractive. We speak of red wine and white and so do the Italians, though the wine is either dark or clear, rarely red and never, in my experience, white.

The local (Trastevere) folk-poet Giuseppe Giachino Belli has a nice sonnet about the perfection of the world as God has made it, that He made only one mistake, wine should be clear and water dark, so crooked tavernkeepers wouldn't be able to add water to wine without your seeing it.* And the bar downstairs is called Ombre Rosse, "Red Shadows" (or "shades"), a vernacular poetic term for red wine.

Today the orange juice is blond, not red; I prefer the latter, but as Lindsey points out the blond is also really quite delicious. And this weekend the piazzas in Rome are full of citrus, both red and blond, for there's a promotion going on all over town to raise both money and consciousness for cancer research, a subject I'm enthusiastic about. These surprised us yesterday morning; we had no idea why a tuba and a bushel or two of oranges should have been dumped into the flowerpots in front of a cafe which had until now been closed all month.

We found out later, when we walked past a bunch of schoolkids, say ten or twelve years old, boys and girls with a couple of teachers in attendance, manning (childing?) card tables with cancer-research literature displays. Give them eight euros for cancer research and you get three kilos, that's six and a half pounds, of oranges. We gave them the money, but declined the fruit; there was no way we were going to carry it about for the day.

> * *Sortanto in questo cqui ttrovo lo smanco,*
> *Che ppoteva, penzànnosce un tantino,*
> *Creacce l'acqua rossa e 'r vino bbianco:*
>
> *Perchè ar meno ggnisun oste assassino*
> *Mo nun vieria co ttanta faccia ar banco*
> *A vvénnesce mezz'acqua e mmezzo vino.*

> In my view just one thing could bear improvement.
> Surely, if he had given more thought to it,
> God would have made wine white and water red.
>
> If this were so, no swindling tavern-keeper
> Could get away with swaggering at the bar
> Selling a slop that's half wine and half water.
>
> —tr. Allen Andrews

Mozart and starlings

S. Egidio, Feb. 1—

WE'VE HEARD FOUR CONCERTS here now — two orchestral concerts, one concert of 20th-century music, and an opera. I wrote so many concert reviews for so many years that I never think about doing it any more; don't take notes; don't think "critically" about the music, so don't worry: this isn't going to be a concert review.

What's fascinated me, as I've already reported, has been the halls — at least in two of these cases, when we found ourselves in halls originally built to serve as theaters. But the other two concerts were in very different kinds of places.

The 20th-century concert in what was designed, I think, as a large lecture hall, in one of the University buildings — one of a number of buildings we've seen from the 1930s, when Fascist Art Deco was the rage. The music ranged from quite fascinating to what I've always thought of, privately, as P.D.D., that is, pretty damn dull; but the performances were splendid and the evening was well worth attending.

Last night we went to a concert given by Rome's first orchestra, the Orchestra dell'Accademia di Santa Cecilia, one of the names I used to practice announcing when I worked at the radio station forty years ago. I've always had a fondness for this orchestra; I remember splendid recordings they made on old 78 rpm shellac discs, released by Telefunken, I think it was. And the repertory was perfect; so we made the long bus trip out to a newfangled concert hall that's apparently pretty controversial here.

We went to the concert, and came home, by bus — the dread "H" bus to the railroad station, then the "M" to the concert hall. The "H" has a bad habit of pulling up next to another bus at the train station, and on its left, with only a foot or so between them. This means that the entire contents of a perfectly jammed bus pile out from the middle door with only a foot of space. The result is what used to be called, before the discovery of political correctness, a Chinese fire drill.

The effect was heightened this time by the presence of fourteen million starlings doing their exercises in solid geometry directly overhead. Advanced math was not the only thing they did, of course; they made an infernal racket, and did some other things as well; Lindsey took a direct hit on her forehead, I on my hat — it is an intelligent thing to wear a hat. The most amazing thing of all, to me, was that a number of people were so astonished at the demonstration that they gazed open-mouthed at the sky, like so many peasants in a Breughel painting. The thought of it leaves a bad taste in my mouth.

The concert began at 6:30 p.m., a perfect hour — it allows sightseeing and a rest before, dinner after. Fortunately it was dark by the time our bus arrived; we could only make out the shapes of the new Auditorium center. I call it that because the building seems to be a cluster; there was a big bookstore and a very well-equipped bar-cafe, judging by what we saw through enormous plate-glass windows as we followed the crowd of pedestrians to what would surely be the auditorium itself.

Then we were walking across a vast plaza toward the central part of the complex. Above us loomed three enormous domes or turrets whose shape suggested Turks-heads, billowing turbanlike forms; I have no idea what they were.

The concert hall reminded us of San Francisco's, seating about three thousand, with seating at the sides and behind the orchestra itself. The house was pretty well full, and instead of reading the newspapers as they did last Sunday at the Teatro Argentina, or talking on their cell phones as they did at the Opera, they spent the time before the orchestra came on stage noisily talking among themselves; there seemed to be many parties of four or more, relative to the number of couples and singles, perhaps because the auditorium is so far out, and many people arrive by private auto, so why not fill up the car.

We sat above the contrabasses, which we never saw, but we could hear them; the acoustics were good. What we could not hear very well were the vocal soloists in the first piece, who were placed right in front of the conductor, some distance away from us and facing the opposite direction. And that was a pity, for it was a piece I've never heard live, and that I like very much, Luigi Dallapiccola's oratorio *Job*.

The vocal soloists were fortunately moved for the rest of the program, the Mozart Requiem. This was a very moving performance, with a fine chorus and soloists and a splendid orchestra. The audience response was enthusiastic.

Otherwise it was a slow, quiet day, a day of catch-up. The weather continues fine, cold but clear; we walk about the city, often knowing our way now, stopping in for the right coffee (Tazza d'Oro), looking for gelaterie (often closed because of the cold weather), giving quarters to perhaps every fifth person who asks for money, wishing we hadn't left our pocket computer on the Metro, checking off one sight after another on the to-do list — either because we've in fact seen it, or (more often) because we've decided we'll be back one day, no point in trying to do it all.

We'd had a good meal at midday — I'll write about it later; sorry to keep teasing so many of you — and a light supper back at home. The days leave us quite exhausted and we fall asleep easily, to awaken completely refreshed — a phenomenon I associate also with our long walk across Holland: so we must be doing something right.

Giuseppe Giachino Belli (see page 96)

Finale

Healdsburg, February 5—

AND, A WEEK LATER, what are the final impressions? and What does one do with a final day, a single bright clear cold day, in Rome, after spending close to five weeks there?

The days were getting longer and the stay was getting short. Monday morning we found the sun beaming down into the Via Cinque, turning the top storey of the corner BAR, as it's called, rather generically I think, a particularly intense chocolate-orange against the flawless light-blue sky. If there was a groundhog handy I don't know what he was thinking: he wouldn't have seen his shadow on the pavement of the Piazza, the sun rides too low in the south except toward noon.

(The Italian news programs made much of Groundhog Day, broadcasting a long segment from Puxatawney, Pennsylvania — if that's the right name — showing outlandish mountain men in flannel shirts and long grey beards holding an obviously drugged marmot, as the Italian commentators insisted on calling the poor thing. It's the sort of thing gives Americans a picturesque aspect to European eyes, rather as we look at Austrian girls in dirndls, or for that matter Italians stuffing themselves with spaghetti. Which, come to think of it, is how Italian television shows Italians, much to the general disgust: the Italian press sniffs at the "spaghetti-and-mandolins" image projected by RAI, the state radio-television network.)

After breakfast we did what we'd learned to do so well: we simply walked about the streets, stopping in at a couple of Very Favorite Places, having a last cup of Tazzo d'Oro coffee, looking for the one or two last souvenirs, recovering from the last (and perhaps not too judiciously ordered) lunch, taking the last regretful photographs.

We accomplished one long-postponed tourist assignment: We took the "Archeobus" tour out the Appian Way. I of course would have preferred seeing this from the seat of a motorbike, but I didn't want to see it alone. As it turned out we had the bus to ourselves, sharing it with a disengaged but good-humored driver and a tour-guide, a young woman who perched next to the driver and chanted an all-but-incomprehensible narration into a handheld microphone. Fortunately she delivered this laconic singsong only intermittently, and we simply sat back and looked out the windows, taking a photo now and then, and admired the effects of a long gloaming on the landscape.

Everyone has seen photos of the Appian Way, just as everyone's seen photos of the Grand Canyon. Like the latter, the Appian Way turns out to be unphotographable; the images you've seen prepare you for it, but the effect of its continuing on beyond you as you drive — walk would be better; riding a donkey would be perfect — joins the rhythmic punctuation of pines and cypress, the channeled regularity of the walls and occasional statues and tombs, and the seemingly endless linearity of the road itself, often still paved with the original black volcanic tufa, to make an effect that was heightened, of course, by the light and color of twilight.

That was four days ago, but I still see the peach-ochre of the stucco, the greys of gravel and stone, most of all the heavy dark greens of the trees, whose casually perfected geometry — the flattened spheres of the pines, the cypress exclamation points — seems the ultimate mediation of human esthetic sensibility with innate natural beauty. All this lit, magically — sorry about the cliche — by a twilight that seemed to hold its breath, to hesitate, touching and retouching the unfolding scene with golden yellow, peach, apricot, rose, and lilac.

We drove past tombs and mausoleums: this is the perfect place to spend eternity, nestled between city and country, past and future, day and night. We drove out a few miles to the ruins of an aqueduct running a line miles long in gold-beige limestone arches against the intense green of what seemed a wheat-field just sprouting from this old but still fertile soil.

And then we were back at the Piazza Venezia, and we walked home, one last time across our Ponte Sisto, curiously empty of its usual desultory street musicians and handout artists and purveyors of phony Verace, and we took final photographs of the sky, moving now from almost a robin's-egg blue toward indigo with lavender and dark-rose clouds, glowing above the dark and featureless silhouettes of our Trastevere, quiet but animated by its yellow-gold streetlights.

We had a salad and some fruit and packed our bags and turned in early, for the cab was coming at five o'clock next morning to take us to the airport. And it turned up right on the dot, just as we were opening the front door and wrestling our luggage out onto the piazza, and it took only twenty minutes to drive up the Garibaldi, across the Janiculum, and out the via Aurelia, I think it was, to the airport. From the top of the Janiculum I took a last look at Rome, sleeping under a nearly full moon, and there was some regret, but it was time to go home.

* * *

Thirty hours later I awoke in my own bed, again at night, and stepped outside. We do not live in a city; the light came from the moon, now full; the air was as cold as Rome's but somehow softer, and heavily scented with an aroma I have always loved, having grown up on a farm with my share of milk-cows and poultry. On our ridge stood our three Italian pines: it's time to prune them. Below them stood our cypresses, and at their feet Lindsey's garden, neglected for a month, awaiting her attention, her care.

Daily life here in Sonoma county need be no less humane than in Italy. Our breakfast is the same here and in Rome: Lavazza Rosso coffee (thanks to Traverso's in Santa Rosa, but you can get it elsewhere), organic milk, substantial bread. The climate, the light, the fields and their fruit are much the same. But that's in the country, with the frequent and obligatory trips into town.

It's the city, I think, that must be different; our cities are less conducive to walking, with their straight and measured grids and their careful separation of pedestrians and cars — safer, but directive, mandatory. (I'll occasionally jaywalk,or even (much less frequently) walk in the street itself: I aways feel I'm doing something wrong, deliberately living a 19th-century life in a 21st-century context. And then there's the orientation of our marketing, so generally directed to masses rather than individuals — I think that's a pervasive aspect of contemporary American civic life that's subtle and insidious, pervading far more than just the fast-food business with Big Mac values and motivations. I realize of course that this is spreading throughout Europe, but you don't notice it that much in the Rome we've been spending our days in, nor, now I think of it, in Healdsburg either, except — and this is telling — on the outskirts.

It's funny: my main goal, in spending a month in Rome, was to live a month as a city-dweller. To live without a car, to be continually in the company of other people (not perceived so much as strangers, though of course they were, but as fellow citizens), to be contained within walls and facades, to move constantly on pavements, to be away from any but ornamental and occasional trees, to share the day with men and women, dogs and cats, sparrows and starlings, urban creatures all, and never see a rabbit or a bluejay, to hear church bells constantly punctuate the hours, and never an owl or a bobcat in the night.

Yet though all that was true of Rome it did not feel like a metropolis. It wasn't like spending a week or two in New York or Chicago. It felt, curiously, right, in a sort of atavistic way; as if it were a city that had been gradually adjusting itself to its occupants over the course of three thousand years, patiently watching the building and collapse of thatched huts, brick apartment buildings, stone temples, concrete theaters; the coming and going of men (and, now, women) on foot, on donkeys, horseback, on scooters and streetcars; arriving on foot, by boat, in carriages and trains and automobiles and airplanes; always attuned not to the momentary mode but to the underlying purpose or motive — which has been constant for centuries, for good most often, I think, though for evil more visibly in the waves of oppression, persecution, and abrupt violence.

In thirty days we neglected a lot: the Vatican most amazingly; the Baths of Caracalla; many museums; many restaurants. (A report on the restaurants we did encounter is still forthcoming.) But it was never our purpose to "do" Rome, to tour its collections or study its history. We can always do that. What we did, it turns out, is in an intense and fatiguing way to go on hold for a month, pause between our own lives and those of the millennia — to "get some perspective," to resort to yet another cliche. And the result has been incredibly enriching; we will be reflecting on it, and on its meaning to everyday life, for a long time to come.

POLITICS AND PASTA

Torino and Rome, October-November 2004

Vicolo del Cedro

We returned to Italy in October, partly to attend (for our third time) the Slow Food exhibition Il Salone del Gusto in Torino, partly because we wanted to get to know Rome better — and to introduce her to two grandchildren. Once again we settled in Trastevere for the month, in a rented apartment on the Vicolo del Cedro, around the corner from the Piazza Sant' Egidio. But first we went to the Salone.

Arrival

Torino, Oct. 21 —

THE FLIGHT OVER the Alps, delayed a half hour by morning fog across Europe, was short and spectacular, the fog breaking just as we crested those hard and angular peaks. The Alps, from the air, are more awesome than our Sierra Nevada, and I always wonder why. The effect was heightened (if the word may be used) by our altitude; we seemed to clear the peaks by no more than a few hundred feet. And while the snow was deep and nearly universal, the steepest slopes were bare, bare granite.

Then back into the fog except for one brief break revealing Italian farm country below. After landing and getting our beautiful blue Fiat Punto we drove out into that country, skirting fuel dumps and bleak airport villages and working girls and the town of Novara before hitting the toll road in the full open beauty of the Po Plain, which I always find somehow curiously attractive. It's like part of me knows it from way back; it's resonant; I feel at home there. Flat open country with meandering rivers, occasional stands of poplars, big three-storey farmhouse-barn combinations with tiled roofs, the walls pierced with *grillages* of roof-tiles, the same as those invariably roofing these handsome, utilitarian, stucco-over-brick buildings.

It was perfect country for fighting, back in Napoleonic times (and earlier, of course), and it's perfect for corn, and hay, and — when you cross into Piemonte — rice.

There are two other kinds of landscape in Piemonte, "foot of the mountains": those mountains themselves, the Alps bordering France and separating the province from that of Valle d'Aosta, to the north; and a series of river-valleys tying those mountains to the Po Plain. Lindsey's father was born in a hardscrabble town in one of those valleys, the one Hannibal led his elephants through, over two thousand years ago — unless it's true, as the residents of all the other valleys claim, that it was one of their valleys he descended.

Torino, "Turin" in French and English, is the capital city of the province, and a fine, handsome, moderate city it is — though it's in the midst of preparations for the 2006 Winter Olympics, to be held here and in those valleys and on those mountains. So one of my favorite piazzas, the Piazza San Carlo, is hidden behind opaque plastic windows, for they're digging it up entirely, to install below-ground parking.

The Piazza straddles one of the two principal avenues, whose several blocks constitute a seamless 18th-century architectural unit, arcades lining it with shops and bars and cafes; but all the life has gone out of those arcades and piazzas for the moment, and we haven't had time to find out where it's gone.

For today was given over to the Salone del Gusto, the biennial Slow Food fair that brought us here this time, and the last time, two years ago, and two years before that again. It's as huge and daunting and delightful as ever. We spent hours walking the main floor, inspecting the long aisles of producers of cheese, salame, wine, bread, beer, jam, pastry, spirits, dried beans and peas, poultry, pastas, beef — all of it approved for one reason or another, its artisanality or its rarity, by the Slow Food Authority, however it works.

This year the Salone is preceded by a similarly colossal undertaking, Terra Madre, a gathering of farmers who produce foodstuffs belonging to the Slow Food canon, whether for their traditional persistence in the face of global uniformity, or their threatened extinction, or simply because they have something important to offer to the part of the world most of us belong to, by far the largest part in terms of world culture and material worth and global power, but much the smallest in terms of cultural depth, and the most recent and ignorant in terms of awareness of life-and-death universalities.

Our friends Jim and Lisa, who are staying in our hotel, attended the opening ceremony which we missed because of bad weather. They were impressed by its opening parade of delegates, one person chosen to represent each country. The delegates were encouraged to wear their traditional garb, and that, along with color and stature and gait and demeanor, must have produced an amazingly varied scene, reminding everyone that the world is immensely rich and varied, and emphasizing the dreary sameness our first-world economy has tried to impose on it, like so many airports and shopping malls.

Numbers: 4300 delegates from 130 nations. Breakdown: 15% each from Africa and Latin America; 14% from Canada and the United States; 12% from Asia and Oceania; 12% from Eastern Europe, 16% from Western Europe; 17% from Italy. Seven languages are officially recognized and provided for: English, French, Spanish, Japanese, Russian, Portuguese, and Italian.

Yesterday these farmers were welcomed by the Mayor of Torino, the Governor of the province of Piemonte, and the Secretary of Agriculture; and the welcomes were not token statements, Jim tells me, but heartfelt and sympathetic invitations to the delegates to do their work, share their stories, and open their hearts and minds to tell Italy and, through her, the world, how their small and slow and local and ancient knowledges can correct the tendency of global commercial agriculture to destroy the variety of the world in its search for efficiency and profit.

The Governor of Piemonte, Enzo Ghigo, had a column in today's paper (*La Stampa*): "Why to say 'no' to GMO." A practical politician, he writes that he has reason to believe that the legitimate motives of profit and the marketplace can be joined to the development of biodiversity through sustainable agriculture and thereby represent the guarantee of a market truly free to and a hope for many nations.

And then he adds a remarkable paragraph, the centerpiece of his column:

"The dedication to human concerns has brought us to stripping the earth of its fruits; the love of the earth will make of us a humanity ever more free." (*L'amore per l'uomo ci ha portato a sfruttare la terra, l'amore per la terra ci restituirà un uomo più libero.* More elegant, concise, and striking in Italian.)

* * *

This afternoon and evening Lindsey and I attended to workshop labs, and we're stuffed and sleepy, and further comment will have to wait. Suffice it to say, for now, that I've sampled five fascinating wines of terroir in the first of four workshops investigating the influence of soils on wines, and then in the evening tasted four different preparations of raw beef, all from a single 16-month-old Piemontese cow specially bred for the high quality of its meat, each matched by a magnificent wine ranging from a dry Italian sparkler to a deep and magisterial Barolo. And Lindsey has similar things to report, involving hams from various countries matched to white wines, and four or five blue cheeses accompanied by as many sweet wines.

Lindsey working hard at a wine-and-cheese labaratory

The Salone del Gusto
Torino, Oct. 23—

THE HOTEL LUXOR BEST WESTERN here in Torino is not the Las Vegas Luxor. It is not a pyramid; it lacks slot machines; no Nile wends its lobby. I have not yet seen a Texan among its guests.

On the other hand it is not an American Best Western. The television set is not much bigger than my 12-inch laptop screen. Not every electrical socket functions. There is no bathtub. There is, however, a bidet, compulsory it seems in every Italian bathroom, just as every shower has a mysterious pull-cord said to summon the medics in case you collapse while washing your hair. One understands that a Senator's wife may have done so, resulting in this obligation imposed by the State on all hotels; but how explain the compulsory bidet? Perhaps it has been requested by the porcelain lobby.

Our first hotel in Italy, thirty years ago — no, the second; the first was the Albergo Chiomonte, then in Lindsey's family — our second hotel in Italy was in the hills above Lake Como in a town whose name I forget. It was found in a moment of desperation: all other hotels were unavailable for some unimaginable reason. It was a bare-bones country hotel with no amenities to speak of. But it did have a bidet, a plastic basin of the correct size and shape, on folding wooden legs like those of a camp cot, tucked away underneath the bathroom sink.

The Hotel Luxor is near the railroad station, nicely situated, small, friendly. Its breakfast is more than adequate: granolas, fruit compote, stewed prunes, croissants, fruit juice, fresh fruit. Cappuccinos, of course. But no eggs, ham, sausages, or cheese, which perhaps explains the absence of the Dutch among the guests. We hear plenty of English in the breakfast room, but mostly Italian. It's the kind of place we like.

[Error: I subsequently discovered the animal protein on a table earlier overlooked.]

Not that we'll be spending much time in the hotel. The Salone del Gusto could easily consume all of each day here; on top of that now, there is the Terra Madre to entertain us. Yesterday we made our first visit there, listening to a conference on "Healing the Soil." Farmers from several continents discussed their methods of returning farmlands that have been compromised by technological farming methods to a more natural state.

It occurred to me that Nature in her wisdom has buried most of her injurious matter, and that the history of man has included the systematic digging up of this stuff and its distribution. This is a recurrent narrative among the German Romantics. E.T.A. Hoffmann has a fine story about miners — is it called "The Mines of Falun?" Gold, petroleum, lead, uranium, copper, sulfur, noxious substances all, are dug up and hoarded and passed around and prized for the mischief they can do.

Fertilizer, poison, and explosives are intimately related, and the chemical industry has much to answer for. And humanity is all too gullible. I don't think it's only the advertising industry that explains this; I think this dark trade has an attraction, an appeal which is built into our genetic makeup, an appeal which the advertisers no doubt take advantage of, if only without actually knowing it. Perhaps this use of dangerous substances is the Knowledge the gods wanted to withhold from us, like the Promethean fire.

In any case a farmer from Ontario recounted his decision, forced by economy, to depend on horses rather than petroleum for his farm-power: muscle-power reproduces; diesel power does not. He couldn't afford a tractor until he had sold enough colts, the by-product of his team of horses, to pay for one.

A fellow from Venezuela talked about returning dry tropical land to production of a native plant useful for its fibers, for fodder, for human food, and particularly for its ability to store water.

An Italian microbiologist talked about the absolute need for soil bacteria, billions of them, to prepare minerals for their assimilation by the roots of plants. These bacteria are routinely slaughtered by deep herbicides and pesticides, and it takes years to replace them.

A Greek agricultural economist asks if this may perhaps explain the spread of soil-based diseases, not only plant diseases but also animal diseases: might they not be flourishing in recently sterilized soils because their natural predators are no longer there?

All this goes on in a number of languages, and is simultaneously translated into French, Italian, English, Spanish, and Portuguese. The audience comprises farmers from every corner of the world.

In a large entrance hall, as big as a train station, our friend Lisa points out the Americans and a number of Europeans gathered at the Internet points and picking up their e-mail, while the Third World delegates from Siberia and Kenya and New Zealand (Maoris are still Third World, I think) and such have set up shop at folding tables. The Siberian, a small handsomely dressed man who might pass for a businessman from Milan, offers teas: the taste of one replicates a Siberian meadow; another a birch forest. They make me want to walk the Siberian countryside, a thought that has never come to me before.

A Maori offers abalone chowder, little pieces of abalone he'd dived for, tenderized by a secret process he was glad to share and stewed in coconut milk. A fellow from Ecuador gives us a taste of a fiery hot sauce he's made of pepper seeds: it persists through an emergency drop of Fernet Branca, but is flavorful and sweet and I'm glad I had it.

Among the most colorfully dressed are the Africans, of course, and we move up to a table run by a Kenyan woman, very dark, indeterminably old, wrapped in a brown and white figured cloth. Her table is covered with clear plastic bags of dried herbs, each neatly labeled with copy that on first sight offers very little detailed information. She looks at me for a moment, sizing me up, and shows me one package of very dark twiglike herbs. "This is good for cancer," she says. That's very interesting, I tell her, I've had prostate cancer for nearly ten years now.

She smiles. Good, she says, and I know that what she means is Good, you're still here, you're obviously in good health. I have had cancer for twenty years, she continues; I had breast surgery nineteen years ago.

She has other herbs for HIV, for various immune-deficiency problems, for miscellaneous ailments. She sells them over the Internet. She shows photos of one of the nineteen children she has adopted over the years: at birth, he was so dark and deformed there was little reason to keep him alive. She gave him herb teas and cared for him, though, and another photo at two years old showed a bright energetic little boy.

We swap cards. I ask if I may take her photograph: Yes, she says, but you have to send me one! She wants Lindsey in the photo, and I take their portraits, smiling at one another, then smiling out at me. What handsome women they are, I think; how good they look together.

We skip lunch and go straight to our workshops, saffron for Lindsey, four different-aged Goudas with Champagnes for me; then, at four o'clock, Dutch pecorinos for Lindsey, the second in a series of wine tastings for me. In between we have a little time for a stroll in the food hall, ostensibly to meet a friend but she is detained. Instead we watch a violinist, an accordionist, and a man who plays guitar and mandolin, playing Italian street songs outside the lunchroom set up by the region of Emiglia-Romagna. (Many Italian regions have set up such restaurants, serving characteristic dishes at both lunch and dinner; they offer very good bargains and a rare chance to sit down for a half hour at this fatiguing exhibition.)

Before long two couples are dancing. They dance quadrilles and couple-dances, dances dating back across a century and more. At one point I notice the older man is making mock menacing gestures to his partner, like a rooster with serious business on his mind. He crouches low as he wheels around her, his arms bowed at his sides, his eyes intent on her; and she pretends timidity, backing away, pinching the corners of the bottom of her jacket and holding them away from her like wing coverlets.

I think of the colorful dress of the Africans, the Peruvians, the Mongols, the Ecuadorians; and I think of the colorful crests and wattles of the capons, plucked but proud in the refrigerated showcases of the poultrymen. The Salone, like Terra Madre, is a true celebration of life as well as the death life feeds on, and Italy is a country apparently at ease with the complexities and contradictions of poultry, religion, tradition, and folding bidets.

Terra Madre, 1

Torino, Monday, Oct. 25 —

THESE HAVE BEEN FIVE days absolutely packed with input — conversational, informative, and physical, with two tasting workshops a day, fairly substantial breakfasts in the morning, and dinners in the evening ranging from a fine but unexceptional pizza-by-the-meter with friends to last night's gala dinner, rather a formal one, in a rustic palace an hour's drive away.

The most impressive moment so far was a long one, the two-hour plenary session concluding Terra Madre. We were gathered in the Palazzo di Lavoro, the Worker's Hall, an enormous hall built in modernist concrete in the 1960s when, as one speaker reminded us, the hope of the future lay in huge corporate industrial efficiency.

On the stage a hundred and more delegates were seated facing us, delegates from a hundred and more countries around the world, many wearing the distinctive clothing of their communities — Peruvians in brilliant red hats and capes, sequined or embroidered, Bolivians in their characteristic hats, an Amazonian whose cap sprouted amazingly long brilliant blue-green feathers standing straight up into the air — to name only a few from one of the six continents represented.

Between these delegates and the thousands of us in the audience stood the podium, sleek and elegant as only the Italians could make it, ground and transparent glass hovering over the floor, a seventeen-inch computer monitor almost invisible on it to help the speaker of the moment.

And behind the delegates, and for all I know behind us as well, enormous multi-screen monitors relaying the proceedings of the moment in much-larger-than-life so everyone has an equal chance to see the facial expressions, the demeanor of the speakers, and occasional glimpses of closeups of the audience as it responded.

All of this, of course, simultaneously translated into the seven official languages of the Terra Madre. (I was struck by the fact that six of them were European languages, the seventh being Japanese; the Africans and Asians present seemed little discommoded by this, being able to make do with English or French or Spanish; such has been the domination of the world by those of European extraction.)

We heard a keynote speech by Winona LaDuke, who reminded us that all living organisms are related, that humans share the world with many thousand others having an equal right to their existence, and that we are all mutually dependent.

A Mexican delegate spoke of Terra Madre as an unprecedented moment organizing the food-producer chain from everywhere in the world into a forum in which individuals retain their personal identities, a counter to the more familiar organization of global agriculture into a mechanism of constituent faceless business- and profit-oriented entities.

A Kenyan spoke of the imperatives of food safety, biodiversity, and cultural integrity. Food rights are human rights, he declaimed to great applause; and powerful nations must stop misadvising the agricultures and economies of developing nations, ruining their self-sufficiency in the name of profits elsewhere in the world.

A woman from India thanked Terra Madre for its revalidation of the processes her seed-exchanging community had been developing. Terra Madre had put food production right back on its feet, she noted, and in so doing had shown the world the role of women in agriculture.

An Italian fisherman noted that a failing of his tuna-roe community had been its tendency to guard its methods and knowledge as closely held secrets — the inheritance of an earlier historical imperative. Terra Madre has suggested the greater need for shared information and mutual trust; it counters peasant suspicion and corporate intellectual property with the optimism of pooled knowledge.

A Russian noted that here at Terra Madre we decide if there will be a future or not — whether the world will be committed to technological development or ecological development.

Then came the three important politicians involved, all of whom had spoken at the opening session a few days ago. The Mayor of the city of Torino spoke for the possibilities of an optimistic political culture, citing the United Nations and the example of Brazil's President Lula. The future lies in growth, not development, he noted; and he thanked, quite passionately and earnestly, the huge audience and the delegates for reminding him of the qualities so impressionably conveyed by farmers: happiness, peace, dignity, and nobility.

The governor of the region of Piemonte promised that his region, a proud and historically self-sufficient one, would be GMO-free as long as he was governor, and noted that Terra Madre was a logical extension of the political agricultural policy of Piemonte, whose rice, milk, cheese, beef, wine, and corn , I would add, leave little margin for improvement. And he noted that in this multiversity of languages and local cultures the first language is that of food, uniting us all, rather than separating us.

The Minister of Agriculture and Forestry of the nation of Italy noted that he'd been to many conferences of economics and politics, and that Terra Madre was the first involving the farmers and producers themselves. We must commit to a fundamental issue, he noted: whether to confront agriculture from an international point of view; or to recognize that the production of food is different from other World Trade Organization preoccupations because it must necessarily reflect local differences. We must end pitting farmers against farmers, and we must end non-farmers profiting at the expense of farmers. Trade must enhance farming rather than spoil its lands, for it is difficult in the extreme to recover from the ruins of exploitation.

Further, he argued, the living world must be protected from the demands of profit and intellectual property rights. Geographical *terroirs* must be designated and protected, through international political organizations working perhaps through Slow Food and Terra Madre. And the Kyoto Protocol on environmental issues, now finally signed by Russia, is now in force and will be enforced, and agriculture is a fundamental note in that protocol.

These three speakers lent great political reality and substance to Terra Madre. I think Italy is developing a very interesting role in the community of developed nations. It is after all quite advanced technologically, but of all the most advanced First World nations it has retained most successfully (and proudly) the cultural and agricultural differences of its constituent regions; it has most successfully combined the forward view of technology and the arts with the rootedness in tradition and history of its daily life values. I think it sees itself as a mediator between the developing nations and the developed, and I hope both Italy and the rest of the world remember that an evolving national character is bigger than any momentary political condition within it.

Carlo Petrini, the founder of Slow Food, summed up the final session, and introduced the final two speakers, Alice Waters and Charles, Prince of Wales. But I see I have filled the space for this dispatch, and will write about their comments next time.

Auto ramps to the roof of the old Fiat factory

Terra Madre concluded

Torino, Oct. 25 —

YESTERDAY I WROTE ABOUT the concluding plenary session of Terra Madre, the impressive gathering here of four thousand small farmers and food producers from 130 countries on six continents, all gathered here to share notes and methodologies and tactics and to brace one another for the coming struggle all feel must inevitably be made if they are to prevail in competition with global corporate agribusiness.

I ran out of steam before getting to the most memorable part of the evening, the concluding address. It was set up by what one might have thought would have been the conclusion: the remarks given by Carlo Petrini, the founder of the international Slow Food movement.

Petrini is a Piemontese, a native of this rather autonomous (though not officially) region of Italy. Piemonte boasts a rich combination of industry (automotive, hydroelectric, printing) and agriculture (wine, fruits, nuts, corn, rice, wheat). Further, it has stood for centuries as the buffer between southern and eastern Italy on the one hand and France to the west. Torino itself, the capital city, is elegant and intellectual, as French as it is Italian; the Piemontese cuisine has marked French influences; the dialect hovers between French and Italian; and the region has been French, Italian, and independent (as Savoia) by turns. Furthermore, it was the first part of Italy to move toward the integration of the modern Italy.

Petrini draws on this heritage of pride in region within a framework of internationalism. He was active in the Italian Communist party, as I understand it; and as I understand it that party was always more Italian than communist as we in the United States think of international communism.

But he has always been a gastronome as well. A journalist, he wrote for years on food as well as politics in a left-wing journal. A few years ago, revolted by the opening of yet another Big Mac in Italy, he had the happy idea of countering fast food with Slow

Food, and ever since he has been working tirelessly in true leftist fashion to gather around him the populist forces of farmers, fishermen, butchers, dairymen, orchardists, vintners, and restaurateurs in a cordial but politically active gathering of local, independent "presidia" dedicated to local, traditional, artisanal foods, often endangered ones threatened with the extinction of the resources or methods on which they rely.

He has folded this activity into a constantly expanding network of "convivia," local gatherings of people who share his enthusiasms, either as producers themselves or, more often, as "consumers" — those of us who admire and desire such products, and resist seeing them disappear under increasing piles of hamburgers, tacos, and take-out. (In Sonoma County, where I live, there are at least four of these convivia.)

So Carlo is the founder and the patron saint of Slow Food, and it was his place to conclude this historic first gathering of the presidia and convivia he has invented. He began by admitting that he didn't know if this conference could be repeated with the same passion and force: everyone who attended — press, politicians, visitors, and delegates — were struck with the great lesson in life the conference had presented: the life, dignity, work, and methods of these independent producers, gathered from Siberia and New Zealand, Peru and Finland, Wisconsin and Kenya, Great Britain and India and all points in between. Other debates he had witnessed have been harsh, Petrini said;; this one was relaxed. And this was not an exercise in folklore: the delegates all exhibited a pride in their identity.

The building we were in, the Palazzo di Lavoro, a striking Pierluigi Nervi monument, had been built in 1961, when industrialism was paramount, when the "First World" was drawing its wealth from the resources of the Second. Now, Petrini said, we are living in a postindustrial age, and there are three worlds: one is poor, ruined, needy; another is balanced and sustainable; yet another is rich but committed to an unsustainable lifestyle. Beware, you of this rich world; you can no longer profit by exporting your poisons to the south. Farmers and scientists must begin to work together.

Then he moved into his conclusion: We have played an overture: now the opera must begin. Its libretto, its words, will not be written by Slow Food; it will be written by all of you. It will be your history: what you do. You are twelve hundred communities, around the world. When we proposed this gathering, this Terra Madre, many said it was madness, utopian. But: Who sows utopia will reap reality.

This drew a lot of applause. But then Carlo Petrini introduced Alice Waters, who quieted the audience, asking them to give a warm welcome to a radical guest who would conclude the session. Radical may seem a strange word to use to describe him, she said; but it is an accurate one: radical means rooted. And in the next moments we heard a remarkable address, elegantly written and eloquently delivered by Charles, Prince of Wales.

He began by asking for indulgence: he had been eating and drinking his way through the Salone del Gusto, the huge exhibition of foods and beverages Slow Food has invited to fill Torino's vast exhibition hall.

"Despite the best intentions of many," the Prince said, "we have to face up to the fact that often, the consequence of globalization is greater unsustainability... Left to its own devices, I fear that globalization will — ironically — sow seeds of ever-greater poverty, disease and hunger in the cities and the loss of viable, self-sufficient rural populations...

"If all the money invested in agricultural biotechnology over the last fifteen years had been invested in developing and disseminating genuinely sustainable techniques — those that work with, rather than against, the grain of Nature — I believe that we would have seen extraordinary, and genuinely sustainable, progress."

Bagna cauda

I Mandorli, Oct. 26—

I'VE MENTIONED THAT Piemonte boasts rather an autonomous culture, and nowhere more readily, apparently, than at the table. There are many reasons for this: its characteristic products, its climate, its history, its blend of French and mountain influences on the more centrally Italian culture it has adopted.

So there are characteristic Piemontese dishes, many of which tend to be heavier, more peasant-like, more cold-weather oriented than those of Tuscany, say, or Emilia-Romagna, or the Veneto. *Bollito misto*, which we had today here at Franco and Gabriela Rampi's idyllic bed and breakfast. *Tajarin* with white truffles, which graced last night's table in an otherwise ordinary restaurant around the corner from our hotel in Torino.

And nothing is more characteristically Piemontese than *bagna cauda*, also spelled *bagna caoda*, literally "hot bath." It's a dish we like a lot, and have eaten in various settings, in restaurants and at home and once, memorably, in the kitchen of a second-cousin twice removed of Lindsey's, in her father's home town Chiomonte, a couple of hours west of here near the French border.

So when we signed up for our workshops at the Salone del Gusto one of the first we chose was on *bagna cauda*. It was particularly fitting, because it would be the final workshop of this year's Salone.

We generally attend two workshops a day. They came at one, four, and seven o'clock, on each of the five days of this fabulous food show: laboratories devoted to a specific area. This year I attended a series of five tastings of "natural" wines, wines made without chemical intervention of any kind in the vineyards or the wineries; and I worked my way around a series of aged farmhouse Gouda cheeses (for not everything here is Italian), and a platter of raw beef (another Piemontese specialty).

We decided, with two friends, that a four o'clock laboratory in *bagna cauda* would serve us for dinner, and we weren't far wrong. But the workshop gave us more than we bargained for.

Perhaps I should begin by explaining what *bagna cauda* is. That's how the workshop began, in fact, with a sort of culinary-historical contextualization, to speak criticese, of this fine traditional meal.

We were told that *bagna cauda* began in the city of Asti (though no doubt other localities would contest the claim), six or eight hundred years ago, when Asti was a central city to the international trade that flourished in those days between the present-day Italy and France. Even then it took imported ingredients to fashion a local cultural tradition, and merchants drove their donkeys through this waypoint on the road from the gulf of Lion in France to Milan and elsewhere in Italy carrying olive oil from the Ligurian coast, garlic from wherever it happened to be growing, and anchovies from Provence and Spain.

And, most important, salt. Many towns will say they were on the authentic salt road from France into Italy, our speaker told us, but in fact it was Asti that was the principal town; it lay on the main road from Provence to Milan and beyond, and all the merchants came through Asti.

(In fact that is a fascinating road, well worth traveling and considering, leading up from Nice by way of San Remo, the pass at Tende, dropping into the fine French-flavored provincial capital Cuneo and the several fertile valleys between it and Torino to the north, Asti to the northeast.)

It occurred to one of those donkey-driving merchants to smash up anchovies and garlic in a mortar, then cook them in some sizzling oil. Into this "hot bath" one dipped whatever edible came to hand, and most of it was vegetable matter. We've done this many times, as I've said, at our home and at others'. But at this *laboratorio* our *bagna cauda* was prepared for us by a noted chef, I don't have his name at hand, and brought out in individual bowls surrounded, on paper plates, by a wonderful array of vegetables all from Slow Food "presidia," farms and producers chosen by the Slow Food organization for the quality and authenticity of their produce.

We had raw and cooked peppers, revisionist accompaniments to *bagna cauda* dating back only a few hundred years; and savoy cabbage so mild and supple one would think it a lettuce of some sort; and chicory blanched of all bitterness; and sweet onions that had been steamed to lose their aggressiveness (which would otherwise argue unpleasantly with the garlic in the *bagna cauda*); and slices of astonishingly subtle and insinuating turnip; and peeled *topanambour* or Jerusalem artichoke; and, most important of all to a proper *bagna cauda*, cardoon, that curious vegetable that looks like celery but tastes of artichoke, which in fact is what it is — a variety of artichoke grown for its stems, which are bent over and buried underground to trade their bitterness for the redolence of the soil.

All of these we tasted methodically, thoughtfully, and with great appreciation, turn by turn, dipping them into...

But was this really a *bagna cauda*? Its flavor was reminiscent; there was anchovy there certainly, and a little garlic (though I would say in fact very little), and olive oil; but it looked like a vichyssoise: it was bound with cream, of all things, and bereft of any other texture.

We tasted it in silence, listening to the lengthy and detailed discussion of the history and preparation of *bagna cauda* being provided by this chef, haltingly translated for us anglophones (we were many) by a translator who seemed indifferent. (I suspect she was not partaking of it herself.) The chef often mentioned the Third Millennium; he felt it necessary to respect this great traditional dish by lifting it out of the farmhouse kitchen (let alone the donkeybacks) and moving it into the future. And he was proud of the result, and so was the rather defensive commentator from Slow Food who had introduced the chef to this audience: it is a true *bagna cauda*, it has great respect, it moves the dish forward, no one else could have made this.

At one point I raised my hand: In the valSusa, I said (the valley Lindsey's father was born in, where we had a fine *bagna cauda* two years ago), they use a little butter in the preparation... The chef went into an explosion of commentary, some of which was ultimately translated. I must be getting old, he said, I forgot to mention that I did use a little bit of butter at the beginning.

Still, I was thinking to myself, there isn't really a lot of garlic in this *bagna cauda*. The chef had insisted over and over that this was a social *bagna cauda*, you didn't feel that you had to avoid polite company after eating it, the garlic was greatly muted to bring this *bagna cauda* into the Third Millenium, whose social values have evolved beyond those of (he did not use this term, at least it never appeared in our headphones) a somewhat more primitive time.

Nevertheless, this was a delicious thing, whatever it was, and the vegetables were out of this world — sweet, complex, varied in texture between the fingers and between the teeth, utterly fresh. All but the cardoon, which seemed a little tired, a little scraggly — a farmer brought a bit against his will into a dining room a little more polite than he was used to.

At this point a woman in the audience made a comment of some sort by way of asking a question, and all hell broke loose. The chef went into a frenzy of retort. She spoke rapidly and at full voice in reply. They both spoke simultaneously.

Gioacchino Rossini composed many brilliant *imbroglii* in such operas as *The Barber of Seville*, but he did not invent the form, he inherited it from the natural way of speaking Italian when you are in passionate disagreement with another native speaker of the language. Voices arise, respond, and join in quick crescendos, the volume naturally rising quickly to keep one's own voice in one's ears. The pace quickens similarly, and parallel passages develop as arguments are supported, paraphrased, analyzed, and recombined.

Through all this a good-natured fellow to the left of the chef smiled in his grey beard and looked down into the four glasses of Barbera with which we had all been thoughtfully armed. The master of ceremonies ultimately turned to him as a sort of judge between the chef and the lady in the audience, and this fellow turned out to be a chef himself.

He seemed to dissociate himself from both, though I suspect his allegiance was with the woman. Certainly it was with tradition. My own *bagna cauda*, he said, is more traditional than this, and I make no apologies for this, you can find my restaurant (La Donna Rossa, in Nizza Monferrato, a town we must visit one of these days) by following your nose.

Which perhaps we will do tomorrow. In the meantime we are visiting our friends Franco and Gabriela Rampi at their farmstead B&B, along with four California friends. Yesterday we visited an agricultural school to see the first pressing of Franco's olives, and today we visit a goat farm, or perhaps an antique apple orchard.

And I still have to tell you about the five wine workshops I attended last week. But all this can wait .

Agricultural school
I Mandorli, Oct. 27—

"I MANDORLI" MEANS "the almond grove," but Franco does a few other things on his ten or twelve acres of land here in Monferrato. He makes a nice Barbera, for example; we had one yesterday with our *bollito misto* and another, aged in wood, with the cheese. And when we arrived Tuesday morning I noticed a small bin of olives in the back of his pickup truck.

We sat down first to lunch, though, Jim and Lisa and Lindsey and I, for that celebratory *bollito misto* — pieces of head, flank, and tail of beef, and pieces of chicken, and *cotechino*, that delicious loose moist uncooked salame, all boiled up with carrot and bay, eaten cool with basil sauce and tomato sauce.

Then we asked about the olives. They had been mysteriously driven away by someone, I still don't know who, to be pressed; this would be Franco's first olive oil. Did we want to see the press? Of course!

By now two more friends had arrived, Lou and Susan; Lou grows olives as well as grapes in Dry Creek Valley and is of course much interested in the press. Franco explained (as well as I could follow) that it was a small press, brand new, and he was as interested in it as any of us.

So we four men piled into Lou's car and drove for what seemed an hour through the gathering night, east, past Moncalvo, then north to skirt its hill, and east again, and turn off onto this little road, no, not this one, back up a bit and continue further, stop here and ask this good-natured young man waiting for a bus whether this is the way to San Martino, yes, straight ahead, and finally we turn downhill and find a fair-sized parking lot outside what seems to be an old convent or something.

It is not a convent, it is the V. Luparia Professional State Institute for Agriculture and the Environment — "a school in the countryside to maintain the countryside." A secretary directs us down the institutional hallway, damp plaster walls (it has been raining) and dimly lit, to a staircase: Down and to the right, she calls out, and we emerge into what I think must be a basement, walk past a shiny new stainless-steel grape crusher and into a cement room housing a brand new stainless steel olive crusher.

A beaming young man with shiny curly black hair immediately congratulates Franco: Your olives are truly excellent, he says; the oil is magnificent. We have arrived just in time to see the first few tablespoons emerge; three or four are already in a wineglass which is passed around. We admire the color and above all the fragrance of this new oil, and Lou quickly lifts the glass to his lips. (I do too, seeing him: the oil is new, fat, complex, very floral, and very very good.)

The crusher is about the size of two refrigerators lying on their sides atop one another. The olives go in a hopper on top and are fed into a vertical cylinder: inside, three blades turn slowly, forcing the olives against the walls of the cylinder. The resulting paste is fed to a chamber where water is combined with them, and the now much more fluid paste is then spun very rapidly in a centrifuge. This separates the oil, water, and paste, much as the cream separator worked when I was a boy (though it makes much more noise), and the oil collects in its own chamber to drain in a very slow stream into a plastic pitcher set on the floor under a petcock.

It's a funny combination of ultramodern technology and peasant farm practicality, but it works. Lou looks with envy at the machine, juggling the figures in his mind: How many pounds of olives, how many liters of oil, how many dollars of machine.

Franco's olives are not only exceptionally tasty; they are exceptionally productive. The young man, who turns out to be Ferrucio Battaglio, a head teacher at the school, says it is the best yield he has seen. The oil continues to accumulate in the pitcher and we begin to discuss the school.

It's a boarding school for boys (and a few girls) from fourteen to eighteen years old. They come from all over the country, many of them from the city, to learn agriculture. They're interviewed and chosen not so much by their previous school grades, though that's important, as by the passion they show for this field. They study agriculture in all its aspects: horticulture, soil sciences, entomology, plant pathology, weather, accounting, marketing, distribution. Also the production of agricultural products: wine, cheese, olive oil, honey. And, of course, the required general education subjects: literature, history, mathematics, religion, physical education, foreign language.

They study nine months of the year, then work two months in the summer on assigned farms; for farming can be studied intellectually, but must be learned with the muscles and the senses. They have one month of vacation.

By now we are tasting some of the experimental wine made here, an Albarossa, a varietal with a long tradition in these parts but one that had fallen out of favor. The Institute is conducting studies on varietals and *terroir*, making wines in very small batches to isolate varietals, soils, and microclimates. Grapes are brought by the farmers, labeled as to exactly which vineyard they come from, how steep it is, what the soil is, what direction they face, and so on. These are crushed and developed in perhaps fifty or sixty miniature stainless-steel fermenting tanks stand, each capable of holding maybe twenty gallons at most.

The Albarossa is an interesting wine, very dark, earthy, fragrant, full-bodied, smooth, and complex. The flavors seem medieval to me; I taste cloves and the soil as well as grape; it would be delicious with a slice of *panforte*, or just the right cheese. Or a *bagna cauda*, Battaglio points out. It is a local wine: it has *terroir*.

We admire the great cellar, centuries old, now used primarily as a meeting room and a lecture hall. The walls are local stone and cobble and brick. They were brought up, underground, to twelve or fourteen feet high; then the room was filled with soil and layered with sand, in the time-honored way, so the vaulted brick ceiling could be laid on the sand and mortared from above, after which the entire room was again dug out and the building continued above it. It's a time-consuming way of building, but the building maintains an absolutely even temperature, and of course it lasts many centuries with little additional maintenance. What you spend making something excellent at the beginning, Jim muses, you save in maintenance and correction later on.

This is something better known by the kinds of people who stay in the place of their forefathers, I think, than by the kinds of people who move on; and we Americans are descended from the latter. This dialectic is familiar to me; I rehearse it every time I come to Europe. We have invented much, we Americans, in our need to develop a culture and a political and social body quickly on virgin territory (let's overlook the native population for the sake of argument) and with the means that come easily to hand. But we have done this at a certain cost, and have threatened older traditions with extinction in our dependency on global networks for our resources and our profits. In our insistence on modernity and efficiency we are losing the distinctions of *terroir*.

Castello di Rivoli, Piemonte

Wines I have tasted

I Mandorli, Oct. 29—

AMONG THE HIGHLIGHTS of the biennial Salone del Gusto, at least for me, are the taste workshops. Here you have the opportunity to taste rare and unusual items and to learn how they are produced. Even more gratifying to me, in the course of concentrating on such things you are reminded how to taste analytically, to take the sensation of taste apart, to separate the flavors and aromas so as to enjoy and appreciate them more fully, to fit words to them and to fix them in memory — to the extent possible.

So in the past we have learned about tuna, from brains to eggs; about raw beef; about parmesan cheese whether from high pastures or low; about pecorino from this breed of sheep or that. We have focussed on gelatos, on pastries, on pastas. As I wrote yesterday, we have argued over *bagna cauda*. This year I even compared and contrasted farmhouse Gouda cheeses of four different ages.

All these, of course, matched to the correct wines; and in the course of drinking those wines with the foodstuffs new aspects of taste and aroma have developed. It's as if you hear an oboe; then several oboes of different manufacture, played by musicians from different countries; all playing the same piece of music solo, then accompanied by a few other instruments; and then you listen to orchestral music for the oboe passages: Haydn, Berlioz, Ravel.

I was particularly looking forward this year to a series of taste workshops on wines and soils. I've been thinking a lot about the mysterious subject of terroir lately, partly unprompted, partly after reading Lawrence Osborne's fascinating book *The Accidental Connoisseur*. Osborne suggests that connoisseurship can be "accidental"; and that the gathering of this accidental connoisseurship is, perhaps, "the one consolation of growing old." (Of course connoisseurship would have evolved in the human animal for practical reasons, as part of the necessary learning and remembering of which ingestables are nutritious, which pleasurable, and which are dangerous.)

"*Terroir*" is of course a French word; I can't readily think of an English equivalent. (That says something; never mind what.) It refers to the local specificity that contributes to (and results in part from) products which, like wine, remain close to the earth. In the case of wine it is part climate, of course, but also (and perhaps more so) part soil. There is no question that minerals are taken up by plants, and that mineral content affects flavor.

But the awareness of *terroir* is both intuitive, I think, and learned. The intuitive awareness is fundamental: without it, learned connoisseurship is merely taste. But the learned component is significant: without it, intuitive connoisseurship is blinkered. Taste may well be the product of cities, but *terroir* is by definition an expression of soil. What alarms Osborne, and alarms me too, is the extent to which the "value" expressed by *terroir* is, at the present moment, threatened with extinction — it's not too strong a word — by the exigencies of Taste at its most extreme, which Osborne encodes, reasonably enough, as Brand. In the case of wine, the men Osborne quotes blame journalism and subsequent marketing for this. Over and again he records conversations with aging connoisseurs who grow resigned to the idea that they may not be survived by the values to which they have dedicated their lives.

The series of five workshops I took on wines turned out not to be about the influence of soils and minerals on the qualities of wines made from the vines that grow in them, as I had hoped, but simply an introduction to wines of *terroir* — a panorama of wines all made in a natural style, without chemical interventions in the vineyard or the fermenting and storage rooms. These were all wines from a single collection, or catalogue: the "Triple 'A'," *Agrigoltori, Artigiani, Artisti*.

The catalogue opens with a manifesto by the man who conducted our workshops, Luca Gargano — a manifesto which speaks directly to the points Osborne raises in *The Accidental Connoisseur:*

MANIFESTO

This manifesto arises with the statement that the larger part of the wines now being produced everywhere in the world are standardized, that is obtained with agricultural and enological techniques that compromise the quality of the vineyard, the influence of its terrain, and the personality of the producer.

Standardization is resulting in wines which are similar in

every corner of the planet, flattened in their organoleptic character and unable to stand up to age.

According to this manifesto, to obtain a great wine, three basic assumptions must be shared by every producer:

• A as in Agriculture: Only the person who directly cultivates the vineyard can obtain a correct rapport with the vines, and obtain healthy and mature grapes with exclusively natural agronomic methods.

• A as in Artisan: There are "artisanal" methods and qualities that activate a viticultural and enological process that doesn't modify the original structure of the grape, and don't alter that of the wine.

• A as in Artist: Only the "artistic" sensibility of a producer, respectful of his own work and ideas, can give life to a great wine in which the character of the terrain and the vineyard reach their peak.

From these initial considerations follow ten commandments, which must be respected by any producer of "Triple A" wines.

DECALOGUE

Triple A wines can develop only:

• from a manual selection of future vines, through a truly husbanded selection.

• through farmers who cultivate the vines without using any synthetic chemicals interfering with the vines and their natural cycles.

• from perfectly healthy grapes harvested at their physical maturity.

• from juice to which neither sulfur dioxide nor any other additive is added. Sulfur dioxide may be added only in minimal amounts at the moment of bottling.

• with the use of only indigenous yeasts and the exclusion of selected yeasts.

• without chemical or physical intervention before and during the fermentation other than the simple control of temperature.

• when matured on their own fine lees until bottling.

• when not corrected by any chemical parameter.

• when neither clarified nor filtered before bottling.

Very well, you might ask, a pretty strict set of rules excluding nearly every well-known wine in the shop. So what did I taste, and how did they strike me?

Of the twenty-six wines, all seemed exceptionally true to their varietal, whether Muscadet, Riesling, Chardonnay, Viognier, Sauvignon Blanc or Moscato; Pinot Noir, Cabernet Sauvignon, Tempranillo, Merlot, Grenache or Gamay. In addition, nearly all seemed to me to express something specific beyond the varietal, something identifying the wine as having a character, a personality all its own; and often that something had a mineral or soil-suggesting quality that one can only think of as *terroir*.

Not all the wines were what I would call really sound. One, for example, was indeed corked, and had to be replaced; two or three had a volatility that suggested they were going through bad phases. At least three were wines that simply didn't interest me: but then we all have our likes and dislikes, and I've never been interested in Muscadet or Merlot.

(Of course if I'd had a plate of oysters in front of me that Muscadet would indeed have been welcome, and that made me think that a parallel survey of these wines, this time matching them to the right foods, would be even more instructive.)

Some of the wines were memorable, and a few were truly outstanding. In the former category, the 2002 Ribolla from Movia, on the Slovenia side of the Collio hills, beautifully direct and fruity; the 2002 Molino Real moscatel from Malaga, with excellent character; a Pinot noir from Stephane Tissot, in the Jura (but my notes for this are missing: was it 2000 or 2001?); and the Matallana Ribera del Duero 2001 Tinto fino, with its gorgeous deep garnet color and fine balance of fruit, wine, and soil.

Six wines were among the best I have tasted. I'm no wine expert, and my wine memory is erratic. Of course I can reconstruct tastes in my mouth-memory: the Zinfandels I have made (and those Lindsey's father made); the Preston wines I drink when we splurge; the ordinary Trader Joe Pinot grigio we drink every day in the summer.

But true taste memory is different — it comes unbidden, simply when a name is mentioned. I remember the exceptionally old California wines I have tasted, a Zinfandel and a Cabernet sauvignon from the 1890s. (Beringer, I think.) I remember my first premier cru, though it wasn't really, a 1953 Haut-Brion at a special dinner in the early 1960s. I remember the first Sauternes I tasted and can distinguish in my memory Chateaux Rayne-Vigneau, Suduiraut, and Climens of the late 1950s and early 1960s; and I remember fondly the great Naudin burgundies of the early 1960s.

To these now are added six more wines, though of course the memories may fade. They are:

• Touraine "La Tesniere", Puzelat, 2003: Dark garnet, unfined, thick legs; red fruit, plums, very dry, dirt; cloves, the nose continuing to the palate; finishing in excellent balance, length; very accessible though complex and integrated — final impression violets: the intersection of violets, plums, and figs. This is from the Pineau d'Aunis grape, a traditional one that had fallen out of favor decades ago but is being reconstructed now by the Puzelat brothers. 1800 bottles were produced in this vintage.

• Clos de Rouge Gorges Cote Catalanes 2002: straw-color, bright, heavy legs; some slight brass; solid mature fruit similar to Viognier, oak, balanced; quite mature yet lively. This was from 65-year-old Maccabeo vines, made in an edition of only 2000 bottles, and it was superb.

• Pouilly-Fuisse 1999, Clos Ressié, réserve particulier: honey-gold, very bright, slow legs; fine full nose, balanced — from 70-year-old Chardonnay vines, thirty months in the barrel, 80% new wood, finishing in a long perfect balance of fruit, minerals, and vanilla — the most satisfying Chardonnay I think I can remember ever having tasted. 1700 bottles.

• Domaine Gramenon "La Sagesse," 2002, Cotes du Rhone: Garnet, unfined, thin at edge; fruit, stems, alcohol on nose; goes deliciously soft, with peppery fruit on palate; from a 65-year-old Grenache vineyard.

• Beaujolais, Fleurie 2003, Domaine Yvon Metras: Garnet, unfined, heavy legs; direct fruit nose, changing quickly, ending in violets; finishing slightly sweet with fruit, very soft, full, a lingering sense of roses, from 75-year-old gamay vines

• Ribera del Duero Matallana 2001, Telmo Rodriguez: black garnet, thick, slow sheet; serious nose, fruit and wine; completely integrated. I'll give you Luca Gargano's notes: "elegant, warm, enveloping, spicy, concentrated, meaty, and minerals; creamy tannins. This is from 65-year-old Tinto fino vines which are attended, in Gargano's words, in a "culture of abandonment": the seven acres of vines are treated biodynamically, and the wine fermented in a single vat, then finished for twenty months in small new French oak for a total production of 4546 bottles.

I have don't know how much these wines sell for, but I have an idea they are completely beyond my reach. (The workshops cost about twenty euros apiece and were well worth the price.) And that, of course, brings up a real conundrum: as things stand, only the very wealthy (by my standards) can afford to buy these marvelous wines which are produced by methods and from resources one can only call peasant-like — land values aside.

There is one consolation: if these wines ultimately succeed in spoiling the near-universal present taste for interchangeable "monster" wines, then more small producers will be encouraged to return to these methods. Perhaps the day will come when it will be the usual way to grow grapes and make wine, and enough vineyardists and vintners will be trained, perhaps in schools like that described in the previous dispatch, to be able to spell one another in the exacting and time-consuming profession.

Peasantry will then have become a profession, honored and recompensed. If at the same time it becomes common for society to encourage a narrowing of the presently grotesquely wide range of personal incomes, we will have learned to work for our own and one another's health and enjoyment, and industrial production will have been channeled toward truly useful, efficient, long-lasting, and relatively few products.

Wouldn't it be nice.

Highways and hotels

Monte San Savino, Nov. 1—

AND A HAPPY ALL SOUL'S DAY to you. This is a serious holiday here; the cemeteries are full of people honoring their dead. Hallowe'en, American Style, has been shouldering its way into the European sensibility for a few years now, and nowhere more enthusiastically than in Italy. Italy, after all, has embraced Coca-Cola and blues and American pop lit for a number of years; why not Hallowe'en? But as usual the Italian assimilation of American pop culture seems a little superficial; these things are enjoyed as playthings rather than taken seriously, and they leave room for the Italian traditional way of life, *la vita quotidiana*.

Chrysanthemums here are invariably associated with the dead; they are the flowers you take to the graveyard. We drove over to Chiomonte Friday to visit Lindsey's grandfather, who has been lying comfortably, we trust, since May 1947, in a plot in the village cemetery. We visit him fairly often, I'd say every three or four years somehow. He's the only close relative of Lindsey's there; all the rest have remained in the United States, where they emigrated nearly a century ago.

They settled in the coalmine country southeast of Seattle, where Luigi, the grandfather, mined coal, and Luigia, his wife, ran a boarding house. They raised five children, of whom the youngest was Bob, Lindsey's father. (He, for some reason, was left behind for a year when the others emigrated, and didn't come until 1914, when he was ten years old; he made the trip by himself, in steerage from Genoa to Bedloe's Island, then by train to Seattle.)

In the 1920s the grandparents returned to Italy; I'm not sure why. They had lost their home in the company town after one of the IWW strikes, and perhaps they wanted to spend their retirement back home. Perhaps it was the Depression that sent them. In any case Luigi, by then an old man, basically had to hide out during the Second World War; his health suffered (it must have been pretty badly compromised years earlier in the mines); and he died before he and Luigia were able to fit into the immigration waitlist to return. Luigia did return, to the family farm Lindsey's father and uncles and aunt had by then bought near Healdsburg.

There are more distant relatives still living in Chiomonte, and we always visit Rosa, whose husband Ernesto was a first cousin of Lindsey's father. We stopped in for lunch, which she insisted on serving us — *salume*; raw beef; *vitello tonnato* which she knows is my favorite; Russian salad — all the Piemontese staples. No *bagna cauda*, but a bottle of this year's Barbera da Chiomonte, which can't be bought, and another a year older that's been aged in wood; and a bottle of Arneis that we didn't touch.

Then we went down to the cemetery to find the family tomb, beautifully washed and polished by Giancarlo, Rosa's son. We set the chrysanthemums in their green-shirted pot on the grave, under Luigi's photo — an old one, I'm afraid, a man clearly younger than the man they buried, sober and not quite at home with himself under a soft Italian hat. He may have been uncomfortable in the plot, which is otherwise Rosa's family — Ernesto, their daughter Anna Maria who died only fifty years old of Legionnaire's disease; other older relatives.

Afterward we walked down the narrow main street lined by brooding dark houses, all three or four storeys high, most capped with haylofts, crouching over "cantinas" or cellars for wine and eggs and potatoes and the like, and hiding from the street behind very large, very old pairs of oak or maybe chestnut doors. There are no longer donkeys in town, but there is still the occasional three-wheel utility vehicle, for some of the citizens are still *contadini*, still spend their days in the outlying vineyards and orchards and gardens, while others work in carpentry shops and the like.

Once inside these buildings, though, you're surprised to find living apartments that are completely up to date, with satellite TV and computers and shelves of books and encyclopedias and the latest magazines. We visited another distant cousin, one we hadn't known before, who'd been e-mailing genealogical information to a childhood cousin of Lindsey's in Sonoma County, practicing our Italian and learning a little more of the immensely complicated family relationships.

We thought of spending the night in the Napoleon, the hotel we always stay in in Susa; the man at the desk recognized us immediately and welcomed us back. I like Susa, a town going back to Caesar's day — there are two arches from those days, and the ruins of a theater and an arena, and there's a church said once to have been a temple dedicated to Venus. Like the much smaller Chiomonte, Susa is essentially a mountain town, all paved, with plastered stone buildings roofed in flagstones. But the street life is growing gayer; there are more cafes and bars lately; color is making its way into town, and everything's getting spruced up for the Winter Olympics next year — an important ski run will be in Chiomonte, the first major event to hit the town really since Hannibal marched his elephants through, two thousand years ago.

But we didn't stay in Susa. We got away in time to head further, for the next day we were to be clear across the top of Italy, in Verona. We'd come a long drive west from the Rampis, in Monferrato, but we drove right past Asti again, retracing our way, and overshot Alessandria and settled for the night in Tortona.

We found a good enough hotel, though a bit too expensive; and, since we'd been eating and drinking far too much and I was getting a cold, we ate light — just a bowl of broth with a few ravioli and a green salad for me, with a half bottle of pretty good Chardonnay from the Alta Adige. Then, next day, on to Verona.

The Italian *autostrade* are a bland pleasure to drive. I stay in the right lane except to pass, and drive between 120 and 140 — 75 to 87 miles per hour. This is possible because the pavement on these toll highways is uniformly excellent, the curves gentle, the grades easy, and the on- and off-ramps few and far between. There are trucks, but they are readily passed, even though there are rarely more than two lanes in each direction.

And the landscape! From Torino to Alessandria we were in the familiar Monferrato, whose hills, hilltop towns and castles, and mixed agricultural use (though heavily planted in those fabulous Piemontese grapes, of course) contrast with the brooding, serene Po plain that comes next, all the way to Brescia — flat grainfields, bare by November, and long serious lines of sepulchral poplars, and large, dark, ample, aging farmsteads, brick with tile roofs, all hazy and romantic in the nearly always present mists rising from the river.

It's always a shock to approach the big cities, with their warehouses, factories, superstores, parking lots, and miscellaneous dumps. The route between Brescia and Verona is particularly distressing, I think; and the surroundings of Verona, the produce markets, the industrial showrooms, the *fiera* or commercial exposition that's been a major part of the Veronese economy since the Middle Ages.

But we parked within a block of Richard and Marta's flat, and spent the weekend on foot in the center of the city, walking up and down the Adige, rather high and muddy Saturday from upstream storms, though we were never actually rained on. Richard was showing his sculpture in a community gallery, elegantly recycled out of a former slaughterhouse that still sports its nicely carved testamentary ox-heads contrasting with his smooth, biomorphic, abstract bronzes and terra-cottas.

They are old friends; our reunions are always both fond and eventful, with much to catch up on, whether food or music or art or politics or, best of all, family. We ate at Greppia, a fine traditional restaurant whose *fegato veneziana* (calf's liver with onions and polenta) is as good as I've had even in Venice; and we ate at da Ugo, a brand-new trattoria whose *osso buco* Richard said was very good, but I changed my mind at last minute and had venison prepared in a sauerbraten style.

And then this morning, after listening to the church-bells, and walking into town for a cappuccino, and through the market in the Piazza dell'Erbe to say hello to The Artichoke Lady (who looks much better, Richard says, having survived a bought of bad health and returned to the pink of enthusiasm), we packed up and drove south, through the Po plain, up into the Apennines, past Bologna and Firenze, and then turned away from the highway (twelve euros for the 150 or so miles Verona to Florence) for a smaller road through the hills past San Gimignano, whose towers we admired but withstood detouring to savor again more closely, and through Siena also ignoring it, to take an unfamiliar road toward Arezzo.

Here the hills recall the Var in Provence, with pines and oaks and occasional groves of olives planted in *restanques*, terraces set apart by low stone walls. I was startled at one sharp turn to see an African woman standing off the road, barely visible for the camouflage flak-jacket and head-scarf she was wearing, a tribal kind of costume rather spoiled by her high heels and fishnet stockings: for she was a working woman, waiting for a customer to drive by.

Who would, I wondered, and then realized that there were many jeeps and sport vehicles on the road, and more parked on shoulders here and there, and then single men and then groups of them standing about, some armed. It is mushroom season, we saw a number of people purposefully sauntering along the road carrying baskets and sharply pointed digging sticks. But it is also hunting season, and perhaps tonight I'll have venison again, or, better yet, *cinghiale*, the wild boar that animates these woods.

We're in the Hotel Sangallo here — can that really mean Saint Rooster? Lindsey's napping, having just watched a news special on, of all things, the Tuscan participation in the Salone del Gusto. We wonder what will happen tomorrow, of course. We'll lift a glass to the Red Sox and the middle class, with Jim and Lisa in Rome, and then we'll settle down to life in Trastevere again, and I'll let you know how that goes.

Pure heart and paranoia
Monte San Savino, Nov. 2—

ON, THEN, TONIGHT, after a short nap (Lindsey, suffering from a cold) and a short fit of writing the previous Dispatch (disfigured by, if nothing else, referring to Lindsey's father as her mother), for a quick walk all the way across town and back and then to dinner.

Monte San Savino is a walled town on the top of a hill. You really don't need to say a lot more than that. The hill is fairly symmetrical: I don't know enough about geology to guess how such hills are formed. I could imagine, having traveled ten years ago or so in Sardinia, that such hills are in fact simply piles of dirt and garbage people have piled up on their town to hide it from the invader. We used to have shell mounds in northern California, formed by the thoughtlessly compulsive stacking of used oyster-shells. Perhaps Monte San Savino is something like that.

In any case it is a fairly symmetrical hill surmounted by a walled town. If that town is bisected by a main street running west to east, we are in a hotel just outside the western gate. A lovely moon hung low in the sky ahead of us as we walked across the town, and it was invisible on the way back.

It was a question of dinner. We have eaten a great deal in the last week or two, a great deal more than we are used to, or than we deserve to, or than probably, if you listen to the current advice, is good for us to do. But it has mostly tasted very good indeed, and my usual approach to this matter is, if you want it, and it isn't poison, and you're not likely to get a chance to have it two or three months from now, at least not more than once or twice a week, why then go ahead and give it a try.

Long, long ago, so long ago I can't really think how long ago, except that a girl in her early twenties was with us who is now a nationally renowned chef in, oh let's say her very late forties, Lindsey and I were in Firenze (Florence, if you must) for a week or two. There I did some things I still remember. I wrote a fair amount of a violin concerto. I bought a pair of shoes. I had an excellent haircut. We visited a fine garden.

And I had *bistecca Fiorentina*.

Bistecca Fiorentina is a threatened meal, or should be. I mean, first of all, it depends on a particular kind of animal, and that breed — *razza* in Italian, only translatable by "race" in English — is the Chianino bovine, and some say it is threatened with extinction, whether by gene modification, or corporate greed, or innate human laziness, or the supremacy of the petroleum industry.

The Chianino is a large, rangy, placid, white, horned, cow of a sort. If it gives milk it's a cow, in English; if it pulls a cart it's an ox; if it gives meat, presumably it's a steer. I'm not sure about too much of this, because when we checked into the hotel tonight there was a television news documentary on about the Salone del Gusto, where we spent a few days a week or two ago, and it was done from the local point of view (that is, the Tuscan), and it said, what I could hardly believe, that scientific tests had proved that the Tuscan Chianino was definitively the bovine animal the lowest in cholesterol and fat of all bovines. And I knew, of course, that that could not be true, because in fact it was true of the Piemontese breed (*razza*) of bovine.

But. A look in the Slow Food Guide to the Osterie d'Italia, the Inns of Italy, showed that while the only recommended restaurant in town was closed on Mondays, there was in the vicinity a butcher who was particularly recommended for his *salume* from biologically (read: organically) raised pigs. On our walk across town we saw this butcher shop, and a sign in the window also recommended his Chianino beef. And of the three restaurants open tonight, a holiday night, one boasted that their beef was exclusively Chianino.

Since it is now (or was when we entered the restaurant, of course I write this a little while later) twenty or thirty years since I last had *bistecca fiorentina*, it seemed only reasonable to give it a whirl. In fact it wasn't all that good the last time, at a heavily recommended (read: Michelin approved) restaurant in Firenze called the Tredici Gobbi (the Thirteen Hunchbacks) or something of the sort. It seemed to me then, and I recall this now, that it was heavy, greasy, a little thin, too trumped-up with *accoutrements*. But I also recall that there was a promise in the dish. I have tried a few times to approximate it in my own kitchen: rib-eye steak, olive oil, salt, lemon. But none of that ever came together in a dish that made sense.

After walking across town an back, and verifying that there were only three eating places open, of which one served only pasta and featured Illy coffee (not my favorite), and that another was playing raucous music, we went to Il Cassero and put ourselves at the mercy of strangers.

Lindsey, not feeling well, wanted broth and salad, as I had had in Tortona a couple of days ago. Neither being available, she settled for fettucine with wild mushrooms and grilled vegetables.

I saw *bistecca Fiorentina* on the menu, and wondered if I could have a small one. *No, signor, non e possible, la bistecca e minime settecento grammi.*

Now seven hundred grams is about a pound and a half, and I regretfully declined.

Well then, the waiter said, in Italian of course, they speak that here, perhaps you'd like the small steak.

Yes, I said, that sounds reasonable. And some grilled vegetables; I'll have those with my wife's pasta.

We negotiated the wine: a half carafe of red, no more, for me. Oh, said Lindsey, but I want white. Very well, a half carafe of white too.

The pasta came, insinuatingly, promisingly, blushing with tomatoes that seemed to have been sun-dried; and blissfully, snugly insulated with a layer of porcini, the wild mushrooms this afternoon's basket-toting poachers must have been hunting. My grilled vegetables came: peppers, torpedo onions, a very thin slice or two of eggplant, ditto zucchini, beautifully sautéed, then grilled.

Then the rather louche waiter returned bearing a plate with an enormous rib-eye lying raw and naked on it. *Sesante grammi*, he promised mendaciously; *va bene?* (Twenty-one ounces, okay?)

A lightening calculation proved to me that at four euros per etto, or hundred grams, this would be a bargain twenty-four dollars, if you believe that the euros and the dollar are coterminous, which works in such moments for me. (It does not for Lindsey.)

Do you ever think about economy, Lindsey asked, unreasonably. Of course I do, I lied; the proof is that I have not ordered a Martini in the last two weeks.

Around us the dining room was festive. There were a great many men eating without women at their tables, as seems often to be the case here in Italy. Many of them were wearing sport outfits that suggested pit mechanics at a racetrack, or standbys in a beer commercial taping.

At other tables there were occasional women. Now and then one would walk past our table toward a room somewhere out of sight, and many of them wore curious local costumes, black skirt-like affairs made of animal skins, ending somewhere between the knee and the hip, often quite oddly tight. The men at their tables set down their knives and forks and paid them respectful attention.

Not too well cooked, I hastily called out to our waiter, I forgot to say, not too well cooked, pinkish. I can never remember the Italian for *saignant*.

A sangue, signor? he asked. *Si.*

And ultimately there it came, an utterly marvelous thing, a rib-eye steak, a teeny bit thin by American standards but rare, beautifully salted, the right amount (very little) of the right kind (floral, buttery, not overly peppery, not too young, retiring) olive oil. Alongside, a quarter of a lemon and a demure leaf of something green, easily ignored.

Well. Dinner and conversation proceeded apace. We had a great deal of fun. Lindsey didn't quite finish her pasta, nor for that matter her half carafe of slightly sparkling very simple and fresh local white wine, but she seemed to like it all.

I managed to get down every morsel of my steak. The red wine proved useful in the exercise.

I called twice for the check, and it finally came. The waiter had already ascertained that our Italian was neither local nor authentic; that we were, in fact, American. He put the check down with a both a flourish and a spoken warning: *Servizio non incluso.*

Well, of course not. The check used to have a line printed at the bottom: such-and-such percent *servizio incluso*; so much tip included. But that's been gone for quite a while. Explanations vary, and the truth will never be known. No one I've spoken to knows quite how to handle this, beyond leaving a little something, perhaps to round up, perhaps to get rid of some excess coins.

But then of course he took forever to pick up the check, and when he did pick it up he immediately put the whole tray, check, credit-card and all, down on a nearby table where three people were having a good time, one of them wearing a Caipirinha tee-shirt with the recipe for that wonderful Brazilian drink stenciled on the back. Caipirinha dropped a heavy-lidded eye on the check, nodded, and Waiter picked it back up and walked off with it. When he returned I signed it and dropped an additional five euros in coin. I hope, though I do not greatly care, that it was enough.

Trastevere, from the window on our landing

Roman arrival

Vicolo del Cedro, Nov. 4—

I WRITE THIS AT a black moment. It has been both frustrating and somehow liberating to be away from current English-language news for the last two weeks. We hear things after the fact, usually via Italian television, sometimes by more surprising means.

We were sitting in the stupid orange-juice cafe in the Piazza Sta. Maria in Trastevere at about five o'clock when Jim and Lisa walked by. Not surprisingly: although they're staying up the other side of St. Peter's, they've been down here a few times. While they sat with us as we finished our $7.50 glasses of orange juice and watched the sunset up the Lungaretta their cell phone rang: Lisa's mother was calling from Los Angeles to announce that Kerry had conceded the election.

This was no surprise to me; I thought months ago that Bush's re-election was inevitable. The Red Sox bounceback over the Yankees, and their subsequent sweep of the Cardinals, gave some of us a little hope: curses can be reversed; records can be broken. On the other hand, we are not really Red Sox fans, Lindsey and I; we are Cubs fans. Our curse was not broken. We were led to believe the impossible might be granted; we might finally rise through all competition and engage in the final contest, possibly even emerge the victor. It was not to be.

An American presidential campaign looks very different from Europe. The other day *La Stampa*, the Torino newspaper I like (though Richard, who favors *La Repubblica*, finds it stodgy), printed an interesting article about the extent to which the American presidential campaign ignores world politics.

> ...it's a disquieting and ultimately contradictory isolationism, of this American empire, the only superpower in the world that engages the least with the world. A self-sufficiency that recognizing only the flank of those few 'true' allies, first among them Blair and Berlusconi, who for having followed Bush have set themselves against 80 percent of their own public opinion (and some of their own parties). A post-isolationism not actually announced by these two

contenders, but is real and substantial.

Not a thought, the other day, on the European constitution. It's over. But not a word, not even by mistake, in these last appearances, on the grand problems of our time. The United Nations, famine, democracy in China, AIDS in Africa, the moderate Arab states. Not a word on Putin, Chechnya, the Pope, the demographic bombs in Mexico and Brazil, the markets and development in India. Nothing. Only America, America, America, the war in Iraq and Bin Laden.

Filippo Ceccarelli goes on to say that this is only an impression, and that an electoral campaign may not be a representative time to assess such national moods. But I think it very important to examine his point. Bush and Kerry did not speak of such matters because their very statement, let alone consideration, bores and annoys a sizable number of voters — sizable enough to lose an election.

I think there is an underlying general American mentality, however much we may learn to moderate it or even overcome it when addressing specific considerations. It was formed partly by the mentalities — the unthinking ways of thinking — brought with them by the first European settlers, and by their "values." Expansion, opportunism, optimism, a certain unconcern for consequence — these are fundamental to the American mentality.

This "post-isolationism" comes of the current address to the rest of the world being the same as the address in earlier times to Native Americans, to American resources, to slaves. To this aspect of the American mentality the rest of the world is a resource or a market when wanted, a nuisance otherwise. To think otherwise is to suggest that American values do not necessarily trump all others.

I knew Bush would win, though I had some hope from time to time. I think the media are to blame, for having alerted a big part of the electorate to the question Ceccarelli raises. To me the key moment in the campaign was Kerry's use of the term "global test." It was of course a phrase quite misunderstood; but the point is that the meaning of the phrase cannot be explained to anyone refusing to consider external concerns.

Over and over again, here in Rome at also at home in Healdsburg, I've been thinking of Gore Vidal's early novel *Julian*, about the emperor of that name who hoped to reverse history by returning Hellenic philosophy in all its subtlety to a world his great-uncle Constantine had ceded to the Christians, suppressing all religions but theirs. It was an intensely interesting time: Rome governed the world from the Scottish border to the north to North Africa, from Spain to the west to Byzantium. Julian was, I think, what we would call a liberal, in other words a man who saw things in shades of gray.

He had studied Greek philosophy and was passionately committed to its mentality, its way of considering the world, human nature, language and thought itself. The rise and institutionalism of monotheism had depended on the suppression of Hellenism, and the necessity of maintaining an international balance of terror, through the stationing of legions of Roman soldiers throughout the colonies, required a constant appeasement of a badly educated and numerically growing underclass in order to prevent insurgencies.

It doesn't hurt Vidal's story to reveal that it ends in the dangerous sands of Iraq.

* * *

Well: we're installed in our apartment, just off the bottom of the Piazza Sant' Egidio where we spent last January. We're at the end of the Vicolo del Cedro, where it turns into the Vicolo delle Cinque. There's a Vespa mechanic's shop next door. The streets are busy with the informal cafe society of students and tourists. Strolling accordionists entertain us as we fall asleep, for it is unseasonably warm, and we leave the front door and the bedroom window open at night.

We spent a few hours yesterday at the airport, where we turned in our car and picked up Simon and Francesca, our grandchildren. The apartment is barely big enough: they have fold-out double sofabeds in the salon; we have a double bed in the bedroom. The kitchen is barely there: a passageway between the two rooms, with two gas burners and a sink and a half-refrigerator.

Our telephone works only when it hangs out the window and there is no internet hookup possible. We will go to to the local internet point, for high-speed web surfing and to exchange e-mails, every day, probably around ten o'clock in the morning.

Last night we had a small supper at one of our favorite Roman restaurants, da Lucia, only a couple of streets away — characteristic Roman food: spaghetti *caccio e peppe*: spaghetti with only grated Pecorino and lots of black pepper (but what Pecorino and pepper!) and a bowl of *puntarelle*, that curious Roman stripped chicory dressed with anchovy dressing, reminiscent of Caesar salad.

And now we're off for the kids' introduction to Trastevere and perhaps a little of Rome beyond. It's never too soon to correct subconscious post-isolationist Americanisms — though of course these kids are European on their father's side, and a quarter European on their mother's!

The Curse of the Zivnys

Barolo del Cardoon
(for so my spellchecker, which has unaccountably picked up a smattering of Italian, has retyped Vicolo del Cedro), Nov. 5—

AFTER READING YOUR E-MAILS regretting the outcome of the election, and spending an afternoon digesting La Repubblica's coverage of the same, and after a simple lunch of *finocchiona* and bread and apple, and a quiet time, and a nice pot of tea, it finally arrived, the moment I had feared: The Curse of the Zivnys.

I won't say too much about this, as I really love the Zivnys who are after all my daughter and her family, and I wouldn't want to embarrass them. Let's just say that no event is entirely negative that teaches you a new word. Today's was *sturalavandani*, from "starer," to unbung or uncork — I have no idea what the derivation might be; unusually, I didn't bring the Italian etymological dictionary along — and "*lavandino*," washbasin, itself no doubt from "*lave*," to wash.

You get a *sturalavandani* at the neighborhood *ferramento*, or hardware store. The *sturalavandani* is an ingenious tool (*geniale* is the Italian word) made of wood and rubber, the wooden part being a simple cylinder about the diameter of a broomstick and a foot or so long, the rubber part looking much like a common trombone mute, a sort of flat cup made of rubber.

It cost two euros twenty, say $2.75, and is worth every penny. Life returned immediately to quasi-normal.

Then we changed into glad rags and walked up to the nearest foreign country and across it to call on our only Roman friends at the moment, Jim and Lisa. They showed us the pearls of the district they had adopted, the Prati, a district that had never attracted me — it's a new part of town, from the 19th century, mostly apartment houses and department stores, wide avenues set in a relentless grid pattern, noisy with traffic and set about with ladies walking dogs, people eating gelato, slow men walking along reading newspapers, and the like.

I like this part of town, Jim said, because it is full of Italians; and it was true that we heard only Italian around us. In Trastevere where we live you hear a number of languages all the time. Trastevere is the Berkeley of Rome, and Prati is more or less the Piedmont. (I refer to the neighbor of Oakland, not the region of Italy.)

But Prati boasts an Apple store, meaning computers; and a wonderful delicatessen featuring Slow foods, La Tradizione; and a slow wine store. And another *ferramento*, this one with a bevy or two of pocket-knives in the window.

I always buy a pocket-knife when I'm in Italy, as I told Jim, partly because you can get really good inexpensive knives here, and partly because I've always misplaced the last by the time I get here. And there in the window was just the one I wanted, a faux-Pattadà with a plastic handle, for seven euros fifty.

Pattadà is a small town in the mountains of Sardinia, where the local trade is knife-smithing. When Lindsey and I were in Sardinia in 1988 we drove there to see it — a remote town in wild country — and Lindsey surprised me with the gift of one of those knives. I will never forget the shop, the small dark young man who had made the knife, his well-matched young wife who had made the felt slipcover for it.

He had made it in the traditional local way, the only concession being the use of imported Swedish steel. Not stainless steel, of course; this makes an inferior blade; instead, a high-tempered carbon steel, forged over a charcoal flame in his home workshop, shaped and sharpened and polished and honed, and fitted with a handle made of wild goat horn.

I treasured that knife as a Sunday knife for a few years, but ultimately it took over as a work knife, replacing one of a succession of lost knives; and of course in its turn it joined its cousins. I think I know exactly where it is, buried in concrete in a fencepost-hole.

In Venice three years ago I bought a replacement, much cheaper because inferior and partially industrial. It was lost as well. Last January in Orvieto I bought another, which met the same fate. I am in the business of redistributing the world's stock of pocket-knives, I'm afraid.

Anyhow we provisioned ourselves at La Tradizione and walked to Jim and Lisa's fine roomy and well-equipped rental apartment where I baptized my new knife on a piece of Castelmagno, which I truly believe to be my current favorite "blue" cheese (it is in fact white, though tasting of and affected by a mold like that of Stilton), and we had a glass of wine, and then we walked past the Macintosh store and the Castell' Sant'Angelo and St. Peter's to our dinner at Le Streghe.

And here the second thing of the day went wrong. Le Streghe had been among our favorite Roman restaurants last January, as you can read below (p. 246). The menu was an interesting compilation of authentic traditional dishes; the cooking was quick and balanced and flavorful; the room was somehow both elegant and comfortable; and the service was outstanding — a young man who was immensely helpful, very friendly without being insinuating, quick to respond to the diner's mood and interests.

This time we ate outside (as it is unseasonably warm) in a four-table setting under a couple of huge umbrellas in a quiet piazza across from the restaurant. Jim and Lisa were flying early in the morning, so we ate as early as we could, at eight o'clock: there was no one at the other tables, inside or out.

We were waited on by a woman in her fifties, I would guess, who had to deal with six people who do not speak Italian and are not necessarily quick to come to a strongly held decision. And the menu was enticing, with tagliarini with white truffles or with artichokes, risotto and spaghetti *alla gricia* and *gnocchi*, guinea hen and beefsteak and *baccalà*, and so on.

When I mentioned that I knew their *fettucine capalbiese* she seemed surprised. It's a delicious sauce, a sort of bolognese without tomatoes — as if tomatoes did not grow near Capalbio! — and not universally made, apparently, outside that corner of southwest Tuscany, really a country suburb of Rome. Do you know our *capalbiese*, she asked; yes, I said; I had it here, last January. Is the restaurant changed since then?

Oh no, she assured us; nothing is changed, except that my sons are not here, they're off at a spa conference center near Pienza. And she took away our orders.

A singing guitarist with a bad cold and a poor gift for mimicry took up his station behind our table. He began fairly modestly, playing a guitar solo and then moving into a couple of vaguely traditional Italian songs. Jim looked annoyed. Is he bugging you, I asked; we'll see how he does, Jim answered.

A man in his forties appeared with a few dishes and with no idea where they were going — nor even a very firm idea of what they were. We sorted them out and he walked uncertainly back across the street to the restaurant. Another party of six appeared and began shuffling their table-positions. The food was good, ditto the local wine, and our conversation was brilliant. Francesca was poised and beautiful in her dark mandarin jacket; Simon relaxed and confident with his share of the table-talk.

The singing guitarist, hearing our conversation in English, moved from Naples to Liverpool, with an unconvincing performance of Let It Be. Then he crossed the Atlantic with My Bodie Lahs Ovrr Thah Oshhahn, to flirt with Texas blues and the like. He would not go away.

We had skipped appetizers and gone straight to our *primi*, or first courses: tagliarini with white truffles for the two *signore*, with artichokes for me, gnocchi for Fran, risotto for Simon, don't-recall-what for Jim. That went well enough, but the *secondi* — the main courses — were more of a problem for our waiter. Two of the group hadn't ordered one at all, other than their *contorni*, their accompanying side vegetable dishes. The man came with Lisa's guinea hen and asked where it went. We told him. He then came with a steak: and where does this go? What is it, we asked. He held the plate close to his face the better to scrutinize it.

Meat, he said. Yes, I said, but what kind of meat? Um, meat, he said. Steak? I asked. Um, *si, signor*, steak, he answered, beefsteak. All of this, of course, in Italian, halting on my side, laconic on his. Simon got his steak; my *baccalà* appeared, bowls of *puntarelle* were distributed as requested, one by one. Jim's plate was yet to be found.

The guitarist finally came to our table, rather sheepishly I thought, and we dug down in our pockets, the ones with the smallest loose change, and dropped a few coins into the cloth bag he carried — mercifully one couldn't readily see how little we gave him, but he seemed disappointed with its heft.

Mio cinghiale, Jim asked, confronting the waiter as he set down the last of the *puntarelle*. *Cinghiale, signor?* Yes, Jim returned, rather firmly, my *cinghiale*, I asked for an order of *cinghiale*. By now the hostess, who had hovered over this hapless waiter before, actively entered the conversation. Yes, she said, *cinghiale*, and the waiter carefully walked across the street again to the restaurant, seeming to expect a flock of taxicabs to run him down, though there had been no traffic on the hidden one-way Vicolo del Curato all night.

Well, things were straightened out. The hostess brought apologetic glasses of vin santo and a plate of biscotti. She refused to take two credit cards, though, only changing her mind after we had obviously given in and retired one of them.

I still think Streghe a fine restaurant, but only for a couple, not for more than four. And rarely have I been shown how important the floor staff is — the difference it makes between a wonderful evening and a frustrating one.

Advertising sign, Via del Moro

Further tribulations of the apartment
Vicolo del Cedro, Nov. 6—

I MENTIONED THAT THE *servizio* had been unbunged. (*Servizio* is the current Italian euphemism for toilet. I first learned the word *gabinetto*, clearly derived from a word allied to the English cabinet, clearly a cousin to the closet of the English w.c. *Gabinetto* is out of fashion; when I used it in a restaurant the other day the girl I was inquiring of was incredulous.)

The *servizio* is unbunged, but problems continue, for this is not the most successful apartment-by-Internet we have negotiated.

It is, by the way, the third we have rented. The first, a three-bedroom (if an entry hall is a bedroom) apartment in Venice, was quite successful, a ground-floor place with a working kitchen and a small garden in a quiet corner of the Cannareggio not too far from S. Maria dei Miracoli.

The second was last January's apartment just around the corner from our present digs. Well, in fact, I'm mistaken: I did not find it on the Internet; I found it in a small advertisement in the New York Review of Books. Fine bedroom with many books; fine useful kitchen; comfortable sitting room.

This time we resorted again to the Internet. We like Trastevere so much we determined to return. The Prati, as I mentioned yesterday, is both a little too petit-bourgeois and a little too far from things; and the center is far too expensive.

But of course last time we were here was in January, when Rome is at its least populated. November isn't exactly the height of the tourist season, but there's a lot more activity than we were used to here. The "streets" of our part of Trastevere — I put the word in quotes because, after all, there are virtually no automobiles on them — are crowded with con men, beggars, crafts tables: you can't help thinking of Telegraph Avenue.

That's okay: these people have to make a living, and most of them are gone by sundown. Then the cafe life surges forth: many people strolling in search of bars, cafes, and restaurants, which exist by the scores. They all have tables in the streets, for it is warm. And the diners at those tables are serenaded by accordionists, klezmer bands, Rumanians with clarinets and violins. And late at night after the wine has flowed freely people's voices rise, naturally.

During the daytime there are other noises. Below us on one side is a motorscooter repair shop: the mechanic there takes delight in attempting to start engines apparently devoid of gasoline or spark. The engines turn, turn, turn, the battery too gradually losing strength. Occasionally, apparently bored with this activity, he runs some sort of electric drill, reminding me of the cruel dentists of my childhood.

On the other side there's a lamp shop. At least I think that's what it is: there are a great many lamps inside — hanging ones, floor models, table lamps; but there are also a good many musical instruments: side drums, tambourines, cellos, violins, mandolins. Two men sit inside and talk most of the day, but occasionally, apparently bored with this activity, they too run some sort of electric drill, reminding me of the cruel dentists of my childhood.

This morning there was a new activity, an air compressor that had been viciously parked on the corner a few meters from our door. It ran all morning, and its exhaust blew in our front window, wafted hesitatingly through the apartment, and regretfully escaped through the door at the stair-landing. When I could take it no longer I followed its hose a full block down the Via della Scala until in ascended straight up an exterior wall to disappear into a fourth-storey apartment window.

Two saucy fellows in worker's blue lounged against a doorway on the street level. The compressor, of course, shut down the minute I noticed them. What's going on, I asked. Need air for the work up there, came the insolent reply. Well it's blowing its exhaust straight into my apartment, I said. But we're finished now, they retorted.

I don't really mind all this very much; it's why we wanted Trastevere. We live in the country; our life is pretty quiet as a general rule. It's nice to be reminded that urbanity involves noise and pollution: we have to understand the lives of quiet desperation lived by the mass of our fellow men.

What I do mind is the great determination with which our apartment is deteriorating around us. The *servizio* didn't surprise me, but it was only the first of a series of things. When we moved in, half the electric sockets were already not working. This didn't matter too much, for half the lamps were missing their light bulbs anyway, and I didn't want to buy the landlord new ones. We don't really need them.

But today another outlet bit the dust. How can this happen? There are two electrical outlets side by side in a single box in the wall. The television set is plugged into one, and it works. The table lamp is plugged into the other, and while it worked yesterday, and the day before that, it declined to work today. Switching it and the television set revealed that the socket itself had stopped working.

This is alarming, for it suggests that a wire has come loose inside. European electricity is twice the strength of American stuff. I can take a shock of 125 volts at home, but I'm not about to experiment with 250 volts here. So I'm just going to let this go.

One of the two sofabeds didn't work when we arrived. It has a broken leg, Veronica explained, when we asked about it. Why not simply shoot the damn thing then, I thought, but couldn't figure out how to put that in Italian. After she left I opened it out anyway, and discovered the frame was bent. Standing on part of it and pulling on another I could straighten it out, but that's about as far as my handyman stuff has gone.

When we arrived the gas stove in the kitchen was inadequate. It took 45 minutes to heat water for tea. I called Veronica, the nice girl who seems to front this place. She said she'd get a man to come over and regulate the burners. He arrived yesterday and fixed things, pretty well. Then he noticed that the bathroom door dragged a little on the floor when you open it.

He tried to lift the door on its hinges, and predictably enough messed up the upper hinge so that the door now has only the one lower hinge. It not only drags, it now flops. It's easiest, in fact, if you take it off the hinge altogether and simply set it in place.

Well, he said, the burners are working better. He explained the gas control lever, which shuts off all gas supply to the apartment. It's best to turn it off at night, he said, to prevent the accumulation of any leaking gas while you're sleeping. I would have thought this simple Italian superstition, allied to the pull-cords universally required in all showers in the event of a broken leg caused by slipping on the soap, but then I remembered the loose wires in the wall. I'll shut the damn thing off at night, all right.

But we went to market in Campo dei Fiori today, and tonight we had a first course of that beautiful spiral green *romanesco* broccoli, long-cooked in oil and garlic; and we followed that with delicious hand-made *tortellini* from the wonderful Sardinian pasta shop on Via del Moro, washed down with cheap local slightly spritzy white wine and followed by some dark chocolate-hazelnut candy for dessert; and you know? Life is Good.

Street Life
Vicolo del Cedro, Nov. 7—

OUT, THEN, AFTER DINNER (prosciutto and mushroom pizzas to go from Da Ivo; *fagiolini*) for a gelato. Now this sounds simple enough; there's a gelateria every fifty meters at least on every business street in our quarter, and most of the streets, though only perhaps ten feet wide (and devoid of sidewalks because with rare exceptions devoid of automobiles), are business streets.

And what business! Around the corner is the Piazza San Egidio, which seemed so empty and placid all January. Tonight — true, a Saturday night — the joint is jumping. When Simon and I walked over to Da Ivo, say about seven o'clock, you could hardly get through the piazza for the card tables. Handmade jewelry, pashmina headscarves, little blocks of wood carved into Christian names and furnished with wheels like toy trains, bootleg CDs, miscellaneous books, Tarot cards.

To get to da Ivo you cross the Piazza Sta. Maria in Trastevere and a smaller piazza and head down S. Francesco da Ripa, which is a fairly important driving street but still lacks sidewalks. Cars park as they can, among the ubiquitous small garbage dumpsters (Rome has no other garbage service) and the small *terrasse*, reserved sections holding three or four tables outside the restaurants. The traffic is, fortunately, one-way — *senso unico* as the Italian has it — but frequently stalled by double-parked cars, their drivers waiting for a pizza or conversing with a pedestrian friend.

On all streets, even the narrowest, there are of course motorscooters to contend with. Often the drivers are amazingly skillful, able to balance and pivot at speeds so slow as to be nearly stationary; then, when a clear space opens up miraculously, like Moses's Red Sea, off they go like gangbusters. Some are incredibly noisy, but most are fairly discreet. You can't generalize about them or their drivers, who may wear business suits, or stockings and high heels, or sports clothes.

Many of these scooters are business vehicles, with big plastic crates fastened somehow fore and aft, delivering messages, or pizzas, or packages. Some carry commuters, or students, or cruisers.

All seem driven by good-natured people, unhurried though determined, aware that in order to gain your way you have as often to cede it. And the same must be said, to tell the truth, about the automobilists: you almost never hear an automobile horn here.

An anecdote: an acquaintance of mine, an American, got a position here a number of years ago. He and his wife established their residency, but she seemed unhappy. It isn't London, she said sadly; it isn't Paris, it isn't New York. Rome seemed foreign and sleepy; she craved cultural excitement.

After six months their car arrived from the United States, and she announced she was going out for a drive. She didn't come back for hours. Her husband fretted: She's finally got her car, she's driven away, she's driven to Paris or Berlin or London and I'll never see her again.

Finally she returned, flushed with pleasure, exhilarated. I love this town, she said; I finally understand the Romans. It's like Venice. They all drive in the same direction, as if they were in boats; they flow in a fluid stream, parting and reassembling as the traffic requires, taking every available space but always aware of one another. It's amazing.

And it's true, that's what driving here is like. Lanes subdivide, then fuse back together; small cars make way for larger ones; people pull U-turns or even turn by backing and filling. If you're determined you get your way, of course; and if you're timid you'll have to wait. It's not exactly dog-eat-dog; there are the occasional unexpected moments of gallantry making the whole thing work.

But it does take a bit of bravery, as does the simple act of crossing a busy street. The traffic will not break for a pedestrian, but if you simply walk out in front of the oncoming traffic it will adjust its velocity, either slowing down or more likely swerving a bit, to accommodate you, and you'll get to the other side.

Well anyway we went out for our gelato after dinner, and that sounds simple enough. There's a gelateria on the other side of Sta. Maria in Trastevere that we know has especially good ice cream. It was closed the entire month of January, or at least when it was not closed it was not selling ice cream, for the very good reason that it was too damned cold and no one was buying.

As we approached it, however, Lindsey realized that wasn't the gelateria at all; the one she wanted was on S. Francesco da Ripa, a block or two away. So like the Epicureans we are we swerved, like cars in a busy stream, to follow our desire and her instincts, and we located the gelateria in question, to discover that it was closed. I don't know why.

Back, then, to the other place, to find it open but not selling gelato. Okay: we know there's a bar back toward Sta. Maria in Trastevere where we bought decent ice cream last January. Through the busy streets we go, me carrying the two bottles of water we'd bought through the traffic and the tables on the *terrasse* to the bar — which had no ice cream.

We ended up at a chain gelateria, Blue Ice I think it's called, and dropped our eight euros on four cups, strawberry for Fran, pistachio and chocolate for Simon, chocolate and almond for Lindsey, and my perennial *crema* and *fior di latte*, the blandest flavors you can buy and therefor excellent tests for the quality of the ice cream itself.

It wasn't bad. We ate it on our feet, listening to a pretty good guitarist quietly singing Spanish songs on the *terrassa* of one of the many Sta. Maria restaurants until we noticed a juggler in front of the church.

He was juggling three torches, quite dramatically, and had drawn a good crowd. After a while he produced three Indian clubs and paced the circle fronting his audience, giving the clubs to three equally distant members of the audience, then pulling them back into the center, hanging little striped vests on their shoulders just like the one he was wearing, and miming instructions to them.

They good-naturedly attempted to follow, trying to toss and catch the clubs, standing foolishly on one foot, grinning on cue. The entire scene, apart from the clothes of most of the crowd, looked like a Breughel painting. It lacked only a sly pickpocket working the crowd, though perhaps he was there after all, though he got nothing from any of us.

We finished our ice cream and slowly walked home, past accordionists, saxophonists, guitarists, violinists — there's enough music in Trastevere to fill a conservatory, and much of it really quite good. We walked past a few beggars: the horribly misshapen old lady, bent nearly double, with the clawlike outstretched hand; and the pretty young girl who had asked me for a coin or two earlier tonight when I walked by carrying two boxes of pizza, a bottle of red wine, a bottle of grappa, a half dozen eggs and a package of butter; and who, when I simply looked at her and shrugged, indicating the impossibility of getting into my pockets, simply smiled at me in return and wished me a pleasant evening.

And now it is eleven o'clock, and the voices are murmuring away, hundreds of people eating and drinking at their *terrassa* tables, or simply conversing while walking the warm streets; and there's the sound of a couple of distant radios, mostly just the beat under some kind of Euro-pop, and an occasional accordion. The sound will continue until after I've fallen asleep. Occasionally I wake in the middle of the night; from two o'clock on it's very quiet, and it will remain still until almost nine. This part of Trastevere is apparently late to bed, late to rise; and that's okay with me.

Italian comments on the American scene

Vicolo del Cedro, Nov. 7—

I WROTE A FEW DAYS ago about the surprise here in Europe that foreign issues were so unconsidered during the American presidential campaign — the war in Iraq excepted, of course. This drew quite a defensive response from one reader, addressing three points:

• Iraq and Afghanistan are enough for now, to consider other crises during a campaign would be entirely out of place.

• The UN was largely our doing; we've demonstrated plenty of humanitarianism.

• Since we're involved in the Middle East, shouldn't the rest of the world pick up some of the other crises — Angola, for example?

• The Brits are upset with Blair because they recall the blood they shed in the middle East years ago. The Italians have their own trouble with radical muslim immigration and are too engrossed with their own *terroir* to be led in difficult causes.

None of these observations quite goes to the point, which was that an Italian journalist was surprised that issues on foreign soil don't interest the American presidential campaign. Why should they? Well, because they are central to a European point of view, because a European is both a citizen of a nation — Italy, Spain, France, Germany, whatever — and also a participant in an international community of (roughly spoken) equals. The European Union exists for a number of reasons: trade, law, agriculture, defense. And it is "run" by a supranational government with input from such smaller nations as The Netherlands and Luxembourg as well as the giants, Germany, France, and Spain.

One of the things we Americans continually forget is the oddity of our governmental organization, neither fish nor fowl. Our government is, after all, a republic comprising fifty states, a rough analogue of the European Union of twenty-three. (I think that's the number.) But over the years we have drifted toward a very strong national government trumping the governments of the states. We didn't originally want that to happen: that's one of the reasons for the Electoral College, and for the equal powers of the House of Representatives vis-a-vis the Senate.

But it's an uneasy balance, Federalism versus State's Rights, and the unease has driven politics for a long time. And while so doing it has distracted many Americans from their larger responsibilities as Citizens of the World. (You can see this in so trivial a matter as our constantly referring to ourselves as "Americans," as if Canadians and Mexicans were not, instead of "United Statespeople," which is, by the way, precisely what the Italians often call us: *Statiunitensi*.)

* * *

La Repubblica, the newspaper I've been reading here in Rome, has devoted several early pages in each day's issue to American politics. Yesterday's paper (Saturday's), for example, runs to sixty tabloid pages. Their front page features "stings" (introductory paragraphs) to the Arafat situation, to Berlusconi's tax-cut plans, and to an extensive commentary on political correctness (written by none other than Umberto Eco).

Below the fold there are stings to two columnists: Vittorio Zucconi who is writing a profile of Columbia, South Carolina; and Federico Rampini, who offers a similar one on San Francisco. (These columnists are permanent correspondents to *La Repubblica* from the United States, and you can read them online at http://www.repubblica.it.)

Pages 2, 3, 4, and 5 continue the Arafat story, reporting on his medical condition and treatment; the mood in Gaza; the obscene position Sharon has taken to Arafat's eventual burial; the likely political reconfiguration of Jihad, Hamas, and Al Fatah; an interview with Dennis Ross, a former Mideast mediator who says only a quick election can avoid chaos; and a report on the positioning of likely candidates in such an election.

I'd guess those pages are no more than forty percent advertising space. There follows a full-page ad; then a page on the current Iraq news (Annan's warning, Allawi's request, the Black Watch crisis in England, and Al Qaeda's warning that the Americans "will soon be seen consumed 'in an unbearable inferno' for having chosen to reelect Bush." The bottom of the page reports on Allawi's cold reception by the European Union leaders at Brussels. Twenty percent advertising on this page.

Next come five pages of Italian news, with no advertising, one column of which reports the Italian center-left's response to the Bush election. Page 13 (perhaps appropriately) is dedicated equally to a story on the U.S. Supreme Court and reports on U.S. journalists being too far from their readers to understand the country's mood, with a sidebar on Michael Moore's recent plea that we not despair.

Then come the two full-page (no advertisements) "jumps" from page one, Zucconi's page describing the mood in South Carolina, Rampini's describing that of San Francisco. I love the opening of Zucconi's page:

> Let's go where God's market explodes into a thousand versions of the same faith, sliced as if in an infinite sushi bar of redemption: pentecostals, presbyterians, adventists, baptists, episcopalians, Christian brothers, Lutherans, methodists, catholics, apostolics, charismatics, independent bible Christians, Jews for Christ, nazarenes, orthodox, universal unitarians and, that no one might be left out, also the "nondenominational." Two hundred twenty churches officially registered here in the county of Columbia, South Carolina, one church for every 500 of 120,000 inhabitants, more than doctors, dentists, hospital beds, restaurants, topless dancers and maybe even of MacDonalds and Burger Kings. The immense, unknown, ridiculed spirituality of heartland America that has overcome the nation, year after year, in this tide of Christian "revival" that the Right has understood how to break, and has overthrown the Left.

Zucconi is very clear about the reductionist "values" that led South Carolina to vote Bush over Kerry, 58 to 41 per cent. He talks to an excited soldier waiting for his posting to Iraq — the two Carolinas and Georgia produce the majority of soldiers in the US Army — who is anxious to tell this foreign correspondent that he's ready to "kick ass, yeah." A sergeant looks on silently. The correspondent asks: why are these kids going to die in Iraq? "For their liberty and that of their children," he answers; and then, in a lower voice, "for our God."

"The Bible teaches that there are always wars and rumors of war; that doesn't concern me," said pastor Ron Laflam who for 27 years has guided the attendants of the Columbia Baptist Temple, in a street prophetically called Faraway Road, "the street we've seen our nation taken in a mistaken direction, sex, lasciviousness, destruction of life, homosexuality above all, the devastation of moral values. We've forgotten that this nation was founded on Christian values and because of this it became the beacon of the world."

And is Bush the man who has again lit the lamp at the top of this beacon?

"That's what we think, because he's a Christian like us."

The journalist asks about Europe.

"Ah, Europe, by now it's a long way from the Word, it no longer interests us. We want to save our America."

He then describes the numbers of Christian novels about the struggle between Good and Evil to be found in the local Barnes and Noble, always featured at the ends of the aisles; and the few books to be found that treat of homosexuality, in the small section devoted to "Sociology." Only the black kid who welcomes him at the desk of the Holiday Inn, who wears a small sticker "I Voted" on his shirt, responds to the journalist with a confrontational voice: "I voted for Kerry." "Ah, these uppity blacks."

And Zucconi ends with a surprising, chilling, but to me persuasive analysis: the fundamentalist Christians who have voted for Bush have done so out of fear of — not Osama, but Sodom. It is the wrath of God they fear, not the blows of terrorists.

**

Being a native of Northern California I take some perverse reassurance from the next page, Rampini's column from San Francisco. The headline: San Francisco's Apology: "I'm Far from the Heart of America."

Dianne Feinstein has thrown down the gauntlet: "The gay marriages celebrated in this city in February sounded the alarm in all of traditionalist America, and has raised the most frightening specter of moral dissolution and the attack on the family. It offered an ideal tool to the right, a whip to mobilize their voters. It's multiplied the energy of the Bush campaign. As it always does, San Francisco has gone too far, too fast."

It's odd: here in Rome, since I only hook up to the Internet a few minutes a day, and get my news otherwise from the television (which I can barely understand), *La Repubblica* (which requires careful study), and the *International Herald Tribune* (which seems to me a bit superficial), my reading of the San Francisco *Chronicle* is filtered through this Italian newspaper.

So I learn of a *Chronicle* service helping readers who want to emigrate — and, by the way, a number of you readers have suggested, whether in jest or seriously, that we keep our eyes out for real estate.

San Francisco, I am proud to read, "simply refuses to assent from its heart; doesn't accept the monopoly of values attributed by the Right. It's the city of the militants of human rights, of the American Civil Liberties Union, horrified by the photos from Abu Ghraib, by the reports of Rumsfeld's generals who go to church to pray for victory because our God is better than the enemy's."

He ends by quoting a student, Adrienne Fodor: "With this president we'll have more environmentally-produced illnesses; less health assistance; more restrictions on individual rights. Out of pure patriotism I shudder when I see my country consigned to a man who does not believe in American values."

***

Neither of these two pages carries any advertising at all, by the way. And in the rest of the newspaper there are still more comments on the American news: but there are also reports from elsewhere. There are pages on France, on Naples, on sports and television and theater and food. There are the full-page ads for lipsticks and cars. There's a page on the 50th anniversary of *The Guinness Book of Records*. There's a page on the crisis at Fiat, and the four-hour general strike it's triggered. There's a page on the European Union's alarm at the decline of the American dollar. (We're a bit alarmed, as well.) There are pages of stock quotes, and classified ads, and so on.

Three full pages are devoted to Umberto Eco's thoughts on Political Correctness, and the responses of a number of people — including Robert Hughes:

> Few things are more absurd, and at the end more counterproductive. We want to make a kind of linguistic Lourdes, where evil and mischance dissolve in the waters of euphemism. The invalid will perhaps arise from his wheelchair... The appeal of politically correct language is uniquely English; it isn't found anywhere else in Europe. In France no one has though of rebaptising Pepin the Short as Pepin the vertically challenged; in Spain Velasquez's dwarfs have not been called The Small People... No substitution of words can reduce the weight of intolerance present in our society or in any other.

La Repubblica devotes several pages to this question because it is a creeping Americanism. America the Unconsciously Priggish and Hypocritical exports its commercial products, its commercial culture, and the language of its "moral values" to the rest of the world, and the more intelligent corners of the rest of the world — and *La Repubblica* represents one of them — tries to understand. To respond to such odd overtures, let alone to defend against them, perhaps to withstand their assault on the "values" of one's own "*terroir*," one must try to understand them. This requires a curiosity, an intellectual curiosity, about the rest of the world.

It is precisely the absence of that kind of curiosity that amazes these Europeans, who — unlike us Americans — are used to living in crossroads. There are other amazements, of course. How did these Americans, who after all descend from Europeans like us, develop these curious anti-intellectual, incurious, ultimately self-defeating, utterly self-assured attitudes? Why don't they see that to participate in global trade, politics, intelligence, one cannot turn one's back on the rest of the world?

And, finally, How do we deal with Holy Innocents who throw their "beliefs" and "value systems" against the rest of the world and refuse to discuss the problems that arise as a result?

In some ways, many here in Europe and there in the United States are beginning to see, the Fundamentalist Right in the United States is acting not so differently from the Fundamentalist Right in the multinational Moslem world.

Nor so differently from the way that radical Christian Europe behaved when they first met the New World. I'm tempted to end: may the gods have mercy on us all.

St. Ivo

Winter and teeth
Vicolo del Cedro, Nov. 8—

LORDY, WHAT A NIGHT. First of all yesterday (Sunday) I lost a filling, one of my favorite fillings, a filling that amply had earned and deserved its name, as it filled virtually every space of a particularly useful tooth. That happened after lunch, which was at Albino il Sard, and before dinner, which was at home.

Of course I was out of sorts after the loss, partly owing to the familiar reminder it brought of mortality, partly because I had determined not to share my little loss with any of the family. I bear my sorrows patiently and alone, I tell myself, though Lindsey may not be of the same opinion.

Then too the lunch had not been what I'd hoped. I begin to think that our visit here in Rome last January was exceptional, perhaps because it was our first extended visit here, perhaps because it was in fact January, when Rome is almost bereft of tourists and embraced the more fondly by its permanent residents. In any case Albino, while to the eye exactly what we had remembered, to the palate and even the mind left a little something lacking.

Oh well. The day wore on, in its rather dreary way — it was the first overcast day since we arrived a week ago or so, even raining at moments, though never while we were out — and then back at home we had some delicious *fagiolini* and bread and *finocchiona* sausage and apples, and so to bed.

But God, what a night. After I had counted the number of ways the tip of one's tongue can explore the interior of one's tooth and finally fallen asleep, a contingent of cretins took up station below our bedroom window, which looks out on the street. (If you have the *DK Eyewitness Travel Guide to Rome*, by the way, you can see our bedroom window. It's on page 206, just to the right of the pair of bloomers hanging from the lower clothesline, on the right. The shutters are open, as they are at this very moment. Our street is one of the most often photographed streets in Trastevere, if not in Rome, precisely because of its hanging laundry.)

I have mentioned before that we do not mind such noises; we

are in a city deliberately; Italians love to express themselves; blablabla. But 1:45 in the morning of a Monday morning is not the time for heated discussions of the most trivial matters, particularly when most of the boys have silly pouting voices, and most of the girls are practicing that exquisitely annoying nasal singsong that disfigures the upperclass Italian female voice.

Some day perhaps I'll have listened to these deliveries enough to be able to describe them. You could make a master's thesis out of the curiously affected ways Italians have of delivering what is otherwise perhaps the most melodious, spontaneous, affecting catalogues of human vocalism. It's as if they feel compelled to take up this God-given instrument, an instrument combining the immediacy of woodwinds and the expressivity of strings, and to use it to play synthesized versions of Lawrence Welk polkas as played by the Tijuana Brass. I do not like it at all.

But I will go no further in the matter. I have learned in sixty-nine years that I can outwait almost any irritation. In time they disappeared, who knows why or where. They left me to consider my mortality, and sleep came once more.

This morning I phoned a woman I know here to ask if she knew a dentist. She did, and promised to call him. I could not: my telephone was nearly empty of time, and I didn't have a recharge card. That would require a trip to the tobacconist, and I wasn't ready to do that, probably because I didn't really want to commit myself. So off, a little after eight, to do the e-mail, and buy the newspapers, and back to fix the breakfast and marvel yet again at the ability of children — grandchildren in this case — to sleep until nearly ten o'clock when the day was bright though cold and all of Rome lay at their feet.

Also we were waiting for Mister Fixit, who the landlady Veronica had promised would come in the morning to re-hang the bathroom door, and explore the enigmatic electrical outlets, and generally convert this dump, through some kind of *bricolage* alchemy, into a place worth something near its price, which I will not tell you lest I tempt the gods into some kind of awful vengeance.

He did not appear, of course, so, since she had in the meanwhile called to say he had a key, we simply bailed. It was a glorious morning, what was left of it, cloudless, incredibly clear for the cold wind. Autumn has been skipped this year, the newspapers marvel; it's cold as January almost; winter has truly set in.

Simon had asked particularly to see the Colosseum, so I decided to tease him. We went first to the Isola, the curious Tiber island which has been a refuge for the sick for the last 2300 years. We walked down the fifty-three steps from its street to the riverbank and walked slowly around the entire island, which the Romans sheathed in marble (actually it looks like travertine to me, but who's to cavil) and then left to disintegrate slowly over the centuries. It's neither big nor small, this island; perhaps two or three city blocks, with a hospital at one end and the Roman navy at the other — you can tell it by the fact that four or five orange life-rings hang disconsolately from its wall, as if anyone would toss one out if Simon should edge too close and fall in.

If he did it would be curtains. The water is swift and, to all appearances, cold. Apart from a few sleek cormorants and a wheelbarrowful or two of empty plastic bottles caught in the undertow below the weir there seems little life here, though now I think about it I believe I've seen people fishing in this churning graygreen river. We are told that Aesculapius, the Greek god of medicine, came downstream on a boat, centuries ago, and that his serpent slithered off his staff and swam to this island, prompting the god to disembark and clear up a local plague. That was some serpent.

We went on to Sta. Maria della Bocca di Verità, uncharacteristically devoid of tourists, allowing Simon and Franny to pose with their hands in the dreadful stone mouth, thereby proving their truthfulness; and we continued to the Circus Maximus, looking up at the bleak brick ruin of the grand palace of the Caesars, and walking the soft grassy track; and we went up the hill across from Nero's aqueduct, and into Cardinal Spellman Way and the Parco del' Celio; and finally down toward the Via di San Giovanni in Laterano. A block before, as we crossed the Quattro Coronati, I asked Simon what he should be doing as he crossed a street.

Look both ways before stepping into the street? he asked dutifully, looking to his left — and his face went round and open with surprise and delight: there was the Colosseum down at the end of the street.

But we stopped for a coffee, and to look at the gladiator's barracks, before charging across the busy piazza and circumambulating the arena itself.

English major that I was, I can't see the Colosseum without thinking of Daisy Miller. To me it will always stand for malaria and loneliness, both of which have long since been banished. Today's Colosseum is barricades, tourguides, busses, cheap souvenirs, and people posing for photos. But it is enormous, and old, and it keeps its own counsel. I have never gone in, and never want to. I like to give it its place, in the hope it and the rest of the cosmos will continue to give me mine, though my dental interiors may crumble to dust.

So we turned our backs and walked on through the Forum, just to acquaint the kids with it, we'll come back another day; and we crossed Mussolini's audacious Via Imperiali toward Trajan's Shoppingmall, and climbed a few more steps to a little pizza-counter we know which we shared with a hundred squealing schoolchildren, and then up the Corso and down to the Tiber and home once more.

I bought the recharge card along the way, and dialed the scratch-off number into my phone, and called the dentist. Tonight, he said, at 1930. And so we had tea and cookies, and went out to shop for dinner, and then it was time for me to Go To The Dentist.

I once walked five miles or so through tunnels and over bridges in the French preAlps to have a wisdom tooth pulled. It was an interesting experience. not entirely unpleasant.

Four years ago or so I drove to the romantic and historical Piemonte town of Saluzzo for no other reason than to visit a dental clinic, having broken a tooth on a piece of stale French bread at lunch in a roadside rest stop above Nice.

This time it was a walk of forty minutes, which is over a mile, clear across Rome to a quarter I don't particularly like, between the Barberini and the Spanish Steps, to open my mouth to another total stranger.

He was reassuring. *Non c'e un problema*, he said, falling back on the global demurral; No Problem. And in fact it wasn't: he shoved some glue in, shone a magic lamp on it, left me to sit for ten minutes with an Italian newsmagazine promising all sorts of magic cell phones in the very near future.

He worked calmly and pleasantly and without an assistant. When we were finished he stepped to his counter, in a discreet alcove off the reception room, and prepared the bill: 110 Euros. I gave him my credit card; he gave me a receipt. I hope my insurance company will understand.

I walked back, relieved, inches taller, younger, more handsome, through the electric, stylish Roman night, bling and luxury on every side, through the Tritone Galleria where a formally dressed fellow unaccountably played the Schumann concerto, minus orchestra, at an amplified grand piano to an audience of thirty; across the Piazza Colonna where the police hunkered down in dozens of squad cars, perhaps guarding against another planned spontaneous redistribution of department-store commodities among the working-class; past the Pantheon with its clot of tourists eagerly listening to a chirping tourguide with a yellow umbrella; past the cat-ridden Area Sacra and its streetcars and trafficlights; and home to have a delicious minestrone Lindsey had prepared in my absence, and to marvel at a short string quartet Simon had composed in my absence, and to type up these notes for you.

And I hope you read them in peace and contentment; and may your teeth hold another few years; and may you enjoy a minestrone as good as mine was.

Cecilia and bagna cauda
Vicolo del Cedro, Nov. 10—

COLD TODAY, QUITE COLD, and threatening sprinkles, though we were rarely moistened. So we stuck close to home, only walking across the Big Street, the Viale Trastevere, to see how the other side lives, and to visit St. Cecilia.

It is one of my favorite spots here. The church itself is a bit of a sleeper, fronting a fairly large piazza with an improbable collection of old attached (of course) houses across from it — a sleeper because the church hides behind a facade. Once through it you're in the forecourt, whose very attractive fountain is alas undergoing repairs at the moment.

We began with the *pièce de resistance*, since its hours were short: the Cavallini frescos in the choir-loft. You pay two euros fifty apiece to see them, and they're well worth it — frescos painted roughly a millennium ago, covered over for some inexplicable reason in the 17th century I think it was, and rediscovered only a century ago.

Painted in a Byzantine manner, with those almond-shaped eyes and rather stiff poses, Christ and the twelve Apostles preside over the Universal Judgment. When you look at these amazing paintings you're about twenty feet above the point from which the painter intended you to see them, because the choir-loft was built in front of them. It's as if you were standing on a scaffold in one of the other similarly frescoed churches here, not that there are many similar frescos. Below the Christ and Apostles there are a few angels herding the wise and the foolish to their respective eternal destinations, but not much of that can be seen — whether because it was destroyed when the frescos were originally covered over, or whether because they are still covered, I do not at present know.

(There's so much I do not at present know, and so much less time, from one year to the next, to do much about that. It doesn't really matter to me: in many ways I prefer my eternal curiosity to any satisfaction of it, not that the questions wouldn't arise again almost immediately, so short does my attention seem to be growing.)

In spite of the early style of this painting, the faces are quite individuated. If you saw one of these guys on the street you'd recognize him. Peter, on Christ's left, looks disturbingly like George W. Bush, narrow-set eyes and all, except that he sports a full beard. Our President would do well to grow a beard, I think. It helped Lincoln's credibility, and it couldn't hurt George's.

I particularly like the archangels at the top of the Cavallini composition, and of them I particularly like the feathered wings. Too often angels' wings seem scaly, perhaps because on the whole scales are easier to paint than feathers. These feathers are stiff, like goose-quills, the better to fly with perhaps; but they also seem soft and upholstering. And their colors are remarkable; the feathers lie in groups like crayons or pastels in a set, with barely perceptible leaps from one color to the next. I suppose all these pigments are mineral pigments, ground stone worked into the fresh plaster; but among the colors their are surprising mulberry greyed violets, and rosy not-quite-reds, colors you just don't otherwise think of.

We went down into the church itself to see Stefano Maderno's portrait sculpture of Cecilia, done in 1600, five years after her body was discovered. You remember the story: Cecilia was a young Roman woman who lived in the 3rd century. She offended the authorities by refusing to marry her boyfriend until he converted to Christianity. One thing led to another until they were both martyred. Her execution was particularly gruesome: she was locked for three days in her Roman bath — she was one of the upper class, and owned such luxuries — but managed to escape both scalding and suffocation by singing hymns throughout the ordeal.

Whereupon she was put to the axe: but she withstood that as well. Three times the decapitation failed. When her body was discovered, in 1595, it was remarkably fresh, as if she had just died — not of decapitation of but of lost blood from the gash in her throat. Maderno's portrait is said to be an accurate portrayal, and while it is immaculate and bloodless, as you'd expect after 1300 years of perfect death, it is nevertheless immensely touching. Cecilia was small, beautiful, chastely dressed. She lies in his marble statue under the altar, and it's hard to resist sympathizing with her.

The church is built above the ground floor of her house. One of the troubling facts about Rome, about all ancient cities, is that the cities of our own time are twelve to twenty feet higher. I have always thought this represented two millennia's worth of fingernail clippings, orange peels, empty packages and the like, but here in Rome it's clearly also a matter of the upper storeys of old buildings being demolished and used to fill in the ground floors.

Cecilia's house has been carefully and instructively excavated, and there are plenty of helpful panels, complete with drawings and you-are-here maps, to guide you through — if you can deal with Italian. Walking around underneath an enormous stone building is of course a little bit creepy, but interesting. Some of the time we're apparently on the original Roman streets on which Cecilia's house had been built; at other times we're within its floor-plan. One room contains a number of cylindrical pits, apparently used like silos to store grain. By a hundred years or so after her time these had been filled in and floored over, still with that serviceable but decorative mosaic system the Romans favored.

We emerged finally to go back and buy some orange marmalade made from the convent's own fruit by the convent's own novitiates, and then went to market, our local market, because we are cutting costs on this trip by eating at home.

Lindsey made a fine minestrone yesterday and added to it today. A little fresh sausage, a quart or two of the famous Roman water, and a few cups of the mixed chopped vegetables available at any market — onion, carrot, a few shell beans, some chopped greens, all ready to toss into the stock for a market-fresh version of instant vegetable soup.

And tonight, special treat, *bagna cauda*. This seemed a little insensitive after visiting Cecilia, but no matter. Lindsey smashed minced garlic, about five cloves, and half a small bottle of anchovies in oil, into a pan with an inch or two of olive oil in it, and heated it. Into these we dipped raw red and yellow pepper strips, blanched small white onions, steamed potatoes, and leaves of Savoy cabbage (you can buy a quarter cabbage at the market) and pale delicate greenish-white chicory.

With this a bottle of cheap local red. It continues to rain and occasionally thunder, clearing and settling at times in between. It's an uncertain life, the newspapers continue to remind us. But these simple pleasures at the table, not so very different from what Cecilia must have known in her better days, send us happy to bed, and there's a lot to be said for that.

Via Appia per cavallo

An uncomfortable moment
Vicolo del Cedro, Nov. 11—

TWO DISPATCHES TODAY, more than you want to deal with, and there's a very simple reason. My usual Internet Points are down.

We're used to the really local one being unreliable. It's a very pleasant place, only a few hundred feet away, but its hours are, well, to repeat a word — and why not? I am no Flaubert! — unreliable. Today being a little bit rainy, we did the laundry. The laundromat isn't far from the local Internet Point, so I thought the efficient thing to do would be to combine errands. Ah, efficiency, such a virtue, so far from Italy, so far from me.

In fact it turned rainy as the day wore on, but it began gloriously. There were tremendous thunderclaps in the night: this was the first night I was not awakened by carousers. But the day began with hard bright blues overhead, and we spent the morning in the nearby Botanical Garden, a pleasant oasis of palms and pines, bamboos and ferns and roses (some still in bloom), decaying monumental staircases and fountains, and an unlikely group of twenty or so national policemen in their rainy-day slickers and their best behavior being lectured about the garden and its plants — I can't imagine why.

And then lunch, and then the laundry. This began badly: Lindsey put a one-Euro coin in the soap dispenser and then pulled open a door on an empty compartment. Goodbye Euro. We scratched together the remaining coins and bought soap and tokens and tossed the clothes and the soap into two washing machines and trooped off to the Internet Point.

It was closed. The handwritten sign on the door, trumping the businesslike printed sign, said clearly that today it would be open from 1400 to 2200, and it was now 2:30 which in Italian is 1430, but no one was there.

So we went on down to the next one, the one we usually go to because the local is in fact usually closed. I walked confidently to the back room with my laptop as I have done for several days, but the manager wagged his forefinger from side to side. *Non posse*: you can't. Why not, I asked. No connection, he said. Why not, I asked. Change of provider. When will you be back on? Hard to tell. Hard to tell, I asked, or No one knows, or only the good Lord knows? Oh, the good Lord, the manager said, I don't know if He knows, but it's hard to tell. Tomorrow? I asked. Oh certainly not, no, not tomorrow.

So we went back to the laundry to put the clothes into the dryer and went home to have a pot of tea. By the time the water was nearing a boil the half hour had gone by and it was time to rescue our clothes from the dryer before someone else did — this has apparently been known to happen.

Back again then for tea, and I recalled another Internet Point, further away, down near the local Standa Supermarket, where Lindsey wanted to go anyway to shop for dinner. So after tea and another half-hour, since one trip through the dryer wasn't enough for some of our clothes, we finally got out of the house for the Internet Expedition.

By now of course I was thoroughly impatient and not thinking too clearly. Some of you will recognize this mood. Jacket, hat, scarf, laptop, wallet, telephone, wife, kids; we were finally out the door, we pulled it to behind us and descended the dangerous staircase and headed across the Piazza San Egidio, the Piazza Santa Maria in Trastevere, the Piazza San Calisto, and down the familiar San Francesco del Ripa.

The Internet Point was not to be found. We noted a promising shop for the pig-cheek we wanted for dinner and continued looking. No Internet Point. Finally we gave up and went to Standa for the things we could not find in our S. Egidio greengrocer's shop: real orange juice, some dry spaghetti, a can of good tuna. Oh: Standa being a typical Italian supermarket there's a decent bookstore, and the clerk knew where the Internet Point was. So after buying our *guanciale* and some pecorino and olives at the pig-cheek shop we went there: but it was full, and would be for hours. And it was full of smoke, too; the first time I've noticed that here.

Home, then, to fix dinner; and it was while nearing home that I reflected that I had forgotten to put the keys in my pocket, and we were locked out of the house. I considered, then dismissed the idea of somehow getting past two locked doors without admitting to Lindsey that I'd forgotten the keys. There was no way to do this.

I called Veronica, the young woman who apparently owns our apartment, but her call diverting was on. Maybe she was at work. She works until midnight: that's a long time away.

Lindsey suggested calling the rental agency we'd dealt with. Fortunately I had their number in the laptop, so I balanced it on my knee, it was now beginning to rain, and found the number. They promised to call right back after calling Veronica.

They did. She was in London. She'd taken our rental money and flown to London to spend it on theater and expensive dinners, I thought bitterly, and left us to stand out in the gathering rain.

Well, Lindsey said, we can ask the police for help. There are always police guarding the Piazza S. Egidio, because it is the home of an important international liberal movement that was threatened with something years ago: once threatened, in Italy, one is apparently guaranteed visible police protection from then on.

The police listened politely and came up with several good suggestions. I might call 155, they said; the firemen would come, and they would break down the doors, both the street door into the apartment house and then the front door into our own apartment. I thought of the likely expense of repairing the damage and dismissed the idea.

Well then, they said, you could see if someone can break in. I looked at Simon, a healthy fifteen-year-old American boy. The police looked at him as well. Maybe a boy from Naples would be a better choice, they said. Then one of the cops suggested the old credit-card trick, and I brightened.

The street door refused to open to my credit card, but this didn't slow me down. I pressed several of the doorbells, and two people answered at once on the intercom, while another leaned out his window and asked, reasonably enough, Who was there. I am here, I answered, I live in the apartment below you, I'm renting it, my keys are in the apartment and I am not.

Someone buzzed the door lock open and we quickly shouldered our way into the lobby, as you might call it. We went up to our door and got out the credit card.

Again, no luck. I began to reconstruct the design of the lock and the bolt; I closed my eyes (after rudely suggesting that the kids give me a little silence) and tried to visualize the length and design of the key. I realized quickly that the bolt was a good way behind the door, further than any credit card of mine would reach.

I detached a strip of metal that hangs purposelessly from the ornate wooden door and tried using it as a jemmy. I tried my shoulder. I returned to the credit card. Nothing worked.

Oh well, I said, I'll go down to the hardware store and see if they can recommend a locksmith. They did, in incomprehensible Italian, describing the location of his door on the next street, but I could not find it. But just then the telephone rang: a friend of Veronica's would be at our door in an hour with the key.

I went back to the apartment to break the good news to the others, and we trooped off to the one remaining Internet Point I knew of here in Trastevere, way down by the river. Everything worked fine here, except that a filter on their system prevented my sending e-mail out. I could of course do this using webmail, but all my outgoing mail was already on my machine, and time was now running out, no time to cut and paste it into a website.

And anyway the hell with it; nothing I have to say is that important. So we walked back home and waited five minutes; the nice young woman came with the key; we got into our apartment; Lindsey cooked up some spaghetti *carbonara*; and all's well that ends well. And from now on Lindsey carries the key.

Haircut (not mine)
Vicolo del Cedro, Nov. 12—

THE FIRST TIME WE CAME to Rome was in November 1988, and the first place I stepped into was a barber shop near the Campo dei Fiori. It wasn't that I needed a haircut, it was that we needed a hotel. We had arrived by car, having driven from France by way of Corsica and Sardinia (taking ferries, I need hardly add), and we had driven straight to the tourist office at the railroad station, where we had found no help in getting cheap lodgings.

But I remembered that Thérèse had told me that you could always find a room near the Campo dei Fiori, so we went there, and I stepped into the barber shop reasoning that the barber would know the locals and could steer me to a good local cheap hotel. He did, and we were very happy with it, and I decided the best way to express my gratitude would be to get a haircut.

I don't like getting them more than once or twice at the same place closer to home. I don't know why this is: I suspect it has something to do with making myself vulnerable near my own home — it's allied, I think, to the primitive instinct we men have not to reveal that we need directional help: it would reveal we are lost and vulnerable. Perhaps a Sunday School lesson about Samson and Delilah, in my horribly vulnerable grammar-school days, left too profound a mark.

But I do like getting haircuts in foreign places. Firenze, Rome, Savigliano, Milano in Italy; La Paz in Mexico; two or three towns whose names I forget in Holland. I regularly get haircuts in Portland, when we're up there. I'll get another here in Rome, next week when I need it just a bit more than I do now. But I thought I'd check the place out, so Simon and I stopped off on our way home from the day's excursion.

Barring the passage of sixteen years — more than Simon has lived — nothing had changed. The same two barbers were there; the same newspaper (*Il Messagero*, not *Repubblica* or *La Stampa*, certainly not *Corriere della Sera* or *Unità*). And the same fellow sweeping the floor, though he, like me and Simon but not like the barbers, looked sixteen years older.

(Barbers, I think, like women, have ways of never looking older. Not all of them, of course, but many; and not simply through recourse to chemistry, though I suspect that happens too from time to time. I don't know of any men other than barbers who manage this. Perhaps that's another reason I try to avoid them, especially local ones; there's something sinister about this; it's like a pact with the devil.)

·One of the things that had endeared this particular barbershop to me, sixteen years ago, was the floor sweeper. He was clearly not right — I mean, he was developmentally disadvantaged, or whatever is the correct term these days. He clearly would not be able to make a living, but he was able, after a fashion, to sweep the floor.

There was something about the way the barbers related to him, and the customers too, that made it clear immediately even to a stranger to the place that the sweeper was a regular — perhaps related to the owner, or one of the barbers. He was accepted and given a way to pass the time.

We had just a few days before been in Sardinia, on that trip, and had eaten at a rather tony restaurant in the capital city, Cagliari. It was a white-tablecloth-and-fancy-flatware place, and nearly all the diners were quite fashionably dressed (not me, of course). Yet a fellow was walking around from one table to another poking his face into the party and acting rather boorish.

It was clear that he too was pathetically disabled; he must have been attached to the restaurant somehow; he babbled and grinned at all the customers (us too); but he was not only tolerated by the clientele, he was greeted and smiled at and accepted for what he was. This was a great lesson to me, one that's been lost on me no doubt, still a lesson, a lesson in humility and generosity and acceptance of things as they are.

My barbershop floorsweeper has improved a bit over the years. He's filled out; he dresses better. He's going a bit bald, but of course he's beautifully coifed. And he's speaking, which he wasn't sixteen years ago. His speech doesn't sound natural, partly because his voice is unnaturally squeaky; and he didn't seem to enter conversations: but he spoke, clarifying requests that were made of him

(open the window a little further; clean off the window of its condensation.)

I need a haircut, but Simon needed it more, it seemed to me. This was aggravated by the fact that he'd just bought himself a hat, a nice soft black felt hat, at a hat shop we passed as we'd walked up the Giolitti, I think it was, near the train station. Borsolino linea, the label said; twenty-six euros. That's no Borsolino, I said to the elderly gentleman who waited on us. *No, signor, non c'e un Borsolino; e un Borsolino linea*, accent on *linea*.

I've never seen an important trade-name used quite like this. I mean, you'd think a hat would either be a Borsolino, or it wouldn't; if not, it wouldn't be allowed to use the name at all — though of course there might be a knock-off: but surely it wouldn't call itself a Borsolino "linea," it would simply and boldly steal the name.

So this must be a lesser-label affair, like the cheap (I mean: inexpensive) wines the major labels sell back home. Yet Borsolino wants you to know they make the thing, cheap though it may be. Maybe this is clever marketing; maybe it's common here in Europe; maybe it's the wave of the future. There's a lot about the fashion industry that escapes my comprehension.

Last January when we were here I went to the Borsolino store, up at the Piazza del Popolo, to buy a hat. I was thrown back on my heels by the prices: you couldn't get out of that store with a hat without leaving nearly two hundred dollars behind. This was in my mind when I observed that Simon's hat couldn't be a Borsolino.

No, the gentleman said, but it's a Borsolino linea — does that mean style, or model, or what? A Chinese Borsolino, I said, and the poor man was aghast: *Oh no signor, non e cinese, è tutto italiano*: this hat isn't at all Chinese, it's completely made here in Italy. Whatever its provenance, it looked good on Simon, and better after the haircut.

We'd been in the morning to the National Museum of Musical Instruments, a collection amassed (or nearly all of it) by a single collector, a tenor prominent in his day — he premiered Rodolfo, for example, in *La Boheme* — but whose day was alas fleeting: his career, for whatever reason, only lasted four years.

But he had money, money and obsessions. He collected corkscrews, cigarette lighters, watches; most of all, he collected musical instruments. He apparently collected many thousand of them, and the best are to be seen in this museum, now run by the State. There are archaeological finds here, musical instruments dating back well before history; whistles and bells and clappers and such. There are lamps and medals and statuettes from the Archaic period, from Etruscan times, and of course from Hellenic Greece, depicting instruments.

There are Roman instruments — bells and trumpets and the like in bronze. And there are fragments in ivory and bone of instruments which, having been made of wood, are otherwise gone forever: tuning pegs and bridges from stringed instruments.

There are lots of folk instruments: hurdy-gurdies, bagpipes, all kinds of mandolins and guitars and whistles and those curious violins called kit-fiddles that are shaped so as to be able to be slipped into a dancing-master's pocket.

There are wonderful instruments from Renaissance and Baroque times: dulcians and rackets and shawms, lutes and theorbos and viols, organs and bells. And there's one of the very first pianos, from Cristoforo's own hand, along with spinets and clavichords and harpsichords. I was a little disappointed that there were no 20th-century instruments; the collection seems to stop in the mid-19th century, with a wondrous array of flutes, one made of solid rock crystal, and an impressive number of harps. You couldn't help hearing the Mozart concerto.

And in our usual undisciplined and completely random way we followed this cultural immersion with lunch in a completely ordinary place, a fish restaurant as it turned out, near the train station, where a liter of decent local white wine cost four Euros, and we had risotto and pasta with scampi (not our prawns, or big shrimp, but small lobsterlike creatures) and a nicely grilled sole. I don't even know the name of the place. It had a very high ceiling, coved at the many corners (for there were a number of columns holding it up), and the usual assortment of pictures apparently obtained at random, and a table of bowls of various vegetables greeting us as we walked in, and a nice English girl who waited on the tables, for the European Union has moved a lot of people around the subcontinent, perhaps also at random, like the Euros themselves, whose obverse sides are uniform, but whose reverse sides are stamped by individual European countries.

The rain has stopped, though as Simon and I walked home in the dark across the Ponte Sisto, and stopped as I always do at night to admire the inky blue sky and the black Tiber and the gold lights on the distant St. Peter's dome we saw lightening in the western sky, far far in the distance, so far there was no thunder to be heard.

Ou sont les neiges
Vicolo del Cedro, Nov. 13—

OU SONT LES NEIGES *d'antan*, old F. Villon asked five hundred years ago: Where are the snows of yesteryear. It seems incredible that things I enjoyed about Rome in January are no longer here to share with my grandchildren ten months later.

But first: I can report that we made the definitive comparison today between the two coffees said to be the best (or at any rate the most special) in Rome. They are the coffee served at Caffe' St. Eustachio and that at Tazza d'Oro.

I quote from a fellow enthusiast, perhaps a specialist: Pavel Zivny, who unaccountably beamed this personal memo from his own traveling PDA to mine:

- the cafés are called 'bars', and not cafés. 1) Sant' Eustachio il Caffe ; (tip -before- you're served); the "Gran Caffe" has super-crema - suspect of additives in roasting.)
2)Tazza d'Oro : the big rival, with smaller crema, but with specialties such as "Caffe Corretto" - corrected with Grappa.
Both close to the Pantheon.
Illy (Illycaffe) Caffetteria Nazionale has food as well.
Not recommended: "caffe lungo" - (espresso with water)

Well, no, I *guess* it isn't recommended. Nor is Illy, as far as I'm concerned. Years ago, when Illy took over the generalized espresso trade here and everywhere, I decided that if an Italian village had only one café — excuse me, Pavel; bar — it might very well offer Illy. If there were two bars, the other one would be the better one. Illy was then, and this is something like fifteen years ago, the Starbucks of Italy (and by the way I have yet to see a Starbucks in this country; I hope I'm not jinxing things by mentioning it).

Anyway today we went out for a long walk, to the Theater of Marcellus and the Ghetto, over to the Campo de' Fiori to have lunch at a fast-food salt-cod restaurant that wasn't there; back toward the Ghetto to the Largo Librari where it was, but it was closed; back to the Ghetto to Giardino da Roma (which we mistook for da Gighetto, where we'd intended to eat) where we did in fact have lunch (artichokes *alla giudia*, fried zucchini blossoms, fried salt cod fillets, *gnocchi al burro*). And after lunch we did the coffee trial.

Sant'Eustachio is on the piazza of that name, and is a legend. There were a number of other tourists there, many clutching guidebooks and most armed with maps; but there were also locals, including laborers in their denim overalls, recently emerged from manholes or climbed down off scaffolds — for Rome is nothing if not a town undergoing constant repair and renewal.

As in every bar and gelateria, you first go to the cash register and pay for your order, then take the receipt to the bar and give it to the barista. At any other bar that would be it: the barista would turn his back to you in order to address his espresso machine, load the coffee-filter with ground coffee, twist it into place, push the button (the days of pull the lever seem pretty much over), and then set the half-filled cup down into the saucer he'd already set out with its little spoon.

Not at Sant'Eustachio. Here everything is cloaked in stealth: you'd think you were dealing with suspicious medieval journeymen anxious lest the secret of their great mastery be discovered by rivals and sold cheaper, thus putting them forever at a disadvantage, or perhaps out of business altogether. At Sant'Eustachio you give the receipt to a barista, who sets out the saucers but — and this is telling, I think — no spoons; and then he murmurs something to a second barista, who manages the machine in the most furtive way imaginable.

And the machine, by the way, is not where it belongs, on the back bar with its handles facing the audience, but on a sort of wing of the bar itself, with a plain board hiding it from view, and two more set at each end to guarantee you'll have no idea what's going on, and, needless to say, no mirror beyond it.

And then the coffee is put down in front of you, with the spoon not on the saucer but in the coffee itself, and the espresso has an impossibly dense "crema," that indescribable component floating atop any well-made espresso; impossibly dense and improbably thick. You can't help yourself: you take a spoonful to taste and discover it's already sweetened, and then you realize there is no sugar on the bar at all.

Sant'Eustachio is famous for this crema, and equally famous

for its being something of a gimmick. It reminds me of nothing so much as the Orange Julius of my childhood, a beverage that shortly after World War II could be found in just about any sizable town. There would be a franchise; it would serve hot dogs maybe, and pie and coffee, but would be attended mostly for its Orange Julius, made of fresh-squeezed oranges blended with a Secret Ingredient that gave it a dense, floury, slightly chemical quality, more pleasant than it sounds.

I think the coffee at Sant' Eustachio is overrated. We went on to Tazza d'Oro, just off the piazza in front of the Pantheon. Here there's no secret: they blend and roast their own coffee, and that's what you get. They also sell the beans, and in fact they have a website from which you can order it — though the freight is incredibly high if you're trying to get it shipped to the United States.

Tazza d'Oro is one of my two favorite coffees, the other being Caffe il Doge, available only in the Veneto, as far as I know — I've only seen it in Venice and in Treviso, where the torrefazione is located. In fact I slightly prefer il Doge, for its somewhat smoky pungency. But Tazza d'Oro is rich and deep and expressive, and we all love the logo, portraying, in silhouette, a dusky maiden casting coffee-beans to the beach in some kind of welcoming ceremony to the noble European visitor.

Franny immediately pronounced Tazza d'Oro as today's winner: it's a nicer bar; the cups are nicer; and the coffee is better. And I agree. But when I pulled my coffee toward me and glanced down the bar for the sugar — for this is a do-it-yourself sweetener, as it should be — I was amazed to discover that the sugar bowl was gone.

It was at Tazza d'Oro that Lindsey and I were struck, last January, by the marvelous sugar bowls on the bar, elegant plastic housings with a bowl of sugar neatly covered by a lid which opened all by itself when you lifted the gold spoon out of its little sleeve, two of which flanked the bowl.

We so loved this contraption that we spent a day or two looking for one to take to Pavel as a present. It was after buying it, in fact, that we boarded the bus on which I was pickpocketed; that's why I knew exactly how much money I'd lost, because I'd just taken it out of the bank to buy the sugar bowl, though in fact I was able to charge it, is why I had the money in my wallet, which was pickpocketed, but I got it all back and then some, as you'll recall if you read these dispatches last January.

Where is the *zuccheriere*, I asked the barman; he pointed at the little paper envelopes of sugar in a receptacle, oddly inelegant in this temple of coffee. Yes yes, I said, I see the sugar, but where is the *zuccheriere*. Another customer at the bar, a real Italian, explained to the barista what I was asking, and clearly he himself realized he'd been missing it too.

It's become illegal, he said to me, after listening to a rapid explanation in Italian from the barman. They both pointed to a notice displayed at the bar, advertising a law of May Something 2004 outlawing sugar bowls on bars, apparently out of concern for public health. Sheesh. You can let people burn diesel oil all over town, dogs can do their business anywhere they like, garbage is allowed to spill at every streetcorner (for there is no pickup, you simply take your household garbage out shopping with you and leave it next to an overflowing public receptacle); but Lord save us if a couple of strangers at a bar might use the same spoon to dip into a general sugarbowl.

I was pretty bitter about this. Simon, I said, let this be a lesson, enjoy what you're seeing here now, when you come back with your grandchildren you'll be telling them there was a time when your coffee was served in a cup, exposed to anything that might be floating about in the air, and not sealed in some sort of plastic container that you had to open with your own hands to protect yourself from public malaise.

There are times I'm not certain Simon cares to hear such comments.

Anyhow we went on from there, up the Via Corso, over to the Spanish Steps where the Trinita del Monte, which crowns that extravagant staircase, was wrapped in an improbable advertisement for Telecom Italia, featuring a Mahatma Ghandi cautioning us to give a message of love if we must give a message.

And we slowly walked back, but not without one last coffee, for the price of a stop at a gent's is a coffee — there are no *pissotières* in Rome, this is not Paris; two thousand years ago the emperor Vespasian realized there was money to be made from calls of Nature.

Every bar has an exclusive with its supplier, and this coffee was Danesi. It's perfectly serviceable: I put it in a category with Lavazza (which is what we have in the apartment for breakfast), and Segafreddo, and two or three others whose names escape me at the moment but which I recognize when I see them. A cut above Illy, in a class with Portland's Torrefazione, but no Doge, certainly no Tazza d'Oro.

Demonstrations: Palestine; farmers
Vicolo del Cedro, Nov. 14—

TODAY'S HIGHLIGHT was a street demonstration — *manifestazione* is the local word — that went on for a number of blocks. We'd walked over to the Trevi fountain, then on to the Via Veneto to see the Capuchin ossuary. The boneyard was closed, of course; there was a sign on the locked gate promising that it would be closed from Dec. 23, 2003, "for works."

In fact the entire Via Veneto was closed, sealed off to vehicular traffic by quite an astounding number of soldier-like police, I think, who stood shoulder to shoulder, armed and backed up by a good many vehicles parked on the sidewalks and adjacent streets.

I asked a bystander what was happening, and he started to explain, then sort of ran down, finally apologizing that he didn't speak very good Italian. Neither do I, I said, still in Italian; what language do you speak? English?

In fact he did, quite well though with an accent: he was from Ukraine. It's a pro-Palestine manifestation, he explained. And they've closed the Via Veneto, because the American Embassy is up there around the curve, and they don't want any anti-American demonstrations.

So we took up stations at the Fontana delle Api, Bernini's charming if badly worn homage to the busy insect featured on the coat-of-arms of his sponsor, Mister Barberini. We hung around to see what would happen, and before too long here came the demonstration down the via Barberini. It took half an hour to go past, at a slow walk, quite peacefully though noisily — bullhorns competed with squawky public-address trucks, most of them broadcasting chants and rants but the last, unaccountably, playing a politicized version of the old Russian song "Katiusha."

In the wake of that truck a number of the demonstrators seemed to be dancing a kind of cheerful two-step, and in front of them, right behind the truck, a very eccentric fellow was prancing and making faces. He reminded me of a man we watched years ago in the town plaza in La Paz, Baja California del Sud, who mimed and pirouetted round and round the bandstand on which the Acapulco Navy Band was playing opera overtures and pasodobles.

That fellow, apparently the town fool, was indulgently approved by the townspeople seated on the park benches, even though he ultimately wound up leading quite a procession of little kids. Our equally strange friend on the Via Barberini attracted no children and was pretty well ignored by everyone around him. But he wasn't the only odd fellow in the parade; two or three other demonstrators carried wine-bottles, one of them at least a magnum, and lurched along as best they could.

For the most part, though, the demonstrators were clearly serious about their mission. Most of the banners spoke for Palestinian recognition, and many equated the Palestinian and Iraqi causes. Palestine for the Palestinians, Iraq for the Iraqis, everyone seemed to agree; let these people choose their own destinies; stop occupying their lands. Bush Sharon Terrorist: Intifada alla Vittoria, one of them proclaimed.

There were a great many Palestine flags, huge ones carried flat by large numbers of people. Some had the familiar image of Yasser Arafat hastily stenciled on them, and many in the crowd wore the keffiyeh, either wrapped around the hair in the usual way, or draped over the shoulders in a distinctly more Italian manner. One young woman wore it like a mask, concealing her face below the eyes.

There were plenty of red flags and banners. The Communist Party is alive and well here. But the people carrying those red flags and banners were far from wild-eyed radicals: this looked like a number of Berkeley street demonstrations we've seen, with little old ladies in tennis shoes, students, and professionals taking part.

Finally the end of the demonstration came walking down the hill, and rather a respectful distance behind them a rear guard of police or carabinieri — I find the Italian distinctions between local and national police, and army for that matter, too nuanced to comprehend. And behind that rear guard, the street-sweepers — first five or six men walking with those long-handled long-bristled willow brooms that are still used here (though in Paris they have been replaced by plastic equivalents), then three or four mechanized street-sweeping vehicles, and finally one last fellow with a broom, who seemed to have nothing really to do, by now the pavement was utterly clean.

Nor was this the only demonstration today. In the morning we set out for the Piazza S. Cosimato, where we like to shop in the daily market. Today is its last day: it's being moved down across the Viale Trastevere to another piazza, and S. Cosimato is being turned into a sort of park: cars will not be allowed to station themselves there, and a lawn is supposed to be planted to set off the majestic plane-tree at its center.

On the way we saw a long table set up in the Piazza S. Maria in Trastevere, culminating in a sort of pavilion where a press table offered a number of pamphlets. The long table was loaded with fruits and vegetables and bottles of oil and wine and jars of honey and jam, for this was an educational demonstration set up by the CIA, not what you think but the Confederazione italiana agricoltori, the Italian Confederation of Farmers, which is celebrating its twenty-fifth anniversary this year.

The displays of fruits and vegetables were beautiful, of course. What was striking was the labels. Each item had a price tag showing two amounts: the average price a consumer pays in the store for these cabbages, onions, tomatoes, and so on; and the average amount that goes to each farmer responsible for providing this food. The farmer's take, of course, is not a very big fraction of the final price.

And even more striking was a smaller display of grapes, olives, apples, and boxes of milk and rice, with a hand-lettered sign accompanying them:

> . *Polish Potatoes*
> . *Chinese Tangerines*
> . *Indian Olive Oil*
> . *German Milk and Cheese*
> . *Chilean Grapes*
> . *Apples from the Czech Republic*
> . *Moroccan Olives*
> . *Indian Rice*
>
> ———
>
> *And Italian Products are Not Sold!*

Well, this is the consequence of globalization and the European Union, of course; but it seems to me it's not a necessary consequence. Adjustments have to be made so that these other countries can export their products, while Italians will still be allowed to consume their own, meanwhile paying a decent amount to their own farmers.

I spoke for a minute to one of the women managing the press table. I'm from California, I told her, and we have the same problem, we grow wonderful food, but the local farmers have to compete with imports from India and Morocco and Chile. And Italy, too, I might add. I said this with a smile, of course, and she smiled too, a smile of sympathy. There are no easy answers to any of this, but there are answers.

I'll have more to say about this, I think, in a later dispatch. Just now it's time for dinner. Lindsey's made our own spaghetti caccia e pepe, spaghetti with pecorino and black pepper; and with it we'll have some broccoli — I think I smell it now. I'll report on it in an hour or so.

* * *

Yes, absolutely delicious. We had to go the the local supermarket for the pepper, which comes in its own little plastic grinder — you've probably seen them; it's by no means the first we've bought. I told Lindsey it should go in her suitcase with the bathtub stopper and the tea ball and, if she finds one, the rubber scraper, the things that are always missing in places like this apartment, not to mention motel rooms. Otherwise it pretty much comes from the market.

And by market I don't mean only the S. Cosimato market. There's a little shop right in the Piazza S. Egidio, with a few crates of apples, pears, onions, potatoes, and other necessities out in front, set up on the piazza outside the shop itself; and, inside the shop, shelves on the other three sides for wine, water, vinegar, oil, and cans of things we haven't found it necessary to investigate.

This is where we buy a lot of our stuff — everything we need outside of bread and milk. The bread's from the local bakery, one of the best in Rome; the milk's from the local supermarket, or occasionally — as this morning — from a latteria-cafe-gelateria-panneteria on a slightly more distant street, say three blocks away, where they make "brioche," meaning croissants, raisin buns, and the like

— breakfast pastries, to put it simply.

The S. Egidio produce stall, as I call it, not knowing what its name really is, has been there quite a while. There are two very nice guys who seem to run it, and I seem to recognize them, much younger, in the color photograph of the place as it looked forty years ago, in the late 1960s. Above that photo there's another, black and white this time, taken in the late 1940s. Then the produce was in willow baskets, whereas now it's in wooden boxes. Otherwise not a lot has changed.

(And that reminds me that this morning, when we came back from the S. Cosimato market, there was a nice flat oval willow basket perched on the garbage can in the piazza, only a little damaged on one end. I picked it up to take home, but Lindsey overruled me, pointing out that our little apartment didn't have a place to put it. When we walked back through the piazza a few hours later it was gone. Someone's making good use of it, and that someone isn't me.)

Jump in mouth
Vicolo del Cedro, Nov. 15—

OFF TO LA STANDA, THEN, this morning, to shop for dinner, Simon and me. And, on the way, to do the Internet thing.

At the risk of seeming to care more about food and eating than any other aspect of human life — nothing really to be ashamed of, and I'll get back to that later on — let me remind you, as I remind myself almost daily, of the range of grocery shopping here:

• the daily markets at S. Cosimato (our neighborhood market) and Campo dei Fiori (the grand market across the river) and elsewhere, I'm sure, but of less utility to us

• the little produce shop in Piazza S. Egidio, our closest provider, who has very good fruit and vegetables and decent ordinary wine (by which I mean no more than 2.50 a bottle) and a limited supply of canned things and juices and water and so on

• the local mini-supermarket, Crai, in the Vicolo delle Cinque, about the equivalent of a block away, with a meat and cheese counter, more canned goods, okay produce though not as good as in the Piazza, milk, coffee, and a small but adequate range of paper goods and soap and the like

• Standa, the nearest supermarket, sharing the basement of a small department store with a fairly adequate bookstore, were I in need of books, as I am temporarily not. Here is a bigger array of precut meat, a wider range of produce, more brands of milk and coffee, and lots of nonfood items — nonprescription remedies, distilled spirits, paper goods, soaps and polishes and waxes. Oh: and sliced bread, which according to a recent newspaper article something like thirty percent of Italians buy, perhaps to clean their typewriters with. Though typewriters are few and far between these days.

I have excluded from this little survey all the specialty stores: oil and wine, what the French call *charcuterie*, cheese, butchershops, pharmacies, and so on. When we want prosciutto or *guanciale* we go to one of them; there are many within three or four blocks.

To Standa this morning because it is my turn to cook, and

Lindsey suggests a saltimbocca, and that requires chicken breasts, though we really should be using veal cutlets here, and perhaps we will later this week.

Standa is laid out in the traditional European manner for supermarkets, which of course are much smaller than the American supermarkets, which have their equivalents here but only in the suburbs, where they are called hypermarkets. That is: you enter through one-way gates, walk through the produce department, past the dairy case, turn at the meat counter, look the other way at the deli counter, then enter the area of the corridors or aisles, where the cans and bottles and paper items are neatly laid out.

(By the way I suddenly realize typing this that I have not noticed any pet food at Standa. Pet food represents maybe twelve percent of American supermarket shelves. Pet food, patent medicines, cosmetics, and wrapping supplies must occupy well over half the space of a typical American supermarket. Add beer and soft drinks and there's hardly any room left for food.)

If you find it necessary to go back to the produce section, say, you get some pretty funny looks from the other shoppers, until they realize as they quickly do that you are no doubt a foreigner. These Italians don't seem to go in for recreational shopping: they come in here with a purpose, they accomplish it, and they get out.

My purpose was chicken, prosciutto, a vegetable to cook; and this required a lot of backtracking and hesitation. There was no appealing vegetable: no problem; I'll get it in the Piazza. I should get the prosciutto at a specialist's, but this San Daniele looks pretty good, and then I'll get some olives too, maybe 100 grams — well, that doesn't look like very much, maybe a few more.

The veal is absurdly thin and expensive so yes, Lindsey, we'll make do with chicken, but how to tell how many chicken breasts are in this package? Oh, why didn't I simply buy a chicken yesterday in the market in S. Cosimato, as we did last January — a fine plump young chicken with yellow feet and a saucy expression on its face. Because the fridge in this apartment of ours is stuffed, that's why.

Then I realize there is another indispensable ingredient in Saltimbocca, and that is sage. Another backtrack to the produce section turns up a styrofoam tray of sage, rosemary, and bay leaves, for

40 cents. But I don't want rosemary and bay; all I need is sage. I'll get it elsewhere.

At the checkstand I look moodily at the stuff the woman in front of me is buying and think about the sage. It will be hard to find elsewhere; I know that. But in January I found it in our store in the piazza S. Egidio, and I think I can count on them again. Besides, to backtrack to the produce section now...

And it's my turn, so I get out the credit card, having also bought another box of blood orange juice because it's on sale, and driven the total up to close to ten bucks. And we walk home, through the Piazza S. Maria in Trastevere, into our Piazza S. Egidio—

Where we find our little shop is closed. It's Sunday. Oh well: we're walking over past the Campo dei Fiori; there'll surely be some sage there.

But there isn't. There's a special market, it being Sunday; lots of stalls offering produce from small organic farms nearby; a few crafts stalls because the Christmas season is in full sway, there being no Thanksgiving to get through first in this country; a fool with an amazingly long and outlandish instrument into which he puts a little water from one of the fountains and then blows, imitating birdsong; three or four flower stands down at the other end of the huge Campo; but the stall that always offers spices and herbs is not here today.

We go on to S. Ivo, the true purpose of today's walk, and admire the chaste intelligent courtyard Borrimini made in front of his eccentric spiral-turretted hexagonal church; and we have a coffee at S. Eustachio, Tazza d'Oro being closed on Sunday; and we walk home. It is very cold; the kids believe they have detected snowflakes in the cold moist air.

I brood about the sage leaves all afternoon. If we have studied one lesson in Italy over the last thirty years it is this: If you see it, and you want it, buy it now. They won't have it over there. They won't even have it here if you wait too long.

So, knowing that Standa will close at two, I make a dash out the door to get that forty-cent box of rosemary, bay, and sage. I shoulder my way past the tourists and students sauntering down the Via della Paglia and lollygagging in front of S. Maria. I easily manage the broken-field quickstep down S. Francesca della Ripa, leaving the cars and taxis and three-wheelers and motos their room, dodging the dog souvenirs, threading the narrow sidewalk, the tables in front of the cafes and restaurants, the temporary police barricades that have been there since January.

But ahead I see the side door to Standa is already closed, locked, and shuttered. I hasten around the corner to the principal entrance, barred by a pleasant young lady who informs me I can't enter. Only for one thing, I promise her: Downstairs? she asks; Yes; and I push past and downstairs and through the gates to the produce section. The herbs are not on their shelf. I ask a fellow with a broom. *Finito*, he says, that desperate word, as bitter and final as "out of print" — in fact it's the other Italian word for out of print, now I think of it, other than *esauro*, I mean.

Up and out. I ask a woman on the street if there's another supermarket nearby. Yes, over there, she says, across the Viale, which is the scene of an incredible traffic jam caused by the moving of all the stalls from S. Cosimato to their new home. I manage to get across the street, but this supermarket is closed; the girls at the checkstands are counting their money; the doors are locked. Anyway there's probably no sage there. It's all been bought, yesterday at the latest, by Roman housewives planning their Sunday saltimbocca.

Home again, emptyhanded. I brood some more until I can stand it no longer. Out at five-thirty to canvass the local restaurants: surely someone here will have a few leaves of sage. By now it is really cold, really cold; and when I stop in at the local wine and oil shop for a bottle of red for dinner, by God we may have no sage to our saltimbocca but we will by God have red wine, I strike up a conversation with a local woman who's taking the cold edge off with a glass, and I join her. Where can I get a few leaves of sage, I ask her.

Very difficult at this time, she says unpromisingly. The markets are closed. Oh but wait a minute, Standa is open. Yes, I answer, but they have no sage; they've sold out. Probably, she says; it's Sunday. We meditate a moment or two with our glasses; then she brightens. Ask at one of the restaurants, she says; surely one of them will have three or four leaves to spare.

Not the first one, and not the second. But on the way back up the Cinque I step into a restaurant whose front door stands beckoningly open, though there's no one to be seen inside. I walk straight back to the kitchen, where a few slices of prosciutto on a plate, absent-mindedly left on a counter, are the only sign of recent human occupancy.

Anyone here, I call, and finally a woman shows up — she'd been eating a sandwich in a dark corner of the dining room with a guy; I hadn't noticed them on my purposeful way in. Have you got a few leaves of sage, I ask, having rehearsed the speech many times in my mind. No, she said. Oh, too bad, I said, I'm making a saltimbocca, and I forgot to buy sage.

She tilts her head to one side and looks at me with frank puzzlement, then says Oh, well, maybe there's something, and we step into the kitchen, she casts a meaningful look at me and I back out of it again, she steps out of sight, then comes back with two fine bunches of rather dried-out sage leaves and offers them to me.

I bring up a handful of change from a pocket: How much do I owe you, I ask, Nothing, she says; and I thank her and walk triumphantly home, a bottle of *novello*, the new wine of this year's vintage, a sort of Italian beaujolais, under my left arm, a spray of sage in my right hand.

* * *

Saltimbocca (chicken version)

Flatten the chicken breasts, using the edge of your fist. Put sage leaves on it, more or less according to taste and, of course, the size of the leaves and the chicken breast. Cover the chicken breast with a thin slice of prosciutto. Pepper it a little.

Fry the chicken breast, prosciutto side up, in a little butter and olive oil mixed. When done on one side, turn over, taking care not to let the three layers (chicken, sage, prosciutto) fall apart. A little salt and pepper.

When done on the other side, remove to serving plate. Add a little white wine to the oil and butter remaining in the pan and cook down to make a sauce, which you then pour over the cooked meat.

With this we had, as a first course, *puntarelle* with an anchovy and oil dressing Lindsey made, and, as our *contorno* or side vegetable dish, *cavolonero*, that delicious dark narrow-leaf kale the Italians grow, which Lindsey simply chopped (the stems finely, the leaves not so fine) and steamed in a little water and salt. And a bottle of *novello*, in this case a Teroldogo from the Alto Adige, Italy's take on the Beaujolais phenomenon — but much less headache-inducing.

Now what I was going to say about it not being anything to be ashamed of, this constant thinking about what you're going to eat, and where you're going to get it, and how you're going to fix it.

I think one of the things wrong with the unthinking majority of the American electorate is just that; they aren't thinking. It's not that they aren't thinking about politics and governance and international relations: they aren't really thinking about much at all. They're believing, or having faith, or being entertained, or going about relatively mechanical occupations; but they're not thinking.

I think one of the reasons for this is that they've been taught to be complacent. Things are pretty easy. They don't, for example, by and large, even think about what they're going to eat, or where they're going to get it. Advertising has taken care of the latter, whether in terms of restaurants — franchises for the most part — or of grocery stores — the major supermarket chains.

As to the former, it's pretty much meat and potatoes in various forms. I know this sounds simplistic, and a little patronizing, but statistically it's not that far off the mark.

Europeans, like northern Californians and some of the people in the other "blue" states, think a certain amount about what they're going to eat. It's an interesting and complex process. It involves inheriting a set of tastes and proclivities and a repertory of dishes; considering new variations and even exotic imports; seeing what's in the market; choosing from a considerable array of restaurants and markets and outlets.

A person who does this, without really thinking about it, is capable of listening, observing, weighing doubts and beliefs, making choices, and executing processes — and on a daily basis. And, of course, talking about it all, not in theoretical terms as I'm doing here, but in direct and practical terms: this is available, that is good at the moment, we used to do it this way, I've heard this other thing can work, and so on and so on.

I call this, for reasons I don't have time to get into now, a sort of unconscious consciousness. It isn't quite rocket science or postmodernist criticism, but it's closer to thinking than simply being imprinted by a few commercials, going out for the same stuff you went out for last week and last month, and disregarding seasons, locales, even personal and family histories.

But enough for now. It's ten o'clock, and tomorrow we've decided to go to the Vatican.

Dome, St. Ivo

God and Cod
Vicolo del Cedro, Nov. 16—

WHAT I MEANT YESTERDAY was: it's by continuing to be alert to the small grain of daily life that the conscious mind is kept working. That's one of today's preoccupations. The other is that it's on the whole better to be connected to the real world than to spend your mental energy on some kind of fantasy, at least if you want to survive, let alone enjoy yourself, without requiring outlandish amounts of money and therefore exploiting a number of other people, usually total strangers.

* * *

It is amazing the sacrifices we will make for our offspring, or in this case for the offspring of our offspring. Today we went to a place we studiously avoided for an entire month last January: the Vatican.

On our first visit to Rome, sixteen years ago, I tried to avoid the Vatican, but the wife of a friend and colleague who lives in Rome — I knew him when he was a visiting professor at Mills College, and conducted my opera — the wife, Jeanne, insisted on our going. She also herded us into the Pantheon, for which I am forever in her debt, and took us to Evangelista for carciofi alla giudea, those wonderful crisp-fried whole artichokes that are somehow flattened while cooking.

But she made us pay for those exquisite pleasures by making us promise to visit the Sistine Chapel, and of course we did. I remember the visit for four things:

- A long wait in a line which ultimately turned out to be for a papal audience, not the Chapel, so we joined another line that went a little quicker
- A long corridor full of sculpture that I deliberately rushed through because it all seemed to be a collection of stolen goods torn out of context and set about any which way
- Signs warning us not to take photographs, speak, sit or lie on the floor, or fall downstairs, all in international-style pictographs with diagonal lines through them

- Michelangelo's ceiling, then half cleaned and restored, so that the contrast between the old dark and dirty state and the present bright and somehow garish condition was heightened.

* * *

Today's visit added little to this, though it did reinforce my aversion to the entire Vatican apparatus. First of all we walked through a fine mist across the river to wait for the number 23 bus which would take us there. We did this because we thought we'd gain time. In this we were completely deluded. A great number of other buses came and went, three or four or five of each of the other buses that stop at that particular point, but no number 23.

Finally we gave it up and began to walk, whereupon two number 23's and possibly a third were right on the spot. We got in one and took it up to the Piazza del Risorgimento.

The line for the Vatican Museums was impossibly long, but we joined it, moving slowly in a half hour to the museum doors. There was a very fine rain, the sort that brings out snails in one's garden, and umbrella-vendors here; it's impossible to imagine how these people spring to life with their umbrellas at just such a moment. They do a good business, of course, charging five Euros apiece for little folding umbrellas that last just about long enough to get to the museum.

Once inside the museum we joined the herd headed for the Sistine Chapel. It's a forced itinerary, up to a point, though one can branch off for the lesser attractions — the Egyptian museum, the Raphaels. We trotted past the Roman sculptures, just as I remembered them from last time, and then entered a gallery I hadn't remembered, the map room.

What a marvelous collection that is! The long gallery boasts huge painted maps on the walls, mural-sized maps perhaps twelve feet high and sixteen wide, over thirty of them, painted in the late 16th century, of the various regions of Italy as they were known at the time. Their detail and their accuracy are astounding: I spent a fair amount of time in front of the map of Pedemontus, as Piemonte was then still known, admiring the depiction of the hills and valleys we'd driven many times, and as recently as a couple of weeks ago.

But from there we were cattle-chuted into the inevitable squeeze to the Sistine Chapel, quite jammed with tourists, all popping away with their flash camera in spite of those clever pictographs, until rather a loud series of recorded announcements was broadcast into the room in Italian, English, German, French, Dutch, Japanese, and a few other languages cautioning us against speaking, photographing, or lying on the floor.

As if we could have found room even to sit on it. And yet what parts of the floor I could see were really among the most arresting aspects of the room — a fine Cosmatesque floor, a mosaic of slices of marble columns set in patterns composed of tiny cubes of stone and glass, all polished by the feet of perhaps thirty thousand visitors a day.

Above, of course, Michelangelo's paintings attracted every face. Taken one at a time and considered as a painting should be they are undoubtedly masterpieces (though they do grow in stature as he continued his work; you can see that he begins as a sculptor somewhat tentatively dealing with the problems of painting, and ends a magnificent painter with all the knowledge of sculpture to draw on).

But there are too many of them; they compete too much with one another; they are too far away; the overall plan is too confused and overwhelming. And they are on the ceiling. Paintings should be on walls, not ceilings; it's unnatural to stand with your head bent back looking at these things. I found myself looking at the lookers, not the paintings. It's amazing how difficult these lookers find it to keep their mouths closed as they gape heavenward; perhaps this is an anatomical imperative, like the one that forces pigeons to bob their heads with each step they take.

I found myself thinking back to the map room, and deciding that I preferred graphic illustrations of real territory to those of Heaven and Hell. And that, of course, led me to wonder why Pope Sixtus would have wanted these depictions of childish tales of Creations and Temptations, Floods and Sermons, and that horrible Last Judgment, when he could have had landscapes and still lifes of real places full of real pleasures.

Well: we left the museum at closing time and stopped in an ordinary restaurant for a bite of lunch — Tavolino Lina, if you want to know, choosing it because 1) it wasn't immediately across the street 2) it was only a block or two away 3) we'd been handbilled by not one but two fellows who assured us that it wasn't bad, and that Italians ate there as well as tourists. We had pizza and a green salad and a half liter of white, and it was okay.

Then we walked home and had *puntarelle* with anchovy sauce that Lindsey made.

Then, after a decent interval, we walked back across the Tiber to what is now my favorite place to eat in all of Rome, Dar Filettaro Santa Barbara (the name is provisional, because various versions of it appear in various places).

This is on the Largo Librari 88, just south of the Campo de' Fiori, and is open evenings only (but from 5 p.m. on), Monday through Saturday. We walked out of a bitter cold night and sat at one of maybe twenty tables for four lining the walls of a long rectangular room. The table was covered with white Formica, then, quickly as we sat down, with paper.

The menu is very short, and I didn't really look at it. Four cod fillets, I said, and a half liter of red. Then Lindsey said Oh, zucchini flowers, and I added them.

The waiters are boys no older than their mid-twenties, rangy and Roman, and they're pretty efficient. The wine came almost immediately, a decent house Abruzzo wine. A plate of four big battered and deep-fried salt-cod fillets arrived next, with eight good-sized sheets of paper folded into triangles. We wrapped a paper around a fillet and began eating out of hand. The zucchini came not long after.

The batter was very crisp, almost brittle; and the cod and zucchini were moist and tender, full of flavor, and heartwarming against the cold night. I don't know why we didn't know about this place last January. I would willingly eat here twice or three times a week, from now until the day, not far off they tell us, that cod is extinct, gone the way of the passenger pigeon, a delicious commodity to tell your grandchildren about with respect and regret for the mortality, general and individual, that confronts us all.

Well, you see where this has led, of course. The popes and their finery, their gold and crystal and enamels, their Roman sculptures and their Egyptian papyruses, occupy themselves with the very real problems of politics and power while impressing their flock with all that apparatus of myth and symbolism and deferred heavenly rewards for present worldly pain and privation.

Meanwhile someone is fishing for cod, and a couple of stalwart women are battering and frying them in the kitchen, and we and a good many others are sitting at plain paper-covered tables eating them with great relish but no sauce, and realizing that really hardly anything could be better.

A Day in the Country
Vicolo del Cedro, Nov. 17—

WE CAME HERE BECAUSE we feel we really need an extended stay in a city from time to time; otherwise we'd rusticate entirely. But this morning was so glorious (though cold) that it was clearly time to get out of town.

Where better to spend a morning in the country than seventy-five feet underground, we reasoned; and the kids, being kids, are fascinated with things grisly (being half Czech reinforces this ghoulish preoccupation, I think); so off we went to the Via Appia for a history lesson.

This involved taking the no. 23 bus to the Piramide stop and transferring there to another bus to get past the city gates. The Piramide is a dislocating sight, even in Rome; a perfect pyramid, 72 feet wide and 118 feet high, made of ordinary brick but faced with gleaming white marble.

Except for the obelisks there's not a lot in Rome in the Egyptian manner, which is a little surprising. Maybe the Christians did away with it all as payback for the nasty treatment Moses got from the Egyptians. Maybe the Goths and the Vandals smashed it all; maybe the alchemists made use of it in the dark ages. Maybe it's all simply been redistributed, either by archaeologists of one kind or another or by dealers in curiosities. I know there's a lot at the Vatican, but we didn't look at it; and I know there's a lot more in the Egyptian museum in Torino, said to be the biggest collection outside of Egypt (which is hard to believe, given the Louvre and the Metropolitan).

In any case there's not a lot to be seen out of doors: just the obelisks and, as far as I know, this very odd pyramid, built to satisfy the last will and testament of one Caius Cestius, who died in 12 B.C. He'd worked for a while in Egypt, at the time when obelisks were being crated up and shipped off to Rome to celebrate Caesar's defeat of Cleopatra; and he wanted to be remembered after his death. He was, by his heirs who had to scratch more money together to pay for the thing; and he is, by all of us who take buses or trams through this part of town, between the Circus Maximus and the Baths of Caracalla.

But the next bus, the 118, was a long time coming. People grew restless, and when one finally hove into view with the depressing sign DEPOSITO on its destination-board — for it was out of service and being driven to the bus rest home, wherever it is — I thought for a while it was going to be hijacked, not by the confused and passive tourists clutching their maps and cameras, but by the few Italian women (none of them under sixty) who had been muttering and expostulating and gesturing and flapping their plastic reticules.

The busdriver got on her phone, talked to someone, and assured us that another would appear in ten minutes. She was wrong: it appeared in only three minutes. But after we got on the driver informed us cooly that this bus had decided not to be a no. 118 after all, and we should get back off. We did, and immediately crossed to the next bus landing and boarded another bus. I don't know how these things are organized. They always make me think of the opening sequence of *Mister Hulot's Holiday*, the one where passengers gather on a train platform, hear an incomprehensible metallic announcement from a loudspeaker, rush downstairs, out of sight, and upstairs back into visibility on another platform, only to hear another announcement as the train pulls in to the ... oh, the hell with it, you get the idea.

In the meantime we'd struck up a conversation with a young woman whose English was beautifully spoken: I wondered where she was from. The north island of New Zealand, it turned out, modified by a number of years living in London, where she is a costume builder for ballet and theater. She accompanied us to the catacombs where we joined a group being herded through the bone mines by an informative and meticulous guide.

Here the highlight was the tomb in which St. Cecilia's body was found. I wrote about her a few days ago; her church is one of our favorite spots in Trastevere, partly for the magnificent Cavallini frescos, partly for the fascinating Roman house in its basement (Cecilia's own house, from the third century). Because Cecilia was martyred in her own *caldarium*, or steam bath, I had always assumed, without really thinking about it, that she had been buried here, but of course that was not at all the case. Like all Roman Christians who died before Constantine legalized their cult she was buried in a catacomb, an underground cemetery, outside the Roman walls.

These were dug out of soft volcanic rock, underground galleries and rooms with niches in the walls just big enough to lay the cloth-wrapped bodies. Some of the richest could afford sarcophogi and even family rooms; most were simply shelved. The catacombs were abandoned when Christianity was legalized, in the fifth century I think it was, and by the ninth they were completely forgotten, and not rediscovered until much later.

But Cecilia's body was found in 1595, I read, or in 1599, the books don't agree on the point; and when it was found it was in perfect state; I've already described the affecting statue made from direct observation of her body when it was found. A copy of this statue is in the catacombs, placed, they say, just where the body was found, so long ago, and it is very dramatic and a little creepy. She was only sixteen, small for her age we would say today, and very pretty; and a teen-aged girl in our group took one look and fainted dead away, and a woman next to her quickly crossed herself, and the parents of the girl caught her and laid her down gently on the floor of the tomb, and reassured the guide that everything would be okay.

Attendants were called, who unaccountably talked among themselves in French, and we moved on to finish our explorations, and then walk down the idyllic avenue of cypresses and pines back to the old Appian Way and on to lunch — *tortellini*; risotto — in a country restaurant beside a fountain gushing a particularly tasty mineral water.

And then through the afternoon sunlight to a couple more sights: St. Sebastian's church, where his body is buried; and another Cecilia's, a big drumshaped brick tower, a perfect cylinder open at the top and conical at the subterranean floor where she was buried. And then, just as we were wondering how to get back to our bus stop, we found a man with a horse and buckboard who offered to take us on a forty-minute ride along the old Appian Way and to finish by dropping us off at the stop.

This was a glorious conclusion to the afternoon. We jolted and bumped over the stretches where the original Roman paving has been revealed — I can't believe they didn't smooth it out with a layer of decomposed granite — and then trotted along on the mercifully smoother *zampietri* and the occasional stretch of asphalt, through the pastoral suburb known as Paradiso, where (the coachman told me) we passed the residences of Gina Lollobrigida, and the designers Armani and Versace, and the man who got rich introducing the song "Nel blu dipinto di blu."

We passed an American military installation, presumably inactive since the end of the Cold War; we passed quite a large farm producing vegetables and salad and fruits, all of them organic; we passed the Russian Embassy, where an old woman in the ubiquitous dark cardigan and blue print skirt and dark stockings, with a kerchief on her head, was sweeping the driveway at the entrance gate, and where an elderly man wearing corduroy jodhpurs and holding a walking stick was sitting, knees crossed, on a bench, smoking a pipe, and lifted a hand to greet us with a smile as we trotted by.

And then we sped down a final hill, asphalt-paved by now, and were dropped off, and paid our twenty euros and crossed to the bus stop to wait for another no. 118 bus, behind us a beautiful meadow, partly plowed for the next planting, green grass and raw siena loam beneath a pale blue sky, Tivoli in the distance and Frascati, whence comes the cheap but tasty and honest white wine we drink every day.

And dinner at home: tuna, *cannelini*, raw chopped onion; and good bread from "our" bakery, warmed and toasted in a little butter in the frying pan. We watch the news, in Italian, and learn of resignations and appointments, and decapitations and distress; and we read about all this in the newspapers; and it sounds pretty damn terrible. But Rome and its three millennia continue to put it in perspective, at least for me. Enjoying our harmless pleasures seems almost a responsibility in times like ours. We won't be here that much longer.

Politics and pasta
Vicolo del Cedro, Nov. 18—

IN SPITE OF WHAT you may think it's not all eat, eat, eat, you know. We continue to pay attention to the larger issues. We read the papers — the *International Herald Tribune* and *La Repubblica* — and we listen to what people in the street are talking about.

They don't have that much in common, the newspapers and the people in the street. That's partly because I can't understand the language, except when I overhear some English, which I do pretty darn often, because we go to touristy places, and because our quarter, near Piazza S. Egidio, is home to a number of students.

(I also hear a lot of Spanish, a certain amount of French, a tiny bit of German, a little more of Dutch, a fair amount of something that sounds like Arabic, and now and then a little Tagalog.)

La Repubblica has been running a series about State and Religion. It's in the news for a number of reasons: first, in chronological order, because of the perceived influence of Religion (of some sort) on the outcome of the American elections; then because of a flap here concerning an Italian nominee to the European Union who felt his personal attitude toward homosexuality, an attitude somehow prompted by religious feelings (I have trouble understanding that, but then I'm from California) would have to be expressed in his governmental role; then more urgently following the nasty mood that's taking hold in The Netherlands since the murder by a Muslim extremist of Theo van Gogh, the Dutch film director who was outspoken (to understate the matter) in his opinion of radical Islam.

Mario Pirani, in today's *Repubbica*, points out that Europe is pretty sensitive to the historical problem of religious wars. They are in the European, um, blood. The Thirty Years' War, for example, which ended in 1648, killed eight million people, not to mention the pestilence that accompanied it, simply because a few papal envoys to Prague threw a few Protestants out the window to their deaths because they wanted to build a few more Protestant churches.

Well, 1648 may seem a long time ago. But religious wars continue. One was settled, or perhaps only set in abeyance, just a few years ago in the former Yugoslavia, and another continues today in Ireland. And, as Pirani notes,

> religious wars are different from 'traditional' ones; they are difficult to conclude, they go on without solutions, the combatants are dominated by absolutism, not easily satisfied by mediation or compromise. For the same reasons they are exceptionally cruel, partly because the combatants think themselves fighting for Good against Evil. And finally they don't recognize any distinction between civilians and the military.

All this resonates pretty resoundingly with the news from Iraq: an unarmed wounded enemy executed in a Mosque. And the news from Washington: the former National Security Advisor (which amounts, it seems to me, to a parallel Secretary of Defense, as the Secretary of War has been called for the last fifty years) promoted to Secretary of State.

* * *

All of this preoccupied me this morning, after I'd bought and scanned the newspapers; but I set it aside as we crossed the Tiber yet again, doing a little shopping and visiting the National Museum of Pasta. I promise you that there is such a thing. And it's rather an ambitious affair, in its engagingly silly way. For a relatively minor admission charge you get headsets and a CD player to guide you through the many smallish galleries on two floors — Rome is no place for the mobility-challenged — and even a microphone so the Head of Family can speak to the others in the group through their headsets.

The museum is pretty cagey about the origins and age of pasta, only noting that the first written record seems to date from the 12th century, well before Marco Polo. (It's in Arabic, by the way.) There are of course two kinds of pasta in Italy, hard pasta and soft pasta; but this museum quite ignores the latter. Tortellini, ravioli, *malfatti*, above all gnocchi have no place here. This museum celebrates the irrational but inevitable and certainly useful technological evolution by which semolina flour, which is ground from a grain quite different from the wheat that gives us Americans our cake and bread flour, is mixed with water, kneaded to a fare-thee-well, and pushed through holes in metal plates to extrude the more than three hundred shapes known to Italians — long hard pastas like macaroni and rigatoni and spaghetti; short hard pastas like *orecchieti* and *stelle* and *farfalle*. (And evasively in-between ones like *penne*, which begin as long pastas but are cut short before they are dried.)

The museum offers prints and photographs, texts and drawings, machines and working models, and all the while it's explained in delightful detail in Italian on the wall-panels, which are glossed in a maddeningly British accent by the voice in your headphone. (None of us can abide hearing "pasta" rhymed with "faster.")

We left the National Museum of Pasta hungry, of course, and stepped around the corner to San Crispino, the gelateria on the via Pannetiere, which Lindsey feels is the best in Rome to her knowledge, and I'm not going to argue. It was our second trip here: we have made a second trip to no other gelateria. (At least not on this trip, not so far.) San Crispino has two very distinctive features separating it from all other gelaterie so far consulted: the gelati are covered, of all things; you can't see them; they're in stainless-steel ice-cream cans with stainless-steel lids, and you have to make your choices by simply reading the labels.

(At least so I thought the last time we were here: but this time there were a couple of Italian men ahead of us, and they were asking about flavors, and being given sample tastes on little plastic spoons to help them make up their minds.)

The other distinction is that the woman behind the counter, and yes, exceptionally it is a woman, it's usually men serving up the gelato, I don't know why that is; the woman behind the counter is black, Nigerian I suspect from the roundness of her face; and she has a glorious voice with which she speaks a beautifully clear Italian — and, last time we were here, sings a fine deep baritone blues.

We walked slowly home for lunch and a desultory afternoon which I spent making webpages — I'll steer you to them next time; all these dispatches and a good many photos will soon be online — and thinking about the political situation.

By "political" I don't really mean the immediate situation, pressing as it is. This city, as you'll have noticed, puts me in a detached frame of mind. Bad as the immediate situation is, it's just another swing of the pendulum. It's amazing how easily the enlightened and the sympathetic can co-exist, I mean exist at the same time as, the close-minded and the hateful.

Yesterday I bought a book by Federico Rampini, a columnist for *La Repubblica*. He's been living in San Francisco for four years, and contributing a weekly column from there to his paper, and he's just brought out this collection of columns, *San Francisco-Milano* (Rome, Editori Laterza, 2004). In the first thirty pages he sounds like many newspaper columnists, a bit like Herb Caen for his celebration of the Bay Area, a bit like Myles naGopaleen (who wrote as Flann O'Brien, as well as other *noms de plume*) for his louche humor and love of language, a bit like my friend Gaye LeBaron (who writes for the Santa Rosa Press Democrat, and will be embarrassed by this) for his awareness of the intersection of history, local politics, and human instinct.

But his recent columns have brought achingly home the distance between his San Francisco (and my Bay Area) and the rest of the country.

I used the term "unconscious consciousness" the other day, writing about the manner in which many Italians (and many in Northern California) go about their daily lives, dealing with a fine-grained life offering many choices, many of them delightful. The expression is shamelessly stolen from the marvelous R. H. Blyth, who described four kinds of poetical address in his indispensable book *Zen in English Literature and Oriental Classics* (Tokyo: Hokkaido: don't have the date handy.)

He divided poets among those who are objectively objective, objectively subjective, subjectively objective, and — worst of all — subjectively subjective. It makes a lot more sense than it sounds here.

What I meant was that the ordinary person who is alive and alert is often unconsciously conscious: he (and more often she, I think) makes decisions among choices by using a conscious mind which is operating on an almost subliminal level.

Critics and philosophers, of course, operate with conscious consciousness: they think about their thinking. And a good many people operate with unconscious unconsciousness: than is, they make their choices without using their own minds, their own "values." They have been programmed to choose in certain ways, and they aren't even aware of the extent of that programming.

(I suppose there's a small fourth category of people who are consciously unconscious; these would be those who deliberately deaden their own critical faculties in one way or another. It would be academic to consider them any further at this point.)

This all came to mind two or three days ago when Lindsey said, on reading some dreadful development or other in the *International Herald Tribune*, What can they be thinking? And I said You know, I think they are not thinking, they are not thinking at all.

I think it's not a difference between red and blue, right and left, uneducated and educated. I'm beginning to think it's a question of consciousness. It's being here in Rome has led me to this. If you read Julian Jaynes's eccentric book *The Origin of Consciousness and the Breakdown of the Bilateral Mind* (sorry: don't have the publication information with me) — and though the title is absurd and the book itself eccentric I recommend it highly — you'll find a fascinating description of the beginnings of consciousness, which he dates to about the time of Homer, in about the place of Greece.

When it developed there was a huge disjunction between the Leaders and the Led and the Dubious, and this was partly because the Leaders and Led weren't really aware of consciousness, and still thought those raging ideas in their minds were the voice of the gods, while the Dubious, the poets and philosophers, were beginning to realize all this was going on in people's minds.

Well: I've gone on long enough now about this, and I'll undoubtedly go on more about it in the future. If you read these dispatches hoping for descriptions of Rome, or recipes, you'll just have to skim through. If on the other hand you want more theoretical blarney about politics and philosophy you'll likely have to wait.

We ended the day at the museum around the corner, in the Piazza S. Egidio, where we saw stills and, more fascinatingly, film footage from Mussolini's propaganda office, *Luce*. (*Luce* = "light," and rhymes with *Duce*, which = Leader.) Here was all that familiar prelude to war, with little children being taught to act as cogs, manufacturers living like kings, the poor being entertained with machines and national pride, and a not-terribly-tall National Leader walking with a swagger. Lordy, lordy.

Haircut (mine)

Vicolo del Cedro, Nov. 19—

THE TIME GROWS SHORT: we have three days left, including today. A lot has happened since we left, exactly a month ago, and it feels like we've been gone much longer than that. We spent the entire month of January here in Trastevere, and it didn't seem nearly as long, perhaps because we stayed in one place that entire time. On this trip we've been in four distinct places, not to mention the traveling between them; and even though they're all in this one country the result has been to make four sojourns and excursions of one.

You've read enough about each of these places — Torino; the Rampis' in Monferrato; Verona; and Rome — that I needn't describe their differences here. But thinking about them, in the barber's chair on the Piazza Pollarola (or is it the Vicolo de' Bovari? Damn: it's right on the margin of the map, of course!), in response to the barber's friendly question as to where I'd been on this trip, I realized that these have all become Favorite Places, where I feel quite at home.

This is partly because I'm beginning to know my way around these places, of course. That is, I know my way around my part of these places. We have our favorite cafés and bars, our favorite markets and restaurants, our favorite lookout points and walks.

But it's also because an adjustment has taken place between my own internal rhythms and those of the places. Some of this is physical: one knows how to find a toilet, where to drink water, which side of the street or the river is in or out of the sun or the wind, and one's feet instinctively turn in the right direction when some part of the body south of the hippocampus makes a gentle suggestion.

But it's also mental, and emotional, and perhaps spiritual. I've found that in visiting a new place I generally go through three phases: I start out either quite enchanted or quite irritated; then I swing to the other extreme; then I swing back, though probably not so far. Sometimes it takes years to negotiate this: I loved Paris for years, over a number of visits; then one time we spent a night there and decided the next morning to get out of the city and drive south, it just didn't interest us any more. A few years later, of course, we came back to our senses: Paris is a great and charming and generous city; I could cheerfully spend half my life there.

The barber wasn't so sure about Torino and Verona. (He didn't know Monferrato at all.) I think he'd been there — he's been around; hell, he even spent three years in Buffalo, New York. *Molto freddo*, he said; very cold. He'd been parked there with an uncle, and he didn't say much more about it than that; it didn't seem to have been among his happiest years.

When I told him I was from California he said Ah, vino; and I responded that that was where I was from, the wine country. Ah, Noppavallee, he said. No, Sonoma county, I responded, my own territorial pride awakening. Noppasonomah, he smiled; and then suggested we begin to travel further south, to Campania and the Basilicata, where it's warm.

It had been a curious day. We began it at S. Clemente, perhaps the most striking of the archaeologist's churches in this city full of such — a Twelfth-century church, built atop a Fourth-century church, built atop a much earlier temple of the Mithraic cult, Christianity's chief rival in its first four hundred years. As if this isn't enough, each of these places is extremely rich in mosaics, sculpture, and frescos, though the Mithraic temple has only a very few to be seen.

From there to Perilli for lunch — Perilli in Testaccio, a workingclass quarter where the slaughterhouses used to be, and which is still renowned for its workingclass meat dishes, tripe and offal and such: but we had rigatoni alla carbonara, three of us did, and I held out for taglialini with artichokes, with an artichoke solo as an appetizer. What a fine place this is! The room so big and spacious, nicely decorated with murals you can stand to look at; the waiters friendly and attentive without any kind of fawning or nudging; the food beautifully seasoned and perfectly cooked. I was sorry not to have a five-course dinner, but this was midday, and money's a bit tight — the low dollar is really hurting — so we contented ourselves with two courses and went on our way.

That took us to a curious thing we've overlooked until now, Mount Testaccio. This is a hill, 120 feet high, made entirely of empty terra-cotta amphorae and jugs, piled up here for a couple of centuries straddling the birth of Christ. Why was this done? Because this was an important port, or an importing port; oil and wine and grain and rotten fish and who knows what else was shipped here, nearly all of it in terra-cotta jugs and amphorae; and when they were emptied out to be repackaged for the local trade the original shipping containers were tossed on a pile.

I suppose this is something like the mountains of steel shipping containers currently stacking up near container ports. In time, of course, even the ancient Romans realized this stuff could be recycled. You could ship the amphorae and jugs back with some kind of local product in it, though I hate to think what that might have been; or more likely you could pulverize the stuff and use it as a filler in building materials, or even turn it into a slurry to make more terra-cotta jugs and amphorae. So after two hundred years or so they stopped doing this, and soil inevitably developed above the broken crockery, and plants took root, and then trees, and the goats browsed there, and it wasn't until a couple of hundred years ago, I read in one of the eight or ten guidebooks that seem to have infiltrated this apartment, that archaeologists realized what was there.

In the meantime people had burrowed into it, finding the unique constituency of this mound made an ideal place for, what else, wine cellars. Wine and cheese, no doubt; and living-quarters too; it would have been cool here.

We set out to walk a circle around the Mount, but we were sidetracked almost immediately by a big area full of campers and caravans and provisional shacks, many with impromptu but rather fascinating constructions around them. I was reminded of the mudflat sculpture you used to see on the east shore of San Francisco Bay back in the 1960s. And then we came to a large building, dating I'd say from the 1920s or so, that had been taken over and turned into a kind of community center.

This was the Villaggio Globale, a sort of squatter community that apparently dates back to that period. We struck up a conversation with a very bright, earnest, pleasant young woman, a Roman, who confirmed that the community shared much with the Diggers of San Francisco and the squatters of Amsterdam. The Global Village seems well organized: the center has a cafe-restaurant, a library, facilities for the community's children. We learned that there are something under a thousand residents here, old-timers like us (she smiled when I asked that) and youngsters. Someone apparently worked out a deal with the city to take over this former slaughterhouse — for such it is — and set it aside for these free-spirited folk.

I explained that I was asking all these questions about the place because I was born in Berkeley, and she broke into a broad but rather wistful smile, Ah, San Francisco, she said, I hope one day to be able to see it, it must be wonderful, it is everything we hope for here, a place where people of different kinds of energy and belief can live together in peace, can live in the moment, without fear and without oppression.

I was greatly moved by this, and could respond only by thanking her and moving on. We walked home, past the big recent blocks of apartments on our side the Tiber, some of them apparently for low-income families; and I thought again of Federico Rampini's book *San Francisco-Milano*. It is an unabashed love-song to San Francisco, and it's pleasant and a little troubling to read his description of a city where everyone is friendly, life is well organized, the sidewalks are clean, etcetera etcetera. I could write about Rome and Torino and Verona this way, and I have in fact been guilty of that from time to time, the traffic moves efficiently, people give way to one another, the coffee is wonderful, at the restaurants you can eat an entire dinner or just a course or two, the dogs are in general well behaved, etcetera etcetera.

But I know about grass being always greener elsewhere, and I know that many of us are by nature Papagenos, we are so happy to find something pleasant that we fail to see the little problems that accompany it. This morning, for example, we took the Number Three tram to the Colosseum in order to visit S. Clemente. While we waited nearly half an hour for the Number Three tram coming our way, five of them went the other way. You can't help wondering what kind of organization this implies. The end of the line isn't that far down the tracks. Surely these trams have to come back our way once they've got there.

There are inexplicable things in this city, casual slowdowns, orchestrated general strikes, walkouts and sit-ins and parades and such. Any of these could affect a tram schedule. Or maybe there's simply a junkyard down there at the end of the line, maybe four trams out of five are given some sort of desultory inspection and then simply tossed out, tossed on a mound of no longer useful or interesting trams. There are piles of things all over towns: Dorian capitals, hands and feet from old statues, bricks, paving-stones, broken jugs and amphorae. Why not trams?

Piramide di Caio Cestio

The Parmesan lesson
Vicolo del Cedro, Nov. 20—

WITH ONLY A COUPLE of days to go the dynamic changes greatly. We no longer consult maps as we walk about the city; we stop noticing things; we don't care any more when something we set out in the morning to do turns out to be unattainable. Today, for example, we walked up to the Piazza del Popolo — not an inconsiderable walk, especially on these goddam stones, after three weeks of walking these goddam stones (shin splint in left leg, left knee buckling at odd moments, sore on gouty right big toe, etcetera) — to take in an exhibition of mechanical inventions by Leonardo da Vinci, said to be at the Sala Bramante, or something.

Well, of course, there was neither a Leonardo banner nor a Sala Bramante to be seen. Nor did any of the uncaring specialists in tourist information have any ideas: neither at the newsstand, nor the bored young man playing video games on his *telefonino* in the Basilica S. Maria del Popolo, nor the lady at the cash register in the bar where we went for coffee. No matter: we all know what Leonardo's inventions looked like, chariots with scythes at the wheels, impractical helicopters, perfectly ordinary winepresses and all that.

Certain things of course are always attended to. We don't walk past the Pantheon without walking in; we don't walk past Tazza d'Oro without having a coffee. But the novelty is definitely off.

So it seemed appropriate to have dinner at an entirely new place. I was prepared to be disappointed for at least two reasons: the name of the restaurant is distinctly non-Italian, or so at least it seems to me; and the place was recommended, in a curiously unintentional way, by my son-in-law. He was born a Czech, and the name of the place is Monsu Vladi.

I suspect the Slavic ring to the name was what attracted him to it in the first place, three or four years ago. I'm not sure, as we haven't discussed it: I only know of his experience here from a memorandum that appeared one day in my PDA, after he and I exchanged a number of items by beaming them back and forth, either to try out our infrared technology or to demonstrate our prowess at these boy toys. (It occurs to me that such indiscriminate sharing of information is analogous to the marks dog leaves on fire-hydrants, announcing their existence to all and sundry.)

In we went, then, at the ungodly early hour of seven-thirty, the first customers of the evening, and were seated by a nice young man with black hair and a dancer's body, and were asked whether we wanted a bottle of water, and were brought menus.

They revealed that the kitchen here was Neapolitan. After the last three weeks here in Rome, riding atop our experience of a month here in January, the menu looked utterly foreign: it was as if we had suddenly found ourselves in a Chinese restaurant. We had had wonderful potato gnocchi for lunch, bought at the Sardinian pasta shop on the Via del Moro near our apartment, where all the paste are made by hand and sold fresh; and we'd eaten it with the last of our sweet delicious Italian butter, with a good lot of fresh sage chopped into it as it was melting, so we weren't about to order gnocchi here.

What to eat, then? I settled for spaghetti *alla puttanesca*, with tomatoes and olives and garlic; Lindsey had a veal scallopini; Franny had spaghetti with clams and cherry tomatoes; Simon had — swordfish, and then his own *puttanesca*. The boy can eat.

The waiter was very nice, speaking to me almost exclusively in Italian, to the kids in English; approving our requests for wineglasses for them (he had jumped to a conclusion and left them out the first time round), asking Simon if he wanted a big spoon with his spaghetti, then immediately ruling it out, and soon after demonstrating the proper Italian way to eat spaghetti: certainly not by twirling your fork in a spoon (which I suspect has a faintly obscene connotation in Italian).

It was all very good, as Pavel's note had indicated; but it all seemed irrelevant to me, eating the wrong food in the wrong setting. I know: Rome is the capital of the country. I know: one of our first meals here was in a Sardinian restaurant, and I enjoyed it. I know: Naples really isn't that far away. But it seemed wrong: perhaps it was underscoring the fact that in only sixty hours we will be flying away from here, not to return for probably a year or more.

Throughout dinner we bantered, talking as grandparents and grandchildren do, about how things were when we were kids, about the curious habits of the generation between us. I have been particularly attentive to the fifteen-year-old, because he's just at the point where he's hesitating between consciousness and unconsciousness, in the sense I was writing about the other day.

At one point he even mentioned sometimes fearing to read something, a book, say, because it might change the way he thinks about things — not change his opinions, he was quick to explain, or simply enlarge his information, but actually change the methodology of his thinking. This is just what the ancient Greek philosophers feared when reading and writing came in, twenty-five hundred years ago, and it's fascinating to see the process developing before your very eyes.

After dinner I asked if I could have a little cheese and a glass of red wine. The waiter looked immediately concerned: We have some Pecorino, he said, and some Parmigiano. Fine, I said, what more could I want. But the red wine is cold, he said; maybe you'd like another white instead. How cold, I asked. He leaned toward me and spoke frankly but discreetly, and in English lest there be a misunderstanding: It's in the fridge.

Fine, I said, I'll have another white. White's what you should have with cheese anyway, Lindsey said. (White wine with cheese is all the rage these days, especially with dry white cheeses like Parmigiano.) But then, after bringing a plate with several nice chunky slices of the cheeses, he brought a glass and a bottle, and tipped some red into my glass: a bottle had been set aside somewhere, and wasn't cold after all.

I ate a piece of the Pecorino rather inattentively, okay, sheep, dry, pungent, nice red wine, I thought to myself, continuing to listen to the kids and to interject a few comments from time to time; and then I bit down on a piece of Parmagiano.

It was really quite an extraordinary piece of cheese. I stopped what I was doing and simply tasted it for a while, without taking more in, or chewing, or anything; simply aftertasting the mouthful I'd just taken.

You really should taste this cheese, I said to the table in general; it's an amazingly good piece of Parmesan. The others took advantage of the offer.

All the lessons of the Salone del Gusto came washing back over me, the lessons learned at a number of taste-workshop "laboratories," many of them in precisely this substance, Parmesan cheese.

You really can taste the full range here, I said: you taste nuts, and cheese, and butter, and milk, and grass — all the successive stages of tastes that have gone in to the making of this cheese. Everyone tasted, silently; you could see the thought and the appreciation, the analysis and the pleasure in the changing expressions of the faces.

Lindsey agreed. It's so sweet, she said; such a sweet cheese. By now the waiter was nearby, enjoying our enjoyment. Where did you get this cheese, I asked. A quick darker look flitted over his face: he didn't know. I'll have to ask, he said. Doesn't matter, I said; I won't be able to get any anyway. It's really an extraordinary cheese, I added. Not a well-aged one, I went on, no more than fourteen or sixteen months —

Exactly, the waiter said. Was he simply agreeing, or did he know? I'll never know. We finished the cheese and accepted his offer of coffee. It's not a Roman coffee, he added, it's Neapolitan. Doesn't matter, I kidded him, the best coffee isn't Roman anyhow, it's from the Veneto. Oh, but there's Tazza d'Oro.

Matter of taste, the waiter countered. This one's Neapolitan, and very good. He brought it; it looked promising, and had a quick full taste that soon left surprisingly little aftertaste. I like it, Lindsey said, and Francesca agreed. I wasn't so sure, and I could see Simon was thinking about the Tazza d'Oro we'd had a few hours earlier.

There's a hint of chocolate in it, Lindsey said. It's surprisingly soft, I returned. Girly coffee, I thought to myself. Good, but soft on the palate, and short in the finish.

And so a group of Americans looking forward to home, growing jaded with Rome, were snapped back to attention. And once again, as so many hundreds of times before, I learn that it's best to suspend prejudice, to approach what's presented with an open mind, looking for the unsuspected delight rather than the presumed disappointment.

Se vuol ballare
Vicolo del Cedro, Nov. 20—

SUNDAY, AND OUR LAST day in Rome, at least for the time being. So I will post this when the Internet Point opens, at ten in the morning, and catch up on your e-mail, and maybe reply to a few of you; and then put the computer away for a couple of days.

As you know if you've stayed with me through all this verbiage it's been a fascinating trip, more fascinating than usual for a number of reasons — the absorbing experience at the Salone del Gusto and Terra Madre in Torino (it seems like three months ago!); the extraordinary last couple of weeks of the presidential campaign; the ongoing discussion of secular vs. theocratic government in the Italian press; the companionship of two children I haven't traveled with before; the challenges of daily life in a not perfectly adequate little apartment.

And I've thought a fair amount about all this, almost always "aloud," at the keyboard, as those of you who've stayed with these dispatches know. Forty thousand words so far, my computer tells me, almost exactly the same as I churned out in January, from a kitchen table just around the corner. This amounts to logorrhea, some would say. Even when I worked for a daily newspaper I never wrote quite as much, quite as compulsively. My defense can only be that these are, after all, extraordinary times; I've never seen anything quite like them, not even the 1960s, and I have only one way of confronting them and responding to them.

Today, walking home from a shopping expedition, I was happy to be greeted warmly by the hat-passer for a group of musicians on the Via dei Giubbonari, a busy shopping street we often negotiate, leading toward the Campo dei Fiori. He recognized me because I'd struck up a conversation with him a few days ago, when he stuck his paper cup in front of me and rather than ignore it I tossed a little change in, saying *Per i musicisti provo sempre da dare un po'*, for the musicians I always try to give a little something.

He smiled so warmly that I was sorry it was indeed only a little. I keep the one-Euro and two-Euro and even the fifty-cent pieces in one pants pocket, but all the little coins that accumulate in another one; there's never more than a dollar's worth there, and it's easy to fish some up in a situation like this. This time I doubt there was even fifty cents' worth: but his smile was still warm and genuine.

I asked him if they were Rumanian, and he said yes, we are. I told him I'd been there twenty years ago; that it wasn't a happy time, but that I thought the country quite beautiful and the people very friendly.

Si, signor; ma povero; molto povero: Yes, but poor, very poor. And so in fact they were in those days; I'll never forget the bare markets, with only a few half-rotten apples on one table, even in the midst of summer. And I suppose they're still poor today, though not as repressed as then. But they are or can be extraordinarily beautiful people, dark, bright-eyed, demonstrative; and more than their share seem to be gifted musicians — or perhaps it's simply that music is so much more accepted a way of responding, personally, to one's surroundings. Music isn't simply something to bounce around to as it comes out of an MP3 player or out of a loudspeaker; it's something to make one's self.

Anyway we said *ciao* to one another and moved on. But we ran into the band again a few days later, and this time I had a little more for them; and tonight he smiled broadly to me and nodded and did not thrust out the paper cup: I was allowed to listen without paying. This has happened before: the accordionist on the Piazza S.Egidio recognized us the other day, and nodded and greeted us while continuing to play, and was not offended at my failure to contribute to the cause (my left pants pocket being empty at the moment).

The musical experiences are not always that happy. Last week we ate at an emergency trattoria out past the Trevi Fountain, because it was mid-afternoon, and we were famished. It was a beautiful day and we sat on the "terrace," that is, at a table set out on the street. (I should remind you that many of these "streets" are closed to vehicular traffic other than the occasional motorbike.)

After a pleasant appetizer and an introductory glass or two of white wine a wandering violinist hove into view carrying a box. The box proved to be a battery-operated amplifier and speaker. He had a contact microphone on his violin. He was the most wretched excuse for a violinist I've heard since 1940, when I played violin in a children's orchestra at the San Francisco World's Fair.

(It suddenly occurs to me that I don't remember there even being an International Exposition in the last forty years. Have they been replaced by the Olympic Games?)

He scratched and scraped away on his miserable instrument, and the result was evilly filtered and amplified by his despicable hardware, and I think every tooth within a hundred meters was set on edge. The woman who'd seated us, and brought our menus, remonstrated with him. *Per carità, signor*, for the love of charity, for sweet Jesus's sake, leave off your playing and go away. But he would not, until finally two or three people (and I was not among them, Lindsey would have left me on the spot) walked menacingly toward him, and he got up and hoisted his box and skulked down the street.

Tonight we ate at Da Gighetto, a place in the Ghetto that Lindsey wanted to try. We got there early, about eight-thirty, but I hadn't been able to get anyone to answer the phone when I called this afternoon to reserve, and it's Saturday night, and the four Americans who went in ahead of us were turned away: You don't have a reservation? Sorry: it's completely full.

Then it was my turn. Same song. But, I said, I called this afternoon, and the phone rang and rang and I couldn't get anyone to answer.

The man at the door turned and looked quizzically, I think, or maybe accusingly, at the woman seated at a large desk with two telephones and a fax machine and some other assorted businesslike instruments. He said something. She said something. He turned back to me: wait five minutes, he said, there's a party that's just ordered dessert. Five minutes.

So we waited as a number of other parties arrived and were escorted into invisible dining rooms in the Promised Land Beyond, because they'd reserved, and finally we too were ushered into an enormous dining room, a dining room the size of a railroad station. We were shown to the one table of many tables that was not set. We sat and stood about while it was set; and then we ordered, to begin with, four artichokes Jewish style and four fillets of salt cod and a zucchini blossom and a rice ball and a bottle of water and a half-liter of white wine, and It Was Good.

And then, just as the pastas were arriving, a guitarist walked into the room. He and his enormous guitar filled the room. He was incredibly loud. He sang and bellowed, and he strummed and beat his guitar. It was not amplified, praise God with sounding brass and tinkling cymbals, but it was infernally loud all the same; I can't imagine how it had been constructed. Everyone in the dining room, by now full, and in all the many adjacent dining rooms, began talking much louder than before. You still couldn't hear yourself think.

No one in our room offered the slightest encouragement, but two men eating alone and bored with one another responded to him in the next room, just beyond Simon. They applauded one number, and then one of them actually sang along with the next. After that there was no discouraging this fellow.

Well, we got through it of course, though the dinner had dimmed considerably. We finally got the check and got out, and walked home across the two-thousand-year-old Bridge of the Four Heads and up the Lungaretta. And there, in the Piazza S. Maria in Trastevere, at eleven o'clock at night, quite a large piazza full of perambulating pleasure-seekers of all ages (including a great many children, by the way), we came upon an entire theater troupe.

The ringleader was setting out an unnecessary number of props, folding tables and little boxes and hats and buckets and baskets and stools, all covered in black-and-white imitation Holstein skin. One of these props was a ghetto-blaster with an apparently prerecorded mix of background music.

Off to one side another three conspirators stood in Renaissance garb, parti-colored tights and odd scarfs and ribbons and gaily colored berets and the like, lip-synching to the music.

Things proceeded at an amazingly slow pace. There were exaggerated gestures, mimed routines, false starts, tentative approaches to the audience, which continued to grow until maybe two hundred of us stood in the chilly night, gaping like so many bumpkins in a Breughel painting. A girl showed up on a bicycle; the Pierrot fell in love with her, blew up an udderlike rubber glove and deflated it again, produced a slide whistle which he did not play, waltzed over to her and pretended to court her shyly. The other three stood on the sidelines.

Clearly anyone with a semester's Dramatic Arts in junior high school could have done this much. We finally gave it up and went home. Out the window I hear the Piazza S. Egidio is still full: people are selling CDs and scarves and handmade jewelry and gloves and bad reproductions of Gustav Klimt paintings, though no one to my observation ever buys. All of Rome seems to be either on pause or slowly milling, wondering what's going to happen next. And that, except for whatever we go out to do with this last day here, is where we're going to have to leave it.

Epilogue
Healdsburg, Dec. 9—

LET ME SEE: do I remember anything of that last day in Rome, and the trip home? I mean, do I remember anything I'd want to admit to here?

It was a difficult day. There was so much left undone, as there always is; and then it was Sunday, and not everything was open. That didn't keep us from shopping, of course; the kids had gifts to pick up for friends and family, and I was still debating that important last question: does our baggage have room for a bottle of grappa, and a bottle of Fernet? Because both are considerably cheaper here than they are back home. Better, too: unbelievably, the Fernet Branca seems to be made to a different formula in Milan than it is in the U.S.A.

And then, inconceivably, we hadn't taken the kids up the Palatine hill. This is one of my favorite spots in Rome, one of everyone's favorites — high and pastoral though quite close to the main transportation hubs. You can see why from the time of the early kings it was the place to build.

So after lunch — at home: Lindsey had things to clean out of the refrigerator — we set off on what has become one of my favorite urban walks, down the Lungari to the Piazza Sonnino, through the Piazza Belli (smiling again at Mr. Belli's statue, showing the poet meditating on one of his scurrilous sonnets), across the Ponte Garibaldi with its fine view of the detritus roiling in the back-currents of the Tiber at the Isola Tibertina weir, and up the Via Arenula with its tram-tracks and taxis.

But we did not go to the Area Sacra with its ruined cats and temples. We turned instead up the Via dei Falegnami toward the Piazza Mattei, for I wanted to surprise the kids with a fountain they hadn't yet seen, the Turtle Fountain. The guide books always call it "delightful," but I find it sobering, another memento mori (just what you want on a final day on holiday), and at the same time another tribute to the Roman penchant for imagining, building, neglecting, rediscovering, adapting.

Epilogue

Giacomo Della Porta designed the fountain in the early 1580s, a large circular marble basin with four huge conch-shells, smaller dolphins perched on them, and four nude boys (*efebi*, says one of my guidebooks, which my dictionary translates helpfully as "girlish young men") poised atop the dolphins reaching with their arms upward and outward...

The houses (*palazzi*) around here were built by the Mattei family; another guidebook says the Duke had this fountain built overnight to prove to his fiancée's father that he was still powerful though recently impoverished. What did these *efebe* represent to the Duke, with their curious gestures of greeting, or beckoning? And what was Bernini thinking, if indeed it was the famous sculptor, when only eighty years later he added to the fountain, already undergoing restoration, the four turtles which now give an explanation for these upraised arms?

I thought about this, and thought about the unsightly erosion making these youthful arms look eczemic, and thought that in their own innocent youth, four centuries and more ago, they must have looked much like the grandson at my side. And then I shrugged and strode forward to the next goal, the outstanding gelateria on the Via Ara Coeli, just below the piazza of the same name.

We found this place last January and I was eager to try it again, though we'd ignored it up until this final day. The gelato here is entirely *bio*, or organic; and it is very good indeed — of all the *fior di latte* tasted in the last month, the best, I think, though Lindsey remains loyal to San Crispino.

And then up one final time that splendidly pedestrian ramp Michelangelo built to lead the masses to his magnificent Piazza del Campidoglio, another exercise in adaptation and modification. Eleanor Clark, in her fine book Rome and a Villa, suggests that any visit to Rome begin with this climb; I agree, but suggest that it also end with it. Between the drowsy black lionesses, then, and past the hapless Cola da Rienzi, and between Castor and Pollux (if indeed that is who they are), and across the Piazza to the famous suckling she-wolf, and down the steps into the Forum.

* * *

We first saw the Forum sixteen years ago, also in November, and it was empty of people, but peopled with statuary — statues lining the Via Sacra. Now the statues are gone and the Forum is crowded (though it wasn't last January, apparently the best month to see Rome if you don't mind the cold). There were groups and guides on every side, making it easy to eavesdrop on an explanation here and there, but inevitably lending a school-outing air to a place I prefer silent though evocative, mysterious though endlessly annotated.

Oh well. We simply walked through the Forum on our way to the entrance to the Capitoline, the day's real goal; and paid our entrance fees; and climbed the many flights of stairs to the top.

There of course there were many fewer people to be seen, in spite of the fine weather. We ate some bread and cheese on benches, rather silently, overcome I suppose by the beauty, the age, and the pathos of the place. This is where Romulus had his hut — you can see evidence of it in the museum. The entire hill was Nero's palace, and is now simply a hill, gardened here and there, set about with pines and cypresses, then suddenly erupting in another monumental revelation of ancient architecture.

I hid a few fallen olives in my pockets, thinking perhaps to try growing them once home again, and led the family to look down on the poignant Stadium, once noisy with chariot races, now silent like everything here; and beyond it on the Circus Maximus, a jogging track, with one of those bland inert governmental buildings beyond, the type called *griere* here, if that's how they spell it, because with their many windows and their blocky forms they look like Swiss cheeses.

And then it was time to go, and then I made my mistake. Our tickets let us in to the Colosseum as well as the Capitoline, and it seemed a pity not to let the kids see it. Off they went, while Lindsey and I walked homeward, to prepare dinner and to pack. But soon I had misgivings: suppose they should be lost on their way home!

I turned back, hurrying up the Via di San Gregorio VII, past the postcard dealers and the pizza-stands and the faux gladiators posing with tourists' girl-friends, and stood impatiently in line to get in, and rushed through groups clustered round their umbrella-waving guides, and finally penetrated the ancient stadium.

It was my first view of the surprisingly small interior of this im-

Epilogue

mense place. I confess I hardly saw it: I was busy looking for the kids, scanning across the arena into the low sun. I took the prescribed course, hurrying counterclockwise a quarter of the way round, then up the stairs to the upper galleries, further around, back down again, completing the ellipse.

I managed to admire the views out from the Colosseum, if only from the corner of my eye; and to form a general impression of stone, stone, stone; and to note the curious trick of proportion that made the arena seem so distant though the ellipse itself seems small — then realized quickly that that of course is precisely what happens, things look smaller in the distance, why am I marveling at that? I must be distracted. And in fact I was having an attack of anxiety, precisely what I've read occurs in this evil place.

I rushed out, and back down the Gregorio, and along the Circus, and between the beautiful old temples to Portunus and Hercules Victor, and over the Ponte Palatino, and up the Lungaretta and the Lungara and through the crowded Piazza S. Maria in Trastevere, and of course the kids were home, safe and sound, and surprised at my anxiety.

* * *

Next day we were off at five in the morning to the airport. We flew to Zurich, where I fretted while Simon visited the Lost and Found to reclaim his PDA, left on the plane when he landed there three weeks previously. I tried not to show the contempt I had for his carelessness; then reflected, as we boarded the next plane for Dallas, that I had left my own cell phone on the plane an hour earlier.

Lindsey made me call the Lost and Found last week. The phone was there; Swissair flew it to LAX; it arrived last Saturday at our motel, where we spent a few days seeing theater in Glendale. I was overcome, once again, with the utter banality of my life and error, and the hopelessness of ever catching up to the grandeur, the grace, the wisdom, and the detachment of the ancient world and the primitive race we all inhabit.

APPENDIX: RESTAURANTS IN ROME

I took reasonably careful notes on the restaurants we patronized in our first month in Rome, and saw little reason to continue in our second. We are rarely interested in Michelin two- or three-star restaurants; we prefer simpler food, settings and service; and we found places that first month that pleased us so much there seemed little reason to explore any further. Herewith the findings from that January, 2004:

Healdsburg, Feb. 12—

We ate out twenty-six times while in Rome that first time, in January, at twenty-five places, ranging from a quick slice of pizza or a panino (and these can be very good) to a white-tablecloth restaurant with all the amenities. Breakfast was invariably at home — our usual café au lait, orange juice, and toast with jam. Fourteen restaurant meals were taken at midday; eleven at night.

The rest of the time we ate at home — after all, this was why we'd rented an apartment with a kitchen. At home we sometimes cooked: Lindsey made some fine semolina gnocchi, and chicken with forty cloves of garlic, and minestrone; I made a chicken valdostana. Or we just had a slice of pizza from the local bakery, or cold cuts, or salad and fruit and cheese.

We ate outside of Rome, too, at restaurants in Orvieto and Tivoli, and most memorably at a friend's house in Orvieto.

Our first impression was that Rome is not an exciting restaurant town, and that impression wasn't really changed much. The local cuisine seems to be pretty plain, allowing for occasional specialties you don't find elsewhere, like the famous *puntarelle*, chicory stems stripped of their leaves, split, curled in ice water, and served with a rich anchovy sauce — a dish that might be straight out of Apicius, who would have had them with the notorious *frumentum*.

There were other reminders of the basically peasant orientation underlying Roman cuisine. I had a wonderful entree of scraps of roast lamb in a sweet-sour gravy, for example. We had salt cod on two or three Fridays. Our favorite take-out pizza was topped with thin slices of potato.

Rome is famous for its pasta dishes, and we had plenty of them. The pasta is indeed good; perhaps it's the famous Roman water — which may also be responsible for the particularly good coffee you get routinely in Rome, even apart from the coffee at Tazza d'Oro, which is truly memorable.

But in general the eating-out was simply solid and quite good, not trendy or sparkling or experimental. For once we did not rely on the Slow Food guide to restaurants; I'd checked our most recent copy (2002) before our departure, and none seemed attractive (though now that I look them over again I'm sorry I hadn't taken a photocopy of those pages: we simply didn't have the time to do it). We relied on the advice of Sari Gilbert, our landlady, and Gisella Isidori, a food professional we met in Orvieto; and we took note of comments in the various guidebooks we were using).

So these notes should be given even less respect than most restaurant recommendations, which are always subjective and undependable — except that I will mark with ++ the restaurants to which I would certainly return given half a chance. I give for each restaurant first the name, address, and telephone number; then the day and month it is NOT open (if I know it); then my comments; finally the date we were there.

+Al Moro, vicolo delle Bollette 13; 06/6783495; closed Sunday, August. Everyone recommends this place, a favorite of Fellini's. It is in fact very good. We shared an artichoke *alla giudea*; Lindsey liked her spaghetti *al moro* (his version of *carbonara*, with a little hot pepper added to the usual dish), broccoli, and a couple of grilled sausages; and for dessert a macedonia of apples and plums. I had — but it was the day I'd misplaced my pocket computer, on which I take notes, so I cannot reconstruct my dinner. Sorry. (January 27)

++Albino il Sardo, Via della Luce, n. 44-45. (Trastevere); 06/5800846. Sari recommended this, and we ate fabulously the ten days we spent in Sardinia in 1989, so we wouldn't miss this. We had antipasto, *maloreddus* (that special Sardinian pasta), and *porchetto*. But what wonderful pork that was! Suckling pig, it remembered its mother and her milk, and the chop of *cinghiale* on the side, being wild, remembered forest and freedom, and things older and deeper than that. The cracklings were particularly savory and made me think of my father who loved such things, and we had a nice bottle of ordinary Sard Monica red. (January 29)

++**Trattoria da Armando al Pantheon**, Gargiooli Claudio & C, Salita de' Crescenzi, 31; 06/68803034. Friends of ours were meeting a friend of theirs, so we took a table as well, and had a fabulous *bruschetta*; then a rough peasant-looking but unctuous *zuppa di farrò* (L. had spaghetti *alla gricia*, which is *carbonara* without the egg); veal saltimbocca; and a deep nutty *torta*; the wines were a fine house Frascati bianco, and a rich, deep Tenuto Rapitalà nero d'avila. (January 13, midday.)

Augusto, Piazza de' Renzi 15 (Trastevere); closed Sunday and Saturday dinner. All the guidebooks mention this joint as being casual and authentic and a local favorite and it was okay, in fact, but nothing to write home about (though here I am doing just that). It was so cold the cooks were wearing jackets and sweaters in their tiny kitchen. The menu is very small: we had the daily special, *baccalà* since it was Friday, and a nice conversation with three American girls at the next table. No credit cards; drink the house wine. (January 9, midday.)

++**La Campana**, v. Campana 18, /6867820. One of the Gourmet Magazine recommendations, this turned out to be a strictly local trattoria, what in Paris you'd call a *restaurant du quartier*. Very ordinary, and absolutely delicious. Lindsey ate marvelous *borlatti* beans with onion and celery slivers and fine olive oil, then *taglarini ai tartuffi*, and what did I have?

Hosteria Costanza, piazza del paradiso 63/65. Four of us ate here, partly because Sari recommended it, partly because we thought we remembered it from our last trip, fifteen years ago. (We're still arguing about this: Lindsey's journal says we were here; I'm convinced it was the nearby *da Pancrazio*; we'll settle this next visit.) Here I had spaghetti *caccio e pepe*, a fine dish to test a restaurant with, simply pasta, pecorino, and black pepper, with olive oil of course; and Costanza did well by me. I went on with roast kid, also very good; L. had pasta with squid and *bottarga*, then suckling pig. Good, but not the best. (January 12)

++**Ditirambo**, Piazza Cancelleria 74; 06/6871626. Recommended to us by Gisella, this turned out to be very good indeed: I had absolutely splendid slices of both salami and prosciutto made from goose, then my spaghetti *caccio e pepe* and, after, that curious lamb scraps in vinegar sweet-sour gravy, much better than the description sounds; L. had a well-seasoned *arista* ; then we split a very generous cheese plate: gorgonzola, fontina, *tomo*, *robiola*, and *piave*, served with *mostarda* and chestnut honey and perfect pears. (January 21)

+**Fly Bar**, v. Merulana 133, (Laterano): don't have phone number, schedule: This was a very simple place, what you could call Roman "fast food" except that it's all done to order and traditionally. Lindsey had a salami *panino*; I just had spaghetti with tomato sauce, a glass of wine, and great coffee, in the company of very simple people. You can eat a meal here for maybe eight or ten dollars; while you don't often find great or exciting meals in Rome you sure can do well by eating plain.

'**Gusto**, Piazza Augusto Imperatore 9; 06/3226273; www.gusto.it. Much recommended by *Access*, this is a glitzy, Los Angeles-like place, with its punning name, its fashionable kitchenware shop next door, and an enormous dining room with an industrial look. It was also the only place open a little before midnight, at least in its neighborhood — we should have gone straight home; Trastevere was still buzzing when we did. Oh well: we had a simple pizza and a glass of house red, and it was fine. (January 13)

++**da Lucia**, vicolo del Mattonato 28 (Trastevere); 06/5803601. Another trattoria for the locals that seems not to have changed in forty years. An old man sat at one of the tables, drying plates; the waiter took loaves of bread out of a tilt-forward bin, holding them against the bin to slice them. Pasta, of course; a little squid, some peas, the house red. (January 25)

+**Mario**, via del Moro (Trastevere). Don't know the address or the phone number, and no one recommended it but the guy who walked in ahead of us, talking to his friend: That other place is more upscale, you know, but this place is comfortable and the price is right. And it was raining, and we were hungry, so we followed them in. It was crowded in the main room; we sat in a side room, under a number of framed drawings artists had left long ago on the table-papers, and thankfully next to a portable stove, because it had been snowing. We had antipasto italiano, spaghetti *amitriciana*, *stracciatella*, and *baccalà*, and it was perfectly ordinary, and perfectly acceptable.

Miraggio, via Lungara (Trastevere). No phone or address here either. This "mirage" is in fact one of a chain of restaurants, and I don't recommend it — it was perhaps the only real disappointment we encountered. So-so pasta (*strozzapreti Trasteveriana*), tough *gnocchi alla Romana*. (January 11)

+**Ristorante Nerone de Santis,** via Terme di Tito 96. Recommended by the *Access* guidebook (which gave an incorrect telephone number) as "one of the few near the Colosseum that has maintained its quality in spite of heavy tourist traffic." The location's fine, a short walk up the Terme di Tito hill, on the corner, a comfortably tight dining room; and the trattoria menu is what you find everywhere. We had *baccalà in bianco* (salt cod fillets sautéed in oil, with parsley and lemon, no tomato), good *carciofi alla giudia,* rather overcooked spinach. (January 16, midday)

++**Ristorante da Paris,** piazza S. Calisto 7/a, 06/5815378; closed Monday, Sunday dinner, and August: This was really very good — the menu leaning toward the classical Jewish Roman Trattoria but with a personal stamp: there's tradition in the kitchen, but there's someone with intelligence and sensitivity who's adding his own personality to history. (The name is the owner's given name; the food has nothing to do with France.) The dining room is more comfortable and quieter than many; you feel you're in a white-tablecloth restaurant here rather than a simple trattoria. Delicious *bresaola*, fried zucchini flower, spaghetti *caccio e pepe*, *vitello picatella* with just a wedge of lemon; a fine bowl of *stracciatella* with a few drops of Balsamic vinegar; good *tiramisu*, but Lindsey thought her *zuppa inglese* heavily flavored with too much Alkermes. (January 17, dinner)

++**Perilli Testaccio,** via Marmorata 39 (Testaccio); 06/5742415; closed Wed., Aug: We stood around listening to three or four Roman foodies discuss where we should go for dinner after a wine-and-canapé party for food professionals. This was the consensus, and I remembered afterward that Access had raved about it: "This place is an Italian national treasure." It ties with Campana as my favorite Roman trattoria — good thing they're in opposite parts of town! Lindsey tested it with her benchmark request, spaghetti carbonara; I had the lamb "stew," actually chunks of lamb braised, then served with a sweet-sour brown gravy — a hearty peasant dish, very local to Rome, perfect on a cold cold night. (January 30, dinner)

+al **Pompiere**, via di Santa Maria de' Calderari 38 (Ghetto); 06/6868377; closed Sun., Aug: This is an old favorite of our friends Richard and Marta, in the most comfortable, elegant dining room of our visit — the first floor of the 16th-century Palazzo Cenci-Bolognetti. Here we had a fine artichoke *alla giudia*, as you'd expect; but Lindsey's pasta featured canned porcini. (January 14, midday)

+**la Scaletta**, v della Maddalena 46 (Pantheon). This was the most ordinary of trattorie; we chose it because we had no other recommendations in the area, we were hungry, we wanted something simple, and when we walked past we noticed a charming bored little girl peering out the window from beneath one of the tables. When we finally stopped in, quite late for lunch, we found pretty green plaid tablepapers, a personable waiter, and the same little girl, now sleeping while her parents and grandparents finished an interminable meal. Lindsey had *bucatini carbonara* which she liked, I my *caccio e pepe*. (January 19, midday)

++**Ristorante Le Streghe**, Vicolo del Curato 13; 06/6878182; 06/6861381; closed Sun. This was our favorite Rome restaurant, the only one we went to twice — we'd have gone a third time willingly. The dining room is small but there's room enough at the tables, and anyway it turned out to be the kind of place where pleasant conversations develop among strangers (and with the friendly waiters, too). The first night we opened with goat cheese with hazelnuts; then we had *tagliarini capalbiese*, under a "peasant-style" bolognese sauce without tomatoes; guinea-hen fillets "Streghe style" (raisins, black olives); artichoke *millefoglia*, really a sort of elegantly handled lasagna; and we finished with excellent semifreddo and *panna cotto*. (January 24, February 3, dinner)

On our last day in Rome we returned. I abstained from rich foods and meat, thinking of the next day's flight home, and ordered a simple plate of *lardo* (uncooked but lightly cured pork belly-fat) drizzled with honey and Balsamic vinegar; then a marvelous cheese plate with several pecorinos of various ages (up to three years!), *tomo*, *piave*, and Gorgonzola, and an arugula-pecorino-pear salad for my obligatory vegetable. Lindsey had a plate of prosciutto and, curious, the *tagiarini capalbiese* I'd had the previous visit. We had a bottle of Arneis, and the waiter pointed out that I really should have Piemontese cheese with it, so he brought a fat slice of Castelmagno, a magnificent white blue cheese rarely found outside Piemonte. And then there were beignets; and a glass of vino *passito*; and a coffee bavarian, and conversations with other tables — a great scene; a wonderful waiter. (Feb. 2, midday) (But see also p. 152ff, *supra*)

la Tana di Noantri, via Paglia 1 (Trastevere); 06/5806404; closed Tuesdays: This was recommended by our landlady, and is in fact on the ground floor of the building on whose second floor we lived for the month. It was the first restaurant we went to, and though we didn't go back we liked it well enough: vegetable soup was rich and earthy, my *penne all'arabbiata* perfectly cooked (as was all the pasta we had in Rome), Lindsey's scaloppini Marsala straightforward; the side-dish of green beans not too overcooked; a bottle of Corvo a good way to warm up a very cold evening. (January 3, dinner)

++**Dar Filettaro Santa Barbara**, Largo Librari 88: cod fillets, battered and fried and served in sheets of paper to eat out of hand with fried zucchini blossoms and a glass or red; yes yes yes (November sometime, lunch)

Out of town:

In Orvieto our friend Rosella took us to **Trattoria dell'Orso**, via della Misericordi 18-20; 0763341642; closed Mondays, Tuesdays, and weeks at a time throughout the year. This is a Slow Food restaurant, deservedly so, with sixty covers at most in a comfortable, relaxed room distinguished by some really marvelous little paintings. The chef, who looked amazingly like the Virgil Thomson of the 1960s, speaks fluent New Jersey English, because he'd lived there for years; but his Italian and his kitchen are just as fluent and just as authentic. *Strozzapreti* with *tartuffi & funghi* for Lindsey, lamb chops perfectly seasoned and grilled for me, and a fine home-style *crostata* or jam-tart for dessert, with a lot of very pleasant conversation, in both the dining room and the tiny one-man kitchen. (January 10, dinner)

In Tivoli we settled on **Ristorante Sibilla**, via Sibilla 50; 0774335281. This was recommended by a fellow on the street whom we stopped for directions to the temples we were in town to see: curiously, it's not mentioned in any of my guide-books except that, left-handedly, the Lonely Planet book suggests asking its proprietors to let you into their garden for close look at the temples — which are in fact in the back yard. But why not have lunch there while you're at it? The rooms are marvelous, and a dozen or more plaques on the walls will assure you that you're in good company: kings and queens, composers and poets have been there before you. I had decent gnocchi, dressed with shredded *radicchio* and zucchini and a very pleasant gorgonzola sauce; the only disappointment was a watery side-dish of *fagiolini* which had apparently been waiting for us too long. (January 15, midday)

Palatine hill

Afternote, January 2007

A FRIEND WROTE TODAY asking how to spend a single day she'll have in Rome. A single day! What a calamity! And yet, a day in Rome, certainly preferable to no day in Rome, or perhaps even several days in some other place… So I wrote back to her:

Depends on the weather. If I had only one day, and it a nice one, I'd start at the Campo de' Fiori early in the morning. I'd walk down to the Ponte Sisto, cross it, then walk down the Tiber to the Isola Tiberna, where I'd spend twenty minutes walking around it. Then I'd walk across the Ponte Palatino, visit the Tempio Vesta and the Tempio della Fortuna Virile, stop in at S. Maria in Cosmedin to admire the floor (but ignore the Bocca di Verità), stop in at S. Giorgio in Velabro (my very favorite), walk the Circo Massimo, then the via di S. Gregorio to the Colloseo.

I'd have lunch at the Ristorante Nerone de Santis, via Terme di Tito 96. Then I'd take a cab to the Pantheon and stop in for coffee at La Tazza d'Oro nearby. Before or after the coffee I'd go to the Gelateria San Crispino, via Panetteria 42, near the Trevi Fountain. I'd take a cab from there to the Piazza del Risorgimento and then rest by taking a long tram ride from there, through the Villa Borghese, getting off at the Piazza Buenos Aires to walk around the fantastic architecture of the Coppedè district, then resume the streetcar back to the Colosseo.

I'd have dinner at Perilli, in the Testaccio district, incredible spaghetti carbonara; or at Da Lucia in Trastevere, wonderful pasta *cacio e pepe*; or at La Campana, marvelous *borlatti* beans with onion and celery slivers. In the course of the day I'd have several coffees and a couple of grappas, and I'd buy a hat, if possible.

I'd do all that on a rainy day too, of course.

𝓛

senza Lindsey niente

*This book was set in a computer version of the Garamond typeface,
with titles in Herculaneum, on a Macintosh computer, by the author;
and printed by the online publisher Lulu*

all photographs by the author

first edition

2007

www.ingramcontent.com/pod-product-compliance
Lightning Source LLC
Chambersburg PA
CBHW020743100426
42735CB00037B/323